Conventional Versus Non-conventional Political Participation in Turkey

This book focuses on the emergence of different forms of civic and political activism in Turkey. It has taken into account different components of active citizenship, specifically looking at the development of civic and political forms of activism that bridge the realms of conventional and non-conventional participation. Focusing on the effects of the 2013 Gezi Park protests – which originated in Istanbul but spread throughout the country – this book reflects on civic and political participation in Turkey. Specifically focusing on the main dynamics of non-conventional forms of civic and political activism, this volume attempts to understand the impact of non-conventional forms of political participation on voting behaviour.

The internal domestic conditions of the country, as well as its role in the international arena, have dramatically changed since 2013, and are constantly evolving due to the domestic societal and political cleavages, and the regional problems in the Middle East. Yet, the chapters in the book reflect upon the significance of occupygezi nowadays, demonstrating its importance not only in questioning the link between the patrimonial state and its citizens, but also for stimulating participatory behaviours.

The chapters of this book were originally published as a special issue in *Turkish Studies*.

Cristiano Bee is Lecturer in Politics at Oxford Brookes University, UK. Previously he was an Assistant Professor at Kadir Has University, Turkey, and Marie Curie Fellow at the European Institute of Istanbul Bilgi University, Turkey, where he was Principal Investigator in the research project 'The Europeanisation of the organised civil society in Turkey. The case of youth organisations in the prospect of the European integration'. He is author of *Active Citizenship in Europe: Practices and Demands in the EU, Italy, Turkey and the UK* (Palgrave 2017).

Ayhan Kaya is Professor of Politics and Jean Monnet Chair of European Politics of Interculturalism at the Department of International Relations, Istanbul Bilgi

University, Director of the Jean Monnet Centre of Excellence, and a member of the Science Academy, Turkey. He received his Ph.D. and MA degrees at the University of Warwick, UK. Some of his books are *Europeanization and Tolerance in Turkey* (2013) and *Islam, Migration and Integration: The Age of Securitization* (2012).

Conventional Versus Non-conventional Political Participation in Turkey

Dimensions, Means, and Consequences

Edited by
Cristiano Bee and Ayhan Kaya

LONDON AND NEW YORK

First published 2018 by Routledge

2 Park Square, Milton Park, Abingdon, Oxfordshire OX14 4RN
52 Vanderbilt Avenue, New York, NY 10017

Routledge is an imprint of the Taylor & Francis Group, an informa business

First issued in paperback 2019

British Library Cataloguing in Publication Data
A catalogue record for this book is available from the British Library

ISBN 13: 978-1-138-57737-4 (hbk)
ISBN 13: 978-0-367-89265-4 (pbk)

Typeset in Minion Pro
by diacriTech, Chennai

Publisher's Note
The publisher accepts responsibility for any inconsistencies that may have arisen during the conversion of this book from journal articles to book chapters, namely the possible inclusion of journal terminology.

Disclaimer
Every effort has been made to contact copyright holders for their permission to reprint material in this book. The publishers would be grateful to hear from any copyright holder who is not here acknowledged and will undertake to rectify any errors or omissions in future editions of this book.

Contents

Citation Information

The following chapters were originally published in *Turkish Studies*, volume 18, issue 1 (March 2017). When citing this material, please use the original page numbering for each article, as follows:

Chapter 1
Conventional versus non-conventional political participation in Turkey: dimensions, means, and consequences
Cristiano Bee and Ayhan Kaya
Turkish Studies, volume 18, issue 1 (March 2017) pp. 1–9

Chapter 2
A participatory generation? The generational and social class bases of political activism in Turkey
Murat İnan and Maria T. Grasso
Turkish Studies, volume 18, issue 1 (March 2017) pp. 10–31

Chapter 3
Voting Behavior of the Youth in Turkey: What Drives Involvement in or Causes Alienation from Conventional Political Participation?
Ayşegül Kayaoğlu
Turkish Studies, volume 18, issue 1 (March 2017) pp. 32–55

Chapter 4
Between Gezi Park and Kamp Armen: the intersectional activism of leftist Armenian youths in Istanbul
Hrag Papazian
Turkish Studies, volume 18, issue 1 (March 2017) pp. 56–76

Chapter 5
Negotiating 'the political': a closer look at the components of young people's politics emerging from the Gezi Protests
Pınar Gümüş
Turkish Studies, volume 18, issue 1 (March 2017) pp. 77–101

Chapter 6

The weakest link or the magic stick?: Turkish activists' perceptions on the scope and strength of digital activism
Şenay Yavuz Görkem
Turkish Studies, volume 18, issue 1 (March 2017) pp. 102–124

Chapter 7

Europeanization of civil society in Turkey: legacy of the #Occupygezi movement
Ayhan Kaya
Turkish Studies, volume 18, issue 1 (March 2017) pp. 125–156

Chapter 8

Youth activists and occupygezi: *patterns of social change in public policy and in civic and political activism in Turkey*
Cristiano Bee and Stavroula Chrona
Turkish Studies, volume 18, issue 1 (March 2017) pp. 157–181

Chapter 9

Stand-in as a performative repertoire of action
Özge Derman
Turkish Studies, volume 18, issue 1 (March 2017) pp. 182–208

For any permission-related enquiries please visit:
http://www.tandfonline.com/page/help/permissions

Notes on Contributors

Cristiano Bee is Lecturer in Politics at Oxford Brookes University, UK. Previously he was an Assistant Professor at Kadir Has University, Turkey, and Marie Curie Fellow at the European Institute of Istanbul Bilgi University, Turkey, where he was Principal Investigator in the research project 'The Europeanisation of the organised civil society in Turkey. The case of youth organisations in the prospect of the European integration'. He is author of *Active Citizenship in Europe: Practices and Demands in the EU, Italy, Turkey and the UK* (Palgrave 2017).

Stavroula Chrona holds a Ph.D in Politics (University of Surrey, UK). She is a specialist in political psychology, electoral behaviour, and public opinion. Currently, she is investigating the cognitive, affective, and motivational processes of public political behaviour. In particular, she is examining the role of ideological inclinations, political sophistication, value orientations and emotions in the processes of information-processing, decision-making, and motivated reasoning.

Özge Derman is a Ph.D. candidate in the Department of Arts and Languages at the Ècole des Hautes Ètudes en Sciences Sociales (EHESS), France. She is a member of the Centre de Recherches sur les Arts et le Langage (CRAL). Her Ph.D. project focuses on artistic expressions in occupy movements and is supervised by Esteban Buch, Director of Studies at EHESS.

Maria T. Grasso is Professor at the Department of Politics, University of Sheffield, UK. She is the author of *Generations, Political Participation and Social Change in Western Europe* (2016) and co-editor of *Austerity and Protest: Popular Contention in Times of Economic Crisis* (2015). Her research has been published in *British Journal of Political Science, European Journal of Political Research, Electoral Studies, Work, Employment and Society, Research in Social Movements, Conflict and Change, Mobilization*, and other journals.

Pınar Gümüş is a doctoral candidate at the International Graduate Centre for the Study of Culture, University of Giessen, Germany. She is also a researcher at Istanbul Bilgi University Youth Studies Unit, Turkey. Her research interests are mainly in the fields of youth studies, social movements, civil society studies, as well as gender and performance studies.

Murat İnan is a Lecturer in the Politics and International Relations Department in the Faculty of Humanities and Social Sciences, Abdullah Gül University, Turkey. He is particularly interested in quantitative methods, political participation, prodemocratic culture, as well as the modernization theory and theories of socialization.

Ayhan Kaya is Professor of Politics and Jean Monnet Chair of European Politics of Interculturalism at the Department of International Relations, Istanbul Bilgi University, Turkey. He is also Director of the Jean Monnet Centre of Excellence and a member of the Science Academy, Turkey. Examples of his books include *Europeanization and Tolerance in Turkey* (2013) and *Islam, Migration and Integration: The Age of Securitization* (2012).

Ayşegül Kayaoğlu is an Assistant Professor of Economics at Istanbul Technical University, Turkey. She is also a research associate at Economic Research Forum, Egypt. Her main research interests are applied development economics, population economics, political economy, and informal institutions.

Hrag Papazian is a D.Phil. candidate in Anthropology at the University of Oxford, UK. His research focuses on Armenian identity(ies) in contemporary Turkey.

Şenay Yavuz Görkem is an Assistant Professor in the Department of Public Relations and Publicity at Maltepe University, Turkey. She believes in the importance of interdisciplinary work and has many national and international publications. Her latest areas of academic interest are digital activism and political humour.

Conventional versus non-conventional political participation in Turkey: dimensions, means, and consequences

Cristiano Bee and Ayhan Kaya

This special issue focuses on the emergence of different forms of civic and political activism in Turkey. In doing so, we have taken into account different components of active citizenship and looked more specifically into the development of civic and political forms of activism that bridge the realms of conventional and non-conventional participation. As witnessed in many different contexts, conventional forms of political participation such as electoral politics are being replaced with non-conventional forms of participation that take place outside, and sometimes in opposition to, the more traditional channels of representation.[1] The issue of active citizenship has become more and more salient in recent years, with a growing literature discussing the processes that bring about new modalities, which conceive the notion of citizenship as something detached from certain rights, obligations and entitlements embedded in the traditional definition of national citizenship.[2] The active role citizens can play in political and civic life deserves particular attention with regard to the analysis of participatory behaviors that signify new modalities through which citizens relate to civic and political domains.[3] We believe that the argument that more and more people are becoming disengaged from politics[4] proves to be misleading. A key point that drives our argumentation is that instead the crisis of representative democracy has favored the emergence of alternative modalities to engage and participate in civic and political life. Civic and political participation take manifold dimensions, and can be expressed through the activation of participatory behaviors[5] of various kinds, including volunteering, taking part in NGO activities, boycotts, and protests and demonstrations.

1

Demands of active citizenship

In the typology that we developed,[6] we argue that active citizenship can be untangled on the basis of two distinct dimensions (top-down and bottom-up) that provide the basis for diverging definitions: *active citizenship as a practice* and *active citizenship as a demand*. In regard to the former, we argue that public institutions through public policy have strategically promoted the activation of participatory behaviors in order to stimulate engagement among citizens, and ultimately to improve bases of input legitimacy. Under this category, we can include conventional political behaviors such as voting as well as non-conventional forms of participation such as joining a political movement or civil society organization with the scope of interacting with policy-makers through lobbying activities or advocacy work. Various examples in Europe provide evidence of the fact that public institutions foremost promote this form of participation in order to shape participatory behaviors, while at the same time, this is key for improving the efficiency of governance systems.[7] In regard to the latter, we argue that the lack of deliberative and participatory public policies is more likely to result with the emergence of bottom-up forms of civic and political mobilization where civil society groups contest the current status quo by posing distinct claims to policy-makers. Understanding the demands of active citizenship becomes particularly important whenever competing claims are made in civil society through the use of both traditional and alternative channels of mobilization.[8] Active citizenship as a demand is expressed outside formal channels of political participation such as electoral politics, and takes expression by means of various forms of deliberation.[9] At the same time, it takes place when public policy is insufficient or non-existent, and individuals tend to mobilize in collective action to solve a particular problem acting apart from – or in some cases replacing – public intervention. From this perspective, citizens tend to gain ownership of social and political settings by trying to subvert the existing order. Examples include getting involved in protests against an authoritarian government; self-mobilizing for the purpose of guaranteeing the well-being of the community to replace the functions of policy-makers when there is a lack of intervention; or occupying and using abandoned public spaces for the organization of cultural and/or social activities to provide help for immigrants or disadvantaged people in a particular community.

Demands of active citizenship in the Turkish context

The Turkish case is particularly an important context, which could provide the reader with an understanding of the complexity inherent in the transformation of the conventional form of citizenship into active citizenship.[10] Many scholars have argued that in Turkey the notion of citizenship has evolved through a strong attachment to the state and its institutions,[11] which has resulted in the development of both passive and militant citizens.[12] In regard to passive citizens, we refer to those who are mostly adherent to the *status quo*. At the same time, the citizens can be militant as they undertake political action in accordance with an organic vision of society, making them to defer their rights until the moment they serve their duties to the state.[13] Additionally, the Turkish context is characterized by a number of limitations in the promotion of practices of active citizenship. Just to draw on a significant example, the promotion of civil society policies by the European Union (EU) was expected to strengthen democratization and to bolster independent associations in Turkey. However, the result is a bit more complicated than was envisaged. On the one hand, the EU civil society policy has had an important effect on stimulating the development of civil society actors. On the other hand, it has not created a truly independent and autonomous civil society.[14]

However, a number of transformative aspects have challenged this top-down promotion of active citizenship highlighting new dimensions that are worthwhile to explore. This is particularly true with respect to bottom-up dimensions of civic and political participation that radically put the link between the state and citizens under scrutiny.[15] More scholars have been looking, in fact, at the emergence of alternative ways through which citizens participate, frame claims and define their ownership of the public space. Research by Engin Isin on the acts of citizenship is enlightening in this sense.[16] Acts of citizenship imply the redefinition of the spaces of participation and new modalities to shape what is political. This process of redefinition is inherent to the emergence of new struggles to express and gain a legitimate voice in public sphere. In another example, Berna Turam conducted important ethnographic research in Teşvikiye, a notoriously secular-oriented neighborhood of Istanbul. She highlights different acts of citizenship, which are performed by both secular-oriented locals of the neighborhood with more bourgeois lifestyles as well as those of newly arrived, more Islamic-oriented high-spenders. Turam argues that both the government and opposition have failed to regulate and protect the rights and liberties of citizens, which are threatened by the political contestation between the two groups. However, in the absence of the regulatory mechanisms by state actors, both devout Muslims and secularists learn in action how to see, talk, and act beyond the Islamist–secularist duality. These new acts of citizenship are performed and negotiated in the public space in a way that leads to the increasing irrelevance of the Islamist–secularist axis, reshuffling and realigning a wide range of groups across the political spectrum in defense of a deeper liberal democracy.[17]

Locating *occupygezi*

On this basis, in this special issue we frame the emergence of occupy movements as a meaningful example of active citizenship as a demand, where mobilizing agents have operated against the political elites as well as the current ideological frameworks such as neo-liberalism in order to vindicate the ownership of the public space[18] and to advocate for better bases of democracy.[19] In these cases, calls for democracy and social justice have been expressed through means such as street protests, arts, satire, humor, parody, creativity, and different acts of solidarity.

Focusing on the specific effects of the 2013 Gezi Park protests – which originated in Istanbul but spread throughout the country – we reflect on how this experience might re-orient current on civic and political participation in Turkey. To this effect, we specifically focus on the main dynamics of non-conventional forms of civic and political activism. In doing so, we are also trying to make conclusions with regard to understanding the impact of non-conventional forms of political participation on voting behavior. The attempt to gain ownership of the public space in the case of Gezi represents a clear example of a bottom-up expression of active citizenship where different claims were developed and communicated in order to break the strong link with the authoritarian state. This resulted in direct demands to gain ownership of public policy processes and to pave the way to develop forms of deliberative democracy in the country. In a volatile context as in Turkish, it is rather difficult to identify clearly the legacy of *occupygezi* and its long-term effects. The internal domestic conditions of the country as well as its role in the international arena have dramatically changed since 2013, and are constantly evolving mainly due to the domestic societal and political cleavages as well as to the regional problems in the Middle East. Yet, the papers in the special issue reflect upon the significance of *occupygezi* nowadays, demonstrating not only its importance in questioning the link between the patrimonial state and its citizens, but also for stimulating participatory behaviors.

Outline of the special issue

This special issue provides a timely reflection on current debates that are of great relevance in order to understand key issues such the historical determinants of civic and political participation in Turkey, traditional and alternative means of political and civic mobilization, and political behavior. The contributors of the special issue take into account both the determinants and the legacy of *occupygezi*. The papers draw on different methodological traditions and disciplines, touching upon insights from political sociology, public policy analysis, political science, social anthropology, and political psychology. In addition, by combining analysis conducted by junior and senior scholars, it provides fresh empirical research and key case studies supported by strong theoretical frameworks. It combines articles that mix both quantitative and qualitative methods of enquiry in order to provide a deeper understanding of the complexity of political participation in Turkey.

İnan and Grasso focus on temporal and structural mechanisms of political activism in Turkey with a particular emphasis on the centrality of generational and social class bases that help us understand social change. Kayaoğlu presents a dataset from a large-scale survey focusing on different determinants of political behavior in Turkey shedding light on the actual implications of the *occupygezi* movement. Papazian refers to the theories of intersectionality to present the results of his ethnographic work conducted in Istanbul, where he investigates the activism of leftist Armenian youths. Gümüş informs the reader about the results of her field work conducted with young participants of the Gezi protests, trying to understand the processes of social change that produced new modalities of political participation. Görkem, drawing upon a large-scale 2015 survey, looks at a particularly prominent and growing aspect of active citizenship, namely digital activism. Kaya examines the *occupygezi* movement under the light of different models of Europeanization, focusing on the legacy of the movement for various civil society actors such as business associations, media, and trade unions. Bee and Chrona report the results of a field work conducted in 2015/2016 with activists of youth organizations in order to provide an account of the impact of the *occupygezi* on their practices, activities, and values. Derman concentrates on the case study of the 'standing man,' providing an example of one of the many alternative and innovative modalities of mobilization and, in particular, reporting a valuable example of how performative acts can represent a significant expression of participation that combine arts and politics.

These articles provide evidence of different dimensions, means, and consequences inherent to conventional and non-conventional political participation in Turkey by raising critical points in regard to the emergence of demands of active citizenship that are meant to contest the current status quo, while at the same time vindicating the independence and autonomy of the civil society from interferences and manipulations coming from the political level. One could question whether the *occupygezi* movement still has a legacy in Turkey, but the articles in this special issue argue that the movement has made a great impact on the civil society to reassemble the social across ethnic, religious, class, cultural, and gendered identities.

Several individuals have been very supportive during the period in which we edited this special issue, which is the outcome of a very-well attended workshop organized by the European Institute of Istanbul Bilgi University on 21 January 2016. The workshop and the publication of this special issue are supported by a grant received from the European Commission's 7th Framework Programme, Intra-European Fellowships (IEF) FP7-PEOPLE-2013-IEF, Grant Agreement No: 625977, entitled 'The Europeanisation of the organised civil society in Turkey: The case of the youth organisations in the prospect of European integration' (EUROCS). We are grateful to the participants of the workshop, who later contributed to this issue with their articles. They have been very punctual and collaborative in due course. Logistically, we appreciated very much the support of Aslı Aydın and Gülperi Vural, members of the European Institute, who made a tremendous contribution to the whole project with their hard-work and friendship. The anonymous peer reviewers offered many constructive critiques that have helped improve the papers. We would also like to thank our language editor, Burak Eröncel, for working with us in this timely special issue. Finally, we want to specifically thank Paul Kubicek, who, from the very beginning, believed in us and supported us to bring all these articles together in a special issue. We thank him for his encouragement and very prompt responses whenever we needed them.

Notes

1. Marinetto, "Who Wants to Be an Active Citizen?"
2. Bee and Villano, "Active Citizenship"; Boje, "Commentary"; Faulks, *Citizenship*; Heater, *What Is Citizenship?*; Hoskins and Mascherini, "Measuring Active Citizenship"; and Lister, *Citizenship*.
3. Barrett and Brunton Smith, "Political and Civic Engagement."
4. Putnam, *Bowling Alone*.
5. Barrett and Smith, "Political and Civic Engagement"; and Ekman and Amnå, "Political Participation."
6. Bee and Kaya, "Between Practices and Demands."
7. Bouza Garcia, *Participatory Democracy*; and Smismans, *Civil Society*.
8. Verba, Schlozman, and Brady, *Voice and Equality*.
9. Delli Carpini, Cook, and Jacobs, "Public Deliberations."
10. Çakmaklı, "Active Citizenship in Turkey"; and Çakmaklı, "Rights and Obligations."
11. Keyman and İçduygu, "Globalisation," 231.
12. İçduygu, Yilmaz, and Nalan, "What Is the Matter with Citizenship?"; and İçduyğu, "Interacting Actors."
13. Keyman and İçduygu, "Globalisation," 231.
14. Ergun, "Civil Society"; Kubicek, "Political Conditionality"; Kuzmanovic, *Refractions*; Yılmaz, "EU Conditionality"; and Zihnioğlu, *European Union*.
15. Bozkurt, Çok, and Şener, "Government Perspectives"; Chrona and Capelos, "The Political Psychology"; and Gül and Cünük, "Istanbul's Taksim Square."
16. Isin, "Theorising"; and Isin, "Citizenship in Flux."
17. Turam, "Primacy of Space in Politics."
18. Murray, "The Sphere"; Turam, "Primacy of Space in Politics"; and Vatikiotis and Yörük, "Gezi Movement."
19. Abbas and Yiğit, "Scenes from Gezi Park"; David and Totamis, *Everywhere Taksim*; and Karasulu, "If a Leaf Falls."

Disclosure statement

No potential conflict of interest was reported by the authors.

Bibliography

Abbas, Tahir, and Ismail Hakki Yiğit. "Scenes from Gezi Park: Localisation, Nationalism and Globalisation in Turkey." *City: Analysis of Urban Trends, Culture, Theory, Policy, Action* 19, no. 1 (2015): 61–76.

Barrett, Martyn, and Ian Brunton-Smith. "Political and Civic Engagement and Participation: Towards an Integrative Perspective." *Journal of Civil Society* 10, no. 1 (2014): 5–28.

Bee, Cristiano, and Ayhan Kaya. "Between Practices and Demands: Ambiguities, Controversies and Constraints in the Emergence of Active Citizenship in Turkey." *Southeast European and Black Sea Studies* (2016). Advance online publication. doi:10.1080/14683857.2016.1244235.

Bee, Cristiano, and Paola Villano. "Active Citizenship in Italy and the UK: Comparing Political Discourse and Practices of Political Participation, Civic Activism and Engagement in Policy Processes." In *Political and Civic Engagement: Multidisciplinary Perspectives*, edited by Martyn Barrett and Bruna Zani, 436–455. London: Routledge, 2015.

Boje, Thomas P. "Commentary: Participatory Democracy, Active Citizenship, and Civic Organizations – Conditions for Volunteering and Activism." *Journal of Civil Society* 6, no. 2 (2010): 189–192.

Bouza Garcia, Luis. *Participatory Democracy and Civil Society in the EU. Agenda-Setting and Institutionalisation.* London: Palgrave, 2000.

Bozkurt, Sümercan, Figen Çok, and Tülin Şener. "Government Perspectives on Civic and Political Participation of Youth and Women in Turkey: Deriving Insights from Policy Documents." In *Political and Civic Engagement: Multidisciplinary Perspectives*, edited by Martyn Barrett and Bruna Zani, 420–435. London: Routledge, 2015.

Çakmaklı, Didem. "Active Citizenship in Turkey: Learning Citizenship in Civil Society Organizations." *Citizenship Studies* 19, nos. 3–4 (2015): 421–435.

Çakmaklı, Didem. "Rights and Obligations in Civil Society Organizations: Learning Active Citizenship in Turkey." *Southeast European and Black Sea Studies* (2016). Advance online publication. doi:10.1080/14683857.2016.1244236.

Chrona, Stavroula, and Tereza Capelos. "The Political Psychology of Participation in Turkey: Civic Engagement, Basic Values, Political Sophistication and the Young." *Southeast European and Black Sea Studies* (2016). Advance online publication. doi:10.1080/14683857.2016.1235002.

Cornwall, Andrea, and John Gaventa. "Makers and Shapers. Repositioning Participation in Social Policy." *IDS Bulletin* 31, no. 4 (2000): 50–62.

David, Isabel, and Kumru F. Toktamis. *Everywhere Taksim: Sowing the Seeds for a New Turkey at Gezi*. Amsterdam: Amsterdam University Press, 2015.

Delli Carpini, Michael X., Fay Lomax Cook, and Lawrence R. Jacobs. "Public Deliberations, Discursive Participation and Citizen Engagement: A Review of the Empirical Literature." *Annual Review of Political Science* 7, no. 1 (2004): 315–344.

Ekman, Joakim, and Erik Amnå. "Political Participation and Civic Engagement: Towards a New Typology." *Human Affairs* 22, no. 3 (2012): 283–300.

Ergun, Ayça. "Civil Society in Turkey and Local Dimensions of Europeanization." *Journal of European Integration* 32, no. 5 (2010): 507–522.

Faulks, Keith. *Citizenship*. London: Routledge, 2000.

Gaventa, John. "Introduction: Exploring Citizenship, Participation and Accountability." *IDS Bulletin* 33, no. 2 (2002): 1–18.

Gül, Murat, John Dee, and Cahide Nur Cünük. "Istanbul's Taksim Square and Gezi Park: The Place of Protest and the Ideology of Place." *Journal of Architecture and Urbanism* 38, no. 1 (2014): 63–72.

Heater, Derek. *What Is Citizenship?* Cambridge: Polity Press, 1999.

Hoskins, Bryony, and Mascherini Massimiliano. "Measuring Active Citizenship Through the Development of a Composite Indicator." *Social Indicators Research* 90, no. 3 (2009): 459–488.

İçduygu, Ahmet. "Interacting Actors: The EU and Civil Society in Turkey." *South European Society and Politics* 16, no. 3 (2011): 381–394.

İçduygu, Ahmet, Colak Yilmaz, and Soyarik Nalan. "What Is the Matter with Citizenship? A Turkish Debate." *Middle Eastern Studies* 35, no. 4 (1999): 187–208.

Isin, Engin F. "Citizenship in Flux: The Figure of the Activist Citizen." *Subjectivity* 29 (2009): 367–388.

Isin, Engin. "Theorizing Acts of Citizenship." In *Acts of Citizenship*, edited by E. F. Isin and G. M. Nielsen, 15–43. London: Zed Books, 2008.

Karasulu, Ahu. "'If A Leaf Falls, They Blame The Tree': Scattered Notes on Gezi Resistances, Contention, and Space." *International Review of Sociology: Revue Internationale de Sociologie* 24, no. 1 (2014): 164–175.

Keyman, E. Fuat, and Ahmet Icduygu. "Globalization, Civil Society and Citizenship in Turkey: Actors, Boundaries and Discourses." *Citizenship Studies* 7, no. 2 (2003): 219–234.

Kubicek, Paul. "Political Conditionality and European Union's Cultivation of Democracy in Turkey." *Democratization* 18, no. 4 (2012): 910–931.

Kuzmanovic, Daniella. *Refractions of Civil Society in Turkey*. London: Palgrave, 2012.

Lister, Ruth. *Citizenship: Feminist Perspectives*. Basingstoke: MacMillan, 1997.

Marinetto, Michael. "Who Wants to Be an Active Citizen? The Politics and Practice of Community Involvement." *Sociology* 37, no. 1 (2003): 103–120.

Murray, Billie. "The Sphere, the Screen, and the Square: 'Locating' Occupy in the Public Sphere." *Communication Theory* 26, no. 4 (2016): 450–468.

Putnam, Robert D. *Bowling Alone: The Collapse and Revival of American Community*. New York: Simon & Schuster, 2000.

Smismans, S., ed. *Civil Society and Legitimate European Governance*. Cheltenham: Edward Elgar, 2006.

Turam, Berna. "Primacy of Space in Politics: Bargaining Space, Power and Freedom in an Istanbul Neighborhood." *International Journal of Urban and Regional Research* 37, no. 2 (2013): 409–429.

Vatikiotis, Pantelis, and Zafer F. Yörük. "Gezi Movement and the Networked Public Sphere: A Comparative Analysis in Global Context." *Social Media and Society* 2, no. 3 (2016): 1–12.

Verba, Sidney, Kay Lehman Schlozman, and Henry Brady. *Voice and Equality: Civic Volunteerism in American Politics*. Cambridge, MA: Harvard University Press, 1995.

Walzer, Michael. "The Communitarian Critique of Liberalism." *Political Theory* 18, no. 1 (1990): 6–23.

Yilmaz, Gözde. "EU Conditionality Is Not the Only Game in Town Domestic Drivers of Turkey's Europeanization." *Turkish Studies* 15, no. 2 (2014): 303–321.

Zihnioğlu, Özge. *European Union Civil Society Policy and Turkey. A Bridge Too Far?* Basingstoke: Palgrave, 2013.

A participatory generation? The generational and social class bases of political activism in Turkey

Murat İnan and Maria T. Grasso

ABSTRACT

This research aims to understand the extent to which generation and social class determine Turkish respondents' level of political activism. It tests both the macroeconomic socialization effect and the social class effect on political activism as hypothesized by Inglehart and Lipset, respectively. It also strives to understand whether a macropolitical period effect may also some generational implications for political activism. Beyond these examinations, it also raises a challenge to Lipset's working-class authoritarianism thesis – within the particular area of political activism – for those generations which came of age under an authoritarian politico-juridical order as well as for those which did not.

Introduction

The Gezi Protests (GP) put Turkey in the limelight of political activism research. The GP, which took place in the summer of 2013, were sparked as resistance against the Turkish government's decision to reconstruct historical military barracks in Taksim's Gezi Park in the center of Istanbul. In the beginning, a small number of environmentalists engaged in the protests, but the police's severe suppression of the first wave of protests through the use of tear gas and water cannons transformed the protests into a nationwide movement.

This paper aims to investigate the role of generational and social class locations for understanding political activism and social change in Turkey. With this purpose in mind, it generates hypotheses derived from specific elements of Inglehart's post-materialist thesis, Beck and Jennings' thesis linking political periods and political activism, and Lipset's working-class authoritarianism thesis. In addition to testing these hypotheses, it raises its original hypothesis by combining the two previous ones and suggests that the extent to which system-level authoritarianism experienced in the formative years determines the social class effect on political activism. In this way it aims to explain Karl Mannheim's argument on the transformation of 'generation as location' into 'generation as actuality.'

Turkey provides an unprecedented test case to investigate both inter-generational and inter-class attitudinal differences and participatory patterns. Its young and dynamic population, developing economy, economic and social inequalities produced by the fierce application of the market economy model, inefficient redistribution policies and history of democratization punctuated by military coups would be expected to produce large differences across generation and class categories. Another important factor underlying Turkey's selection, as preliminary analysis has shown, is its citizens' low level of political activism, which is dire news for Turkish democracy. However, it should be noted that, despite taking the form of a case study of Turkey, this article employs models which may be generalizable for all societies experiencing similar conditions. Developing countries with long-term socioeconomic development and unstable political histories would be fruitful locations for replication studies testing generalizable conditions. Alternatively, the models that are sketched in this research can be applied cross-culturally within a comparative setting. However, one should note that comparative research would require a periodization of generations unique to each country, meaning that the researchers would have to be aware of the political history of each country being studied.

The remainder of the article proceeds as follows. First, the next section reviews extant literature on political participation, socialization and generational effects. It also presents the hypotheses that we test in our analysis. Next, we introduce our data and methodology. Subsequently, the results of the analysis are presented. Finally, wider implications of the findings are further elaborated in the conclusion.

Theoretical framework

Looking at declining levels of electoral turnout and party membership since the 1970s, numerous scholars have noted that political participation was in decline in the industrialized countries of the West. And that this could result in a crisis of democracy.[1] However, some have challenged this view and argued that, rather than declining, political activism was in fact on the rise when unconventional repertoires of political activism were taken into account. Ronald Inglehart was a strong supporter of the latter view. Basing his analysis on Maslow's hierarchy of needs theory, Inglehart described a shift from materialist to post-materialist needs in post-war Europe. According to Inglehart, individuals who were already born into physical and economic security environment in the post-war period did not need to struggle for their physical and material needs. Instead, enjoying these securities from birth, those individuals seek a higher set of needs, including self-esteem and self-actualization as well as intellectual and aesthetic needs. Eventually, by means of a generational replacement mechanism, those individuals with post-materialist needs were understood to have become far more numerous in the 1970s, paving the way for a sociological transformation in Western European advanced industrial societies, which was labeled by Inglehart as 'the silent revolution.' Inglehart has argued that a post-materialist shift in needs also has implications for political activism. According to his analysis, rising levels of physical and human capital have undermined conventional forms of political activism and introduced new avenues for participating in politics. More elite-challenging, flexible and direct forms of political action have replaced conventional forms since the latter had substantially lost their ability to cater to the needs of a new post-materialist generation.[2]

Looking at the Turkish case from Inglehart's perspective, we can draw an analogy between the periods of economic development in post-war Western Europe and in post-1980 Turkey, a period in which Turkey has seen signifi- cant economic growth and modernization. Making such analogy is important because a possible participatory Turkish generation that was socialized during this period may breathe fresh life into Turkish democracy, as did the post-war youth in Western Europe. During the period from the 1980s to the 2010s, which corresponds to the term in which most of the GP participants spent their formative years, the Turkish economy grew by an average of about five percent a year and the GDP per capita at purchasing power parity quad- rupled. The share of the middle class increased from 18 to 41 percent between 1993 and 2010. Turkey signed the Customs Union agreement with the EU in 1995, which increased Turkish exports to the European region by about 20 fold.[3] By looking at this picture, we hypothesize in line with Inglehart's post-materialist theory that the members of the generation which have enjoyed relatively affluent economic conditions of the post-1980 Turkey during their formative years are more likely to develop an activity-prone characteristic than the members of the preceding generations, who grew up at a time when Turkey was poorer and less dynamic economically (*Hypothesis I*).

As an alternative to the idea of macroeconomic socialization enshrined in the post-materialist thesis that links greater affluence at the time of socializa- tion to increased political activism, particularly more unconventional means of participation, another group of researchers has focused on the role of macropolitical period factors to understand changes in the levels of political activity. The period ranging from the late 1960s to the early 1970s in the US has particularly drawn their attention in this regard. For example, Beck and Jennings, examining data from the 1965–73 Socialization Panel Study and the 1956–76 Michigan presidential election series, concluded that the American youth of the late 1960s and early 1970s, which they recognized as 'a deviant period', constituted a particular generation with respect to their level of political action. The youth of this 'turbulent' period, being influenced by some remarkable political events, including anti-Vietnam War protests and the Civil Rights Movement, developed a more activity-prone profile than both their parental generation and successor filial generations. Rejecting the previous theories of political participation that were based on a curvilinear relationship between age and political activism, which had long served as a guideline to understand the patterns of American political activism, Beck and Jennings concluded that there is no constant relationship between age and participation. Thus, to 'handle "deviance" as well as "normality"' in the relationship between the two, Beck and Jennings advised 'adding an explicit political factor, the opportunities for involvement, into the participation equation.'[4]

As described above, when the development of macroeconomic condition is considered, post-1980 Turkey and post-war Western Europe show some similarities. However, they diverge significantly when macropolitical circumstances are taken into account. Unlike the situation in the post-war Western Europe in which socioeconomic development was accompanied by democratization movements and enhancement of civil rights and freedoms, in post-1980 Turkey, macroeconomic development was accompanied by military and civil authoritarian governments aiming to re-establish state authority and security environment at the expense of violation of fundamental rights and freedoms. Following the 1980 military coup, individual economic, social and political rights that were introduced in the 1962 constitution were largely suspended. Executive power was further strengthened. The Council of Ministers was authorized to pass laws by decree.[5] The Higher Education Council (YÖK) was established as a supreme authority over the higher education.[6] The Radio and Television Supreme Council (RTÜK) was established to control broadcast media.[7] State security courts, the members of which were assigned by the executive authority, were effectively used to suppress political opposition.[8] An anti-terror law was adopted in 1991, which often made way for the violation of fundamental rights and freedoms of the civilians, in particular with regard to the fighting of Kurdish militants in the southeastern part of the country.

Departing from this point of view, in order to investigate what extent a possible macropolitical period effect has for political activism, one can derive, from Beck and Jennings, an alternative to the post-materialist thesis. It should also be noted that while developing this hypothesis, we made a distinction between three political periods in twentieth century Turkish political history by looking at the administrative practices introduced by the incumbent governments and the legal system in power and labeled each of them either as authoritarian or non-authoritarian.[9] In this way we aimed to take 'opportunities for involvement' into account as suggested by Beck and Jennings. Thus, we hypothesize that the members of the post-1980 generation are less likely to develop an activity-prone characteristics than the members of the previous generation owing to their exposure to authoritarian system-level socialization during their formative years (*Hypothesis II*).

So far, we have discussed only the direct generation-political activism relationship. However, it is likely that the generational effect on political activism is mediated by the social class, given the extremely large differences between the living conditions of social classes in Turkey. This thinking implies a potential indirect generational effect on political activism, which presumably operates via the social class structure. To understand this indirect effect, if any, we first need to understand the social class effect on political activism. With this purpose in mind, we will draw upon Lipset's working-class authoritarianism thesis. The working-class authoritarianism thesis is a well-respected perspective of the relationship between class and social attitudes in modern societies. In his seminal 1959 work, 'Democracy and Working Class Authoritarianism,' Lipset raised perhaps one of the clearest arguments concerning the relationship between social class structure and authoritarian propensities. Lipset argued that the working class was the most pro-democratic social segment of the society before 1914. The working-class left-wing parties were strong supporters of civil rights and freedoms, democracy and peace while the middle class ones resisted suffrage movements, promoted nationalistic policies and allied with traditional powers such as the Church. However, since 1914 the working class had become the most authoritarian segment in many countries of the world. Lipset has noted that single-party system preference, political extremism, intolerance against minority groups, intransigence, punitive child-rearing patterns and low participation in politics are but some working-class conditions which are largely underlined by factors including low educational attainment, income insecurity, isolated group existence and lack of sophistication.[10] Hereby, departing from Lipset's viewpoint on the relationship between social class and participation in politics, we hypothesize that the Turkish working-class respondents are less likely to develop an activity-prone characteristic than their middle-class counterparts and this can largely be explained by the former group's low education and income (*Hypothesis III*).

Having clarified the relationship between the class structure and political activism, next we need to test this relationship across generations. We developed our fourth and final hypothesis, arguing that the macropolitical effect has generational implications which determines the individual-level social class effect on political activism. This draws upon Karl Mannheim's argument on the transformation of 'generation as location' into 'generation as actuality.'

Mannheim laid down the foundations of his theory of generations in his 1927 essay, 'The Sociological Problem of Generations.' In this essay, reflecting his relationist perspective, Mannheim upheld Wilhelm Pinder's view, suggesting that the combined effects of constant and transient factors produce historical progress. Thus, according to Mannheim, knowledge about existence can only be achieved by considering spatial and temporal factors together. Within this context, Mannheim has argued that contemporaneity cannot be the only factor playing a role in the formation of generations. Instead, it has to be accompanied by exposure to the same historical and social environment. Moreover, basing his theory on the theories of the development of the human mind, Mannheim argued that this exposure takes place during the early phases of human life, because at this early period human beings are highly susceptible to the formative forces of life. Values that are acquired during this period occupy such an important place in one's value system that they play significant roles in shaping one's future attitudes and behavior in a predicted way and this paves the way for the formation of generations. Mannheim has depicted the generation phenomenon as a combination of three imaginary concentric circles, generation as location (*generationslagerung*), generation as actuality (*generationszusammenhang*) and generation unit (*generationseinheiten*). In this representation, generation as location corresponds to the largest outmost circle which sets the widest criterion of a generation. The first inner-circle symbolizing generation as actuality surrounds the second inner-circle symbolizing a generation unit. According to Mannheim, moving from the outmost circle to the innermost one increases attitudinal homogeneity. However, Mannheim has argued that generation as location transforms into generation as actuality in some particular circumstances. According to Mannheim, social classes may blend in with one another as a result of being socialized by extraordinary time such as a war and this is what happened to German classes during the wars against Napoleon.[11] Keeping in mind our two previously set hypothesis generated to investigate the generational implications of macropolitical period effect and social class effect on political activism (*Hypotheses II and III*) as well as Mannheim's above argument on the transformation of generation as location into generation as actuality a result of being exposed to major scale political events, we argue that Lipset's working-class authoritarianism thesis cannot be applied to the generation which was socialized during the post-1980 period due to its members' exposure to system-level authoritarianism during the age they came of age. Instead, raising a generational challenge to Lipset's thesis, we hypothesize that for the members of the post-1980 generation, social classes were equalized with respect to their likelihood of participating in politics owing to system-level authoritarianism they have faced during their formative years (*Hypothesis IV*).

Data and methods

We utilized World Values Survey (WVS) data for Turkey for this research project. The survey is administered by the World Values Survey Association (WVSA), which is a global network of social scientists. The Turkish survey began in 1990 and was repeated in 1996, 2001, 2007 and 2011. Each wave of the survey was conducted through face-to-face interviews with respondents aged 18 and over.[12] The selection of the WVS is underlined by the fact that it is the only available data set for Turkey involving all the variables of interest. Due to the lack of panel data, five waves of cross-sectional WVS data for Turkey, spanning over 20 years, accomplished our aim to treat the notorious age/period/cohort (APC) identification problem. After removing cases with 'no answer' and 'don't know' responses for the variables of interest, a multi-stage representative sample of the Turkish population, consisting of 6257 cases, was obtained. Construction of the dependent and the two key independent variables are presented below.[13]

Dependent variables

Our dependent variable is based on a survey item asking the respondents to self-report some elements of their participation in politics. The question reads as follows: 'Now here are some forms of political action that people can take. Please indicate, for each one, whether you have done any of these things, whether you might do it or would never under any circumstances do it.' Three forms of political action were given repeatedly to the respondents across all waves of the Turkish survey. They are: 'signing a petition,' 'joining in boycotts' and 'attending lawful demonstrations.' These three unconventional repertoires of action constitute the three dependent variables of the current investigation. While constructing the dependent variables, we dummy-coded the answers. We assigned '1' for actual participation and '0' for non-participation, putting the 'might do' into the non-participation category.

Independent variables

Generation

In order to analyze a potential generational divide in Turkish political activism, generation was employed as the first key independent variable. The generation variable was basically derived from the WVS question asking the respondents' birth years. The following procedure was adopted while generating the variable. First, the 1960 and the 1980 military coups were pinpointed as two major politico-historical events in the twentieth-century Turkish political history. Next, referring to these two noticeable events, Turkish twentieth-century political history was divided into three periods, which we labeled as 'foundation,' 'interim' and 'post-1980'. Having the three periods split apart, following Beck and Jennings' advice, opportunities for involvement were considered by making a qualitative assessment.[14] The interim period (which ranges between 1960 and 1980) was distinguished from the foundation (pre-1960) and the post-1980 periods owing to relatively lower level of restrictive politico-juridical practices during this period. Following this periodization, in order to clarify generational locations, each respondent was associated with one political period by referring to the year of his/her formative age. Our selection of the formative age is guided by some important works in the existing early socialization literature. According to Mannheim the age 17 or thereabouts is the formative time in a person's life cycle.[15] Nie and his collaborators defined the formative period as an interval between mid to late adolescence.[16] According to Powell and Cowart, this period is between ages 12 and 30.[17] Erikson suggested the period from 14 to 15 for the formation of political views and attitudes.[18] Niemi and Hepburn proposed the age range between 14 and 25 as being crucial for the formation of participatory behavior.[19] Following this tradition, 15 was taken as the socialization age. One particular age was preferred to a period in order to avoid overlapping generational locations. Thus, by looking at in which period one spent one's 15th year, the respondent is located in the related generation. The three adjacent generations were thus generated and named after the same names with the political periods.[20] The foundation generation was born prior to 1945; the interim generation was born between 1945 and 1965; and the post-1980 generation was born after 1965.

Social class

Our social class measurement was derived from the WVS question asking respondents' current or last occupation. Following the question, respondents were given 15 alternatives to match with their own occupational status. We collapsed 15-digit occupation measurement into a 5-digit social class variable following Erikson and Goldhorpe's class schema, which is a respected categorization of social classes in the capitalist economies.[21] In addition to 'manual,' 'nonmanual' and 'service/self-employed' classes, we also included 'farmer' and 'unemployed' categories due to the high number of respondents who identified themselves as 'farmer,' 'agricultural worker' and 'unemployed' while responding the 15-digit survey question.

Besides our variables of primary interest, a series of control variables were also included in the analysis. The configuration of this group of variables was guided by the empirical findings of the previous works. Since education and income variables are expected to intertwine with the social class variable, they were included in the analysis to isolate the pure class effect.[22] The education variable was collapsed into three categories by looking at the three basic stages in the Turkish national education system: elementary, secondary and university.[23] The income variable was left in its 10-digit original model. Age was employed in its original linear format to control for the age effect. Age squared was included as a quadratic term to account for the curvilinear age effects. Survey year dummies were included to account for the period effect. Including age, age squared and survey year variables allows us to deal to some extent with the APC identification problem.[24] Gender was included as a classical control variable. Three more variables, namely political interest, importance of politics and self-political positioning were included to control for the respondents' general interest in politics.

Method

A quantitative approach was employed in this research. Three groups of logistic regression were employed in the analyses for estimating probabilities for three unconventional repertoires of political action.[25] The reason underlying the selection of logistic regression is the dichotomous character of the dependent variables. Each group of regressions consisted of four models. The first set of models tested the first and second hypotheses, the next two sets of models tested the third hypothesis and the fourth set of models ran three separate analyses with three samples coming from three adjacent generations to test the fourth hypothesis.

Findings

Before we move on with inferential statistics, we present some descriptive findings first. Table 1 demonstrates the percentage shares of 'have done' answers given to the petition, boycott and demonstration questions for each generation divided by survey years.

The table provides *prima facie* evidence supporting our both first and the second hypotheses explaining generational implications of macropolitical effect and macroeconomic socialization effect in different rounds. As shown in the table, until 2007 for petition and boycott and until 2011 for demonstration, the percentage rates of 'have done' answers generally start off at a low level, reach a nadir in the middle and level off in the end. This lends support to our second hypothesis which is based on the macropolitical effect over the first one. However, by 2007 for petition and boycott and by 2001 for demonstration, percentage rates increase continuously which supports our first hypothesis which is based on macroeconomic socialization effect over the second one. Yet, in average, it seems that the macropolitical effect, in descriptive terms, prevails over the macroeconomic effect in the Turkish case. The descriptive findings reveal that the members of the interim generation seem to participate more than the members of the foundation and the post-1980 generations when average rates are considered.

Table 1. Percentage rates of 'have done' answers pertaining to three repertoires of political action for each generation by survey years.

Generation/Survey Years	Petition			Boycott			Demonstration		
	Foundation	Interim	Post-1980	Foundation	Interim	Post-1980	Foundation	Interim	Post-1980
1990	13.19	15.76	10.64	2.78	8.18	4.26	4.17	9.70	4.26
1995	16.47	24.57	26.24	4.71	14.93	10.74	5.88	13.61	11.57
2001	11.64	18.70	14.08	4.23	9.55	5.25	3.70	11.14	6.58
2007	11.36	12.76	13.42	2.27	5.35	6.16	2.27	7.00	6.44
2011	2.22	6.92	12.57	0.00	2.69	6.55	0.00	2.31	7.18
Average	10.97	15.74	15.39	2.79	8.14	6.59	3.20	8.75	7.20

N: 6.257. Data: WVS, Rounds: 1990/1996/2001/2007/2011.

However, it should be noted that the trend is changing in the recent rounds. For a more robust analysis, three groups of logistic regressions were run for three unconventional repertoires of political action.

Table 2 shows the models predicting signing a petition.

The first model tests the first two alternative hypotheses. After introducing all the necessary controls, the coefficient scores and odds rations pertaining to the categories of the generation variable show that there is no significant difference, neither between the post-1980 and the interim generations ($p = .190$) nor between the post-1980 and the foundation generations ($p = .284$) with respect to their members' likelihoods of signing a petition. When the reference category is switched to foundation, there is also no significant difference between the foundation and the interim generations ($p = .550$). The second and the third models test our third hypothesis which was generated in line with Lipset's working-class authoritarianism thesis. The second model reveals that the members of the nonmanual class are 1.79 times more likely to sign a petition than the members of the manual class ($p < .000$). However, as shown on the third model, when education and income variables are controlled, the significant difference between the two classes disappears ($p = .803$). The fourth model, on the other hand, tests Lipset's thesis across three subsequent generations. When the model is run with the data coming from the interim generation, it can be seen that there is no significant difference between the manual and nonmanual categories ($p = .252$). However, the members of the unemployed category have significantly lower odds of signing a petition than the members of all other classes. Apart from these, there are no statistically significant differences between any class pairs among the remaining four classes. When the same model is run with the data coming from the foundation and the post-1980 generations, no significant difference can be observed between any class pairs except for the difference between unemployed and farmer categories of the foundation generation.

Table 3 shows the models predicting joining in a boycott.

The first model tests the first two alternative hypotheses. It is shown in the table that the post-1980 generation, does not differ with respect to their members' likelihood of joining in a boycott from the foundation and interim generations ($p = .292$ and $.247$, respectively). The second model reveals that the members of the nonmanual class are 1.86 times more likely to join in a boycott than the members of the manual class ($p < .000$). Moreover, as shown on the third model, the significant difference between the classes fades away when the education and income variables are controlled ($p = .306$). The fourth model runs the same analysis for samples coming from the three subsequent generations. As the table shows no significant difference can be observed between the two classes of primary interest, neither in the foundation nor in the post-1980 generations. However, the

20

Table 2. Multivariate logistic regression models predicting signing a petition.

	Socialization Model		Lipset's Models				Socialization and Lipset's models combined					
	Model 1		Model 2		Model 3		Model 4					
							Foundation		Interim		Post-1980	
	Logit	OR	Logit	OR	Logit	OR	Logit	OR	Logit	OR	Logit	OR
Age	0.02 (.01)	1.02	0.01(.01)	1.01	0.02(.01)	1.02	−0.16(.21)	0.84	0.02(.08)	1.02	−0.02(.06)	0.97
Age²	−0.00(.00)*	0.99	−0.00(.00)	0.99	−0.00(.00)*	0.99	0.00(.00)	1.00	−0.00(.00)	0.99	0.00(.00)	1.00
Gender (Ref. male)	−0.22(.07)**	0.79	−0.11(.08)	0.89	−0.13(.08)	0.87	−0.83(.38)*	0.413	−0.03(.15)	0.96	−0.07(.11)	0.92
Survey Years												
1990	Omitted		Omitted		Omitted		Omitted		Omitted		Omitted	
1996	0.63(.14)***	1.88	0.47(.13)**	1.60	0.42(.14)**	1.52	0.26(.38)	1.30	0.25(.22)	1.29	0.91(.27)**	2.50
2001	0.35(.14)*	1.42	0.34(.13)*	1.41	0.24(.13)	1.27	−0.22(.55)	0.80	0.46(.24)	1.58	0.50(.27)	1.65
2007	0.23(.17)	1.26	0.19(.15)	1.21	0.03(.15)	1.03	0.41(.66)	1.51	−0.05(.32)	0.94	0.45(.28)	1.56
2011	−0.09(.17)	0.90	−0.16(.15)	0.84	−0.49(.15)**	0.61	−0.93(1.13)	0.39	−0.77(.39)	0.46	−0.03(.28)	0.96
Political interest	0.46(.04)***	1.59	0.44(.04)***	1.55	0.38(.05)***	1.46	0.33(.18)	1.39	0.41(.08)***	1.52	0.38(.06)***	1.46
Importance of politics	0.23(.04)***	1.26	0.22(.04)***	1.25	0.22(.04)***	1.24	0.15(.14)	1.16	0.20(.07)**	1.23	0.22(.05)***	1.25
Self-political positioning	−0.15(.01)***	0.85	−0.14(.01)***	0.86	−0.13(.01)***	0.87	−0.10(.05)	0.90	−0.15(.02)***	0.85	−0.11(.01)***	0.88
Education (Ref. Elementary)												
Secondary					0.49(.09)***	1.64	0.68(.33)*	1.97	0.45(.15)**	1.58	0.52(.14)***	1.69
University					1.20(.12)***	3.34	0.99(.48)*	2.71	0.88(.21)***	2.43	1.41(.17)***	4.12
Household Income					0.04(.02)*	1.04	0.00(.07)	1.00	0.08(.03)*	1.08	0.03(.02)	1.03
Social Class (Manual)												
Unemployed			−0.14(.11)	0.86	−0.13(.11)	0.87	0.78(.56)	2.18	−0.69(.22)**	0.49	0.00(.15)	1.00
Farmer			−0.07(.19)	0.92	0.04(.19)	1.05	−0.61(.63)	0.53	0.17(.29)	1.18	0.05(.31)	1.05
Nonmanual			0.58(.10)***	1.79	0.02(.11)	1.03	0.16(.48)	1.17	−0.22(.19)	0.79	0.16(.16)	1.18
Self-employed			0.32(.12)**	1.38	0.08(.12)	1.08	0.08(.47)	1.09	−0.09(.20)	0.91	0.14(.17)	1.15
Generation (Ref. post-1980)												
Foundation	0.31(.29)	1.36										
Interim	0.17(.13)	1.19										
Intercept	−3.11(.38)***		−3.02(.35)***		−3.65(.37)***		3.01(6.82)		−3.35(1.88)		−3.35(.92)***	
Log Likelihood	−2430.86		−2403.74		−2341.51		−197.13		−827.27		−1395.76	
N. (obs.)	6257		6257		6257		592		2116		3549	
Pseudo R²	0.1049		0.1149		0.1378		0.1238		0.1592		0.1369	

Note: Entries are multivariate logistic regression logit estimates with standard error values in parentheses and odds ratios (exponentiated B). Data: WVS, rounds: 1990/1996/2001/2007/2011.
Significance levels: *p < .05, **p < .01, ***p < .001.

Table 3. Multivariate logistic regression models predicting joining in boycotts.

	Socialization Model		Lipset's Model				Socialization and Lipset's models combined					
	Model 1		Model 2		Model 3		Model 4					
							Foundation		Interim		Post-1980	
	Logit	OR	Logit	OR	Logit	OR	Logit	OR	Logit	OR	Logit	OR
Age	0.05(.03)	1.05	0.07(.02)**	1.07	0.09(.02)***	1.09	-0.30(.38)	0.73	-0.04(.12)	0.95	0.00(.08)	1.00
Age^2	-0.00(.00)	0.99	-0.00(.00)**	0.99	-0.00(.00)***	0.99	0.00(.00)	1.00	0.00(.00)	1.00	0.00(.00)	1.00
Gender (Ref. male)	-0.45(.11)***	0.63	-0.42(.12)**	0.65	-0.46(.12)***	0.63	-1.06(.70)	0.34	-0.36(.21)	0.69	-0.44(.16)**	0.64
Survey Years												
1990	Omitted		Omitted		Omitted		Omitted		Omitted		Omitted	
1996	0.56(.20)**	1.75	0.43(.20)*	1.53	0.36(.20)	1.44	0.20(.77)	1.23	0.18(.30)	1.19	0.82(.42)	2.27
2001	0.25(.21)	1.29	0.28(.20)*	1.32	0.11(.20)	1.12	-0.24(1.13)	0.78	0.26(.33)	1.30	0.30(.42)	1.36
2007	0.19(.25)	1.22	0.24(.22)	1.27	0.04(.23)	1.04	0.48(1.37)	1.61	-0.63(.46)	0.52	0.63(.43)	1.87
2011	-0.01(.25)	0.98	-0.02(.21)	0.97	-0.36(.23)	0.69	–	–	-1.46(.59)*	0.23	0.31(.43)	1.36
Political interest	0.65(.07)***	1.92	0.61(.07)***	1.84	0.53(.08)***	1.71	0.26(.37)	1.30	0.41(.12)**	1.51	0.70(.11)***	2.01
Importance of politics	0.38(.06)***	1.47	0.39(.06)***	1.48	0.38(.06)***	1.46	0.38(.31)	1.47	0.38(.10)***	1.46	0.36(.08)***	1.44
Self-political positioning	-0.26(.02)***	0.76	-0.25(.02)***	0.77	-0.23(.02)***	0.78	-0.20(.10)	0.81	-0.27(.03)***	0.76	-0.22(.02)***	0.80
Education (Ref. Elementary)												
Secondary					0.76(.16)***	2.15	0.78(.72)	2.19	0.71(.24)**	2.04	0.66(.24)**	1.93
University					1.88(.18)***	6.56	1.67(.81)*	5.34	1.91(.29)***	6.79	1.68(.26)***	5.41
Household Income					-0.00(.02)	0.99	0.18(.12)	1.20	0.05(.04)	1.05	-0.07(.03)	0.93
Social Class (Manual)												
Unemployed			-0.11(.17)	0.88	-0.15(.17)	0.85	1.86(1.38)	6.45	-1.11(.34)**	0.32	0.08(.22)	1.08
Farmer			-1.13(.43)**	0.32	-0.99(.43)*	0.36	–	–	-1.56(.75)*	0.20	-0.40(.54)	0.66
Nonmanual			0.62(.14)***	1.86	-0.17(.16)	0.84	0.97(1.18)	2.64	-0.53(.26)*	0.58	0.05(.22)	1.05
Self-employed			0.13(.17)	1.15	-0.20(.18)	0.81	0.50(1.24)	1.65	-0.43(.27)	0.64	-0.15(.27)	0.85
Generation (Ref. post-1980)												
Foundation	-0.47(.45)	0.62										
Interim	0.22(.19)	1.24										
Intercept	-4.98(.60)***		-5.42(.56)***		-6.13(.61)***		3.93(12.11)		-2.71(2.71)		-5.56(1.40)***	
Log Likelihood	-1304.49		-1285.32		-1220.59		-64.33		-468.44		-661.32	
N. (obs.)	6257		6257		6257		482		2116		3549	
Pseudo R^2	0.1924		0.2043		0.2444		0.2548		0.2875		0.2236	

Note: Entries are multivariate logistic regression logit estimates with standard error values in parentheses and odds ratios (exponentiated *B*). Data: WVS, rounds: 1990/1996/2001/2007/2011.
Significance levels: *$p < .05$, **$p < .01$, ***$p < .001$.

analysis of the interim generation surprisingly shows that the members of the manual class have 1.69 times the odds of joining in a boycott than the members of the nonmanual class ($p = .044$). Yet, it should be noted that the difference is only marginally significant. In fact, our analysis shows that the manual class members of the interim generation have higher odds of joining in a boycott compared to their counterparts from all the other social classes except for the self-employed class.

Table 4 shows the models predicting lawful demonstrations.

The first model shows that the members of the post-1980 generation are significantly less likely to attend lawful demonstrations compared to the members of the interim generation ($p = .007$). It can be seen from the second model that the members of the nonmanual class have 1.79 times higher odds of attending a lawful demonstration than the members of the manual class ($p < .017$) and as shown by the third model the difference becomes insignificant when the education and income are controlled ($p = .053$). The fourth model reveals that the odds of attending in a lawful demonstration do not appear to be significantly different for any of the two classes in the foundation and the post-1980 generations. However, in the interim generation the members of the manual class seem to be more likely to attend lawful demonstrations compared to their unemployed, farmer and self-employed counterparts ($p = .027, .027, .037$ respectively). Nevertheless, the difference between the manual and the nonmanual classes is still insignificant ($p = .190$).

Conclusion

The present research has aimed to investigate the generational and social class bases of political activism in Turkey. Our first and the second hypotheses basically suggested that the post-1980 and interim generations are different from each other with respect to their likelihoods of participating in the three unconventional repertoires of political action. More specifically, we argued that if Inglehart's macroeconomic socialization thesis is applicable to the Turkish case, the post-1980 generation should be more activity-prone than the interim generation. Alternatively, we suggested that if Beck and Jennings' macropolitical effect has generational implications for political activism in Turkey, the interim generation should be more activity-prone than the post-1980 generation. Neither our first nor second hypotheses concerning the relationship between generation and political activism are confirmed for two out of three unconventional repertoires of political action. Only for attending demonstrations did we find limited evidence favoring the *Hypothesis II* over *Hypothesis I*. In other words, neither Inglehart's postmaterialist thesis is applicable nor does Beck and Jennings' macropolitical effect appear to have generational implications for the Turkish case. This finding has a

Table 4. Multivariate logistic regression models predicting attending lawful demonstrations.

	Socialization Model		Lipset's Models				Socialization and Lipset's models combined					
	Model 1		Model 2		Model 3		Model 4					
							Foundation		Interim		Post-1980	
	Logit	OR	Logit	OR	Logit	OR	Logit	OR	Logit	OR	Logit	OR
Age	0.01(.02)	1.01	0.05(.02)*	1.01	0.06(.02)**	1.07	-0.35(.36)	0.70	-0.03(.11)	0.96	-0.13(.08)	0.87
Age²	-0.00(.00)	0.99	-0.00(.00)**	0.99	-0.00(.00)**	0.99	0.00(.00)	1.00	0.00(.00)	1.00	0.00(.00)	1.00
Gender (Ref. male)	-0.44(.10)***	0.63	-0.44(.11)***	0.63	-0.45(.12)***	0.63	-1.56(.80)	0.20	-0.44(.19)*	0.64	-0.35(.15)*	0.70
Survey Years												
1990	Omitted		Omitted		Omitted		Omitted		Omitted		Omitted	
1996	0.46(.19)*	1.58	0.29(.19)	1.60	0.22(.19)	1.25	0.41(.67)	1.51	0.06(.28)	1.06	1.05(.41)*	2.87
2001	0.41(.19)*	1.51	0.29(.18)	1.41	0.15(.19)	1.16	-0.75(1.17)	0.46	0.33(.31)	1.39	0.81(.41)	2.24
2007	0.28(.23)	1.33	0.12(.21)	1.21	-0.05(.21)	0.94	0.18(1.32)	1.20	-0.23(.41)	0.79	0.84(.42)*	2.33
2011	-0.08(.24)	1.09	-0.16(.20)	0.84	-0.44(.21)*	0.63	–	–	-1.42(.58)*	0.23	0.54(.42)	1.73
Political interest	0.57(.07)***	1.77	0.54(.07)***	1.55	0.48(.07)***	1.61	0.49(.38)	1.63	0.34(.11)**	1.41	0.61(.10)***	1.85
Importance of politics	0.35(.05)***	1.42	0.35(.05)***	1.25	0.34(.06)***	1.41	0.25(.29)	1.28	0.26(.09)**	1.30	0.41(.08)***	1.51
Self-political positioning	-0.26(.02)***	0.76	-0.25(.02)***	0.86	-0.24(.02)***	0.78	-0.13(.09)	0.87	-0.23(.03)***	0.78	-0.24(.02)***	0.78
Education (Ref. Elementary)												
Secondary					0.67(.14)***	1.95	1.02(.65)	2.79	0.67(.21)**	1.96	0.50(.21)*	1.65
University					1.54(.17)***	4.66	2.24(.78)**	9.46	1.56(.27)***	4.76	1.34(.24)***	3.84
Household Income					-0.00(.02)	0.99	0.15(.12)	1.16	0.01(.04)	1.01	-0.03(.03)	0.96
Social Class (Manual)												
Unemployed			-0.18(.15)	0.86	-0.21(.15)	0.80	0.90(1.14)	2.47	-0.65(.29)*	0.52	-0.17(.20)	0.84
Farmer			-1.42(.43)**	0.92	-1.30(.43)**	0.27	–	–	1.36(.62)*	0.25	-1.01(.61)	0.36
Nonmanual			0.32(.13)*	1.79	-0.30(.15)	0.73	-0.92(.82)	0.39	-0.32(.24)	0.72	-0.27(.21)	0.76
Self-employed			-0.16(.16)	1.38	-0.43(.17)*	0.64	-0.43(.80)	0.64	-0.56(.27)*	0.56	-0.42(.25)	0.65
Generation (Ref. post-1980)												
Foundation	0.16(.43)	1.17										
Interim	0.49(.18)**	1.64										
Intercept	-3.84(.56)***		-4.32(.51)***		-4.89(.55)***		6.76(11.25)		-1.82(2.48)		-2.93(1.26)*	
Log Likelihood	-1426.89		-1414.59		-1368.94		-70.16		-540.99		-730.13	
N. (obs.)	6257		6257		6257		482		2116		3549	
Pseudo R²	0.1732		0.1803		0.2067		0.2644		0.2120		0.2104	

Note: Entries are multivariate logistic regression logit estimates with standard error values in parentheses and odds ratios (exponentiated B). Data: WVS, rounds: 1990/1996/2001/2007/2011.
Significance levels: *p < .05, **p < .01, ***p < .001.

bearing on the current discussion of a 'rising participatory Gezi generation,' which is examined in some other papers in this special issue. At least for what concerns our analyses – keeping in mind that all of our data pre-date Gezi – we do not find evidence for this pattern in our data. There might be several reasons underlying this. The first explanation that comes to mind is that the macroeconomic and macropolitical effects might have counterbalanced each other in socializing potential generations. Our descriptive findings shown in the Table 1 support this idea. An alternative explanation could be that, the Gezi generation is still too young to appear in our results. Each explanation requires further scrutiny and presents avenues for further research. Yet, even though European Social Survey data asking respondents' participation in the last 12 months also reveal generational patterns similar to what we have found,[26] if there were significant differences between the generations, there would not be any way of knowing with data in hand, except making predictions in accordance with theories, whether socialization mechanism or period effect was primarily responsible of this difference, owing to the fact that the WVS question does not reveal the exact date that the activity took place.

Our third hypothesis was designed as a test of Lipset's working-class authoritarianism thesis. We hypothesized in line with Lipset's thesis that the members of the working class are less likely to participate in politics than the members of the middle class and this is largely due to the former group's low education and to a lesser extent low income. The analysis run with the pooled data coming from all the generations validated Lipset's thesis to a large extent. It was shown that for participating in all the three unconventional repertoires of political action, the members of the nonmanual class outstripped the members of the manual class and the differences between the two classes disappeared when the education and income variables were controlled. However, the whole picture changed when the generation factor was taken into account. Our fourth group of analysis showed that although it does not play a direct one, generation plays an indirect role in political activism operating via social class structure. We found that for all the three unconventional repertoires of action, the total number of significant differences in the interim generation (which is ten) is higher than the total number of significant differences in the foundation (which is one) and post-1980 (which is zero) generations.[27] This finding supports our fourth hypothesis suggesting that for those generations, which have come of age under an authoritarian politico-juridical order, the social classes are equalized with respect to their members' level of political activity. Yet, the most interesting is the finding related to the analysis of the interim generation, for which we expected Lipset's thesis to hold true due to its members' non-exposure to system-level authoritarianism. Surprisingly, our finding run explicitly counter to Lipset's prediction. We found that, in the interim generation the manual class is not less activity-prone than the nonmanual class. By looking at this picture, we can conclude that Lipset's thesis is not invalid only for those generations which were socialized by system-level authoritarianism but also for those which were not. Moreover, for all the three forms of action in the interim generation, the total number of inter-class differences between the manual class and the two low classes (which is four) was greater than the total number of inter-class differences between the manual class and the two high classes (which is two). In other words, the manual class resembles to the two high classes with a greater degree than it resembles to the two low classes. By looking at this extra finding, we can conclude that for those generations, which were not exposed to system-level authoritarianism during their formative years, the main clash regarding political activism seems to be between the traditional and modern classes. This suggests a role for modernization effect. This finding also promotes modernization theory's classification of the social classes that was based on traditional/modern dichotomy against Lipset's categorization of the classes which regards manual/working class among the low classes.

Notes

1. See Crozier, Huntington, and Watanuki, "The Crisis of Democracy"; Putnam, "Bowling alone"; and Pharr and Putnam, *Disaffected Democracies*.
2. Inglehart, "The Silent Revolution"; Welzel, Inglehart, and Deutsch, "Social Capital"; and Inglehart and Welzel. *Modernization, Cultural Change, and Democracy*.
3. World Bank, "Turkey."
4. Beck and Jennings, "Political Periods and Political Participation," and Beck and Jennings, "Pathways to Participation."
5. 1982 Turkish Constitution, Article 87.
6. 1982 Turkish Constitution, Article 131.
7. Established in 1994 in accordance with 1982 Turkish Constitution, Article 133.
8. 1982 Turkish Constitution, Article 143.
9. See for further information the Data and Methods section.
10. Lipset, "Working-Class Authoritarianism," 277–281.
11. Mannheim, "The Sociological Problem of Generations."
12. The Turkish surveys were conducted by Boğaziçi University under the chairmanship of Yılmaz Esmer.
13. A detailed overview of the survey items used in the analyses is presented in the appendix.
14. Beck and Jennings, "Political Periods and Political Participation."
15. Mannheim, "The Sociological Problem of Generations."
16. Nie, Junn, and Stehlik-Barry, *Education and Citizenship*.
17. Powell and Cowart, *Political Campaign Communication*.
18. Erikson, *Childhood and Society*.
19. Niemi and Hepburn, "The Rebirth of Political Socialization."
20. See for a similar method of categorization generations by historical period, see Grasso *et al.*, "Thatcher's Children."

21. Erikson and Goldthorpe, *The Constant Flux.*
22. See, Mishler and Rose, "What are the Origins of Political Trust?", and Evans and Rose, "Understanding Education's Influence."
23. See Bratton, "Critical Mass Theory Revisited."
24. See Grasso, "Age, Period and Cohort Analysis," and Dunn, Grasso, and Saunders, "Unemployment and Attitudes to Work," for the inclusion of sociodemographic controls.
25. See Grasso and Giugni, "Protest Participation," for using conventional, that is, petition, and unconventional, that is, protest, repertoires of political action as separate dependent variables.
26. See Grasso, *Generations,* and Grasso, "Political Participation," or results showing similar generational patterns with 'last 12 months data' from the ESS.
27. All the differences are at the 95 percent and higher confidence levels.

Acknowledgements

We would like to thank to the World Values Survey Association, especially Professor Yılmaz Esmer and his team for the development of World Values Survey data set for Turkey. We would also like to thank to Professor Ayhan Kaya and Dr Cristiano Bee as well as Professor Paul Kubicek and our anonymous reviewer for the efforts they made in the publication process. This work was financially supported by Turkish Ministry of Education Study Abroad Program.

Disclosure statement

No potential conflict of interest was reported by the authors.

References

1982 Turkish Constitution. Accessed August 14, 2016. https://www.tbmm.gov.tr/anayasa/anayasa82.htm.

Beck, Paul Allen, and M. Kent Jennings. "Political Periods and Political Participation." *American Political Science Review* 73, no. 3 (1979): 737–750.

Beck, Paul Allen, and M. Kent Jennings. "Pathways to Participation." *American Political Science Review* 76, no. 1 (1982): 94–108.

Bratton, Kathleen A. "Critical Mass Theory Revisited: The Behaviour and Success of Token Women in State Legislatures." *Politics & Gender* 1, no. 1 (2005): 97–125.

Crozier, Michel, Samuel P. Huntington, and Joji Watanuki. *The Crisis of Democracy: Report on the Governability of Democracies to the Trilateral Commission.* New York: New York University Press, 1975.

Dalton, Russell J. "Citizenship Norms and the Expansion of Political Participation." *Political studies* 56, no. 1 (2008): 76–98.

Dunn, Andrew, Maria T. Grasso, and Clare Saunders. "Unemployment and Attitudes to Work: Asking the 'Right' Question." *Work, Employment and Society* 28, no. 6 (2014): 904–925.

Erikson, Erik H. *Childhood and Society.* New York: Norton, 1993.

Erikson, Robert, and John H. Goldthorpe. *The Constant Flux: A Study of Class Mobility in Industrial Societies.* New York: Oxford University Press, 1992.

Erikson, Robert, John H. Goldthorpe, and Lucienne Portocarero. "Intergenerational Class Mobility in Three Western European Societies: England, France and Sweden." *The British Journal of Sociology* 30, no. 4 (1979): 415–441.

Evans, Geoffrey, and Pauline Rose. "Understanding Education's Influence on Support for Democracy in Sub-Saharan Africa." *Journal of Development Studies* 48, no. 4 (2012): 498–515.

Grasso, Maria. T. "Political Participation in Western Europe". D.Phil. Thesis., University of Oxford, Nuffield College, 2011.

Grasso, Maria. T. "The Differential Impact of Education on Young People's Political Activism: Comparing Italy and the United Kingdom." *Comparative Sociology* 12, no. 1 (2013): 1–30.

Grasso, Maria T. "Age, Period and Cohort Analysis in a Comparative Context: Political Generations and Political Participation Repertoires in Western Europe." *Electoral Studies* 33, no. 1 (2014): 63–76.

Grasso, Maria T. *Generations, Political Participation and Social Change in Western Europe.* London: Routledge, 2016.

Grasso, Maria, Stephen Farrall, Emily Gray, Colin Hay, and Will Jennings. "Thatcher's Children, Blair's Babies, Political Socialisation and Trickle-Down Value-Change: An Age, Period and Cohort Analysis." *British Journal of Political Science*, forthcoming.

Grasso, Maria T., and Marco Giugni. "Protest Participation and Economic Crisis: The Conditioning Role of Political Opportunities." *European Journal of Political Research* 55, no. 4 (2016): 663–680.

Inglehart, Ronald. "The Silent Revolution in Europe: Intergenerational Change in Post-Industrial Societies." *American Political Science Review* 65, no. 4 (1971): 991–1017.

Inglehart, Ronald, and Christian Welzel. *Modernization, Cultural Change, and Democracy: The Human Development Sequence.* Cambridge: Cambridge University Press, 2005.

Lipset, Seymour Martin. "Democracy and Working-Class Authoritarianism." *American Sociological Review* 24, no. 4 (1959): 482–501.

Lipset, Seymour Martin. "'Working-Class Authoritarianism': A Reply to Miller and Riessman." *British Journal of Sociology* 12, no. 3 (1961): 277–281.

Mannheim, Karl. "The Sociological Problem of Generations." In *Essays on the Sociology of Knowledge*, edited by Paul Kecskemeti, 276–322. New York: Oxford University Press, 1952 [First Published: 1927–28].

Mishler, William, and Richard Rose. "Trajectories of Fear and Hope Support for Democracy in Post-Communist Europe." *Comparative Political Studies* 28, no. 4 (1996): 553–581.

Mishler, William, and Richard Rose. "What are the Origins of Political Trust? Testing Institutional and Cultural Theories in Post-Communist Societies." *Comparative Political Studies* 34, no. 1 (2001): 30–62.

Nie, Norman, Jane Junn, and Ken Stehlik-Barry. *Education and Citizenship in America.* Chicago: University of Chicago Press, 1996.

Niemi, Richard G., and Mary A. Hepburn. "The Rebirth of Political Socialization." *Perspectives on Political Science* 24, no. 1 (1995): 7–16.

Norris, Pippa. *Democratic Phoenix: Reinventing Political Activism.* Cambridge: Cambridge University Press, 2002.

Pharr, Susan J., and Robert D. Putnam. *Disaffected Democracies: What's Troubling the Trilateral Countries?* Princeton, NJ: Princeton University Press, 2000.

Powell, Larry, and Joseph Cowart. *Political Campaign Communication: Inside and Out.* New York: Routledge, 2003.

Putnam, Robert D. "Bowling Alone: America's Declining Social Capital." *Journal of Democracy* 6, no. 1 (1995): 65–78.

Welzel, Christian, Ronald Inglehart, and Franziska Deutsch. "Social Capital, Voluntary Associations and Collective Action: Which Aspects of Social Capital have the Greatest 'Civic' Payoff?" *Journal of Civil Society* 1, no. 2 (2005): 121–146.

World Bank. "Turkey: Europe and Central Asia (Developing Only)." 2016. Accessed May 01, 2016. http://data.worldbank.org/country/turkey.

Appendix. Variables in the analyses.

Variable name	Original value	Recoded value	Questionnaire wording
Signing a petition* Joining in a boycott* Attending lawful demonstrations*	1 = Have done 2 = Might do 3 = Would never do	0 = Not done 1 = Done	Here are some forms of political action that people can take. Please indicate, for each one, whether you have done any of these things, whether you might do it or would never under any circumstances do it.
Generation[†]	1910/1994 (birth year)	1910 < Birth year < 1944 1945 < Birth year < 1964 1965 < Birth year < 1994	Can you tell me your year of birth please? This means you are ____ years old.
Social Class[†]	13 = employer manager of establishment with 10 or more employed 16 = employer manager of establishment with less than 10 employed	13/16 = 5 self-employed	In which profession/occupation do you work? If more than one job, the main job? What is/ was your job there?
	21 = Professional worker 22 = middle level nonmanual office worker 23 = supervisory nonmanual office worker 24 = junior level nonmanual 25 = nonmanual office worker 31 = forman and supervisor	21/22/23/24/25/31 = 4 nonmanual	
	32 = skilled manual 33 = semi-skilled manual 34 = unskilled manual	32/33/34 = 3 manual	
	41 = farmer: has own farm. 42 = agrarian worker	41/42 = 2 farmer	
	51 = member of armed forces 61 = never had a job	51 = 4 nonmanual 61 = 1 unemployed	
Age Squared		age*age Dummy coded	
Survey Years	1990/1996/2001/2007/2011		

(Continued)

Appendix. Continued.

Variable name	Original value	Recoded value	Questionnaire wording
Gender (female)	1 = Male 2 = Female	0 = Male 1 = Female	
Education	1 = Inadequately completed elementary education. 2 = Completed elementary education. 3 = Incomplete secondary school (technical). 4 = Complete secondary school (technical). 5 = Incomplete secondary school (university prep.) 6 = Complete secondary school (university prep.) 7 = Some university without degree 8 = University with degree	1/2 = 1 elementary 3/4/5/6 = 2 secondary 7/8 = 3 university	What is the highest education level that you have attained? (NOTE: if the respondent indicates to be a student, code highest level s/he expects to complete)
Household Income	1/10	1/10	Here is a scale of household incomes on which 1 indicates the lowest income decile and 10 the highest income decile in your country. We would like to know in what group your household is. Please, specify the appropriate number, counting all wages, salaries, pensions and other incomes that come in.
Self-political Positioning	1/10	1/10	In political matters, people talk of 'the left' and 'the right'. How would you place your views on this scale, generally speaking?
Political interest	1 = Very interested 2 = Somewhat interested 3 = Not very interested 4 = Not at all interested	1 = Not at all interested 2 = Not very interested 3 = Somewhat interested 4 = Very interested	How interested would you say you are in politics? Are you …
Importance of politics	1 = Very important 2 = Rather important 3 = Not very important 4 = Not at all important	1 = Not at all important 2 = Not very important 3 = Rather important 4 = Very important	For each of the following, indicate how important it is in your life. Would you say it is … (politics)

*Dependent Variables.
†Key Independent Variables.

Voting Behavior of the Youth in Turkey: What Drives Involvement in or Causes Alienation from Conventional Political Participation?

Ayşegül Kayaoğlu ⓘ

ABSTRACT
The decline of conventional political participation of the youth is a serious concern in many countries worldwide. Studying the Turkish example, this paper aims to empirically analyze the determinants of youngsters' (non)voting behavior. The analysis shows that lifestyle is the most important factor, reflecting the importance of the youth's everyday practices on their conventional political participation. Besides, being female, having higher levels of education and residing in an urban area increase the probability of abstaining. Moreover, 'economic voting' exists for youngsters as they are found to be punishing the ruling Justice and Development Party (AKP) for economic prospects unpromising either individually or societally. For first-time voters, lifestyle and the 2013 Gezi protests are the main determinants of voting behavior. Furthermore, there is persistence in abstaining from voting as having abstained in the 2011 general elections increases the probability of abstaining again by 18 percent. The analysis of disillusioned youth demonstrates that Gezi protests have increased the probability of their conventional political participation; they can be associated either with a decline in their probability of voting for the AKP, or of being indecisive and/ or abstaining. A factor change analysis, however, finds that the abstained and indecisive Kurdish youth's preferences have shifted towards pro-Kurdish Peace and Democracy Party post-Gezi.

1. Introduction

The decline in conventional political participation among youth is of serious concern in contemporary societies. Although this problem has been widely studied in established democracies,[1] there is much less evidence for developing countries. In Turkey's case, military takeovers, especially the 1980 military coup, are blamed for the 'apoliticization' of young people. However, the *occupygezi* movement, which started on 28 May 2013 in Taksim's Gezi Park as a protest of an urban development plan before turning into the largest protest against ruling Justice and Development Party (*Adalet ve Kalkınma Partisi*, AKP) policies, proved that the lack of interest among young people in politics, if there was any, was more in the conventional form of political participation as thousands of young people were on the streets in 80 of Turkey's 81 provinces in May and June 2013.[2]

The questions of whether young Turkish people are non-active in conventional politics or not, and, more importantly, what the determinants of them being active in conventional politics are, have not been studied in detail even though young people in Turkey have a notable importance for election results because of their share among voters. In addition, the young population is important to all the political parties as their proportion among the voting population keeps increasing in each election. In 2015, around 15 million voters were aged 18–30, yet they are still underrepresented in parliament. When we look at the socio-economic situation of Turkish youth, the picture is also not bright. Youth unemployment is higher than overall unemployment in Turkey. According to recent Organization for Economic Cooperation and Development (OECD) statistics,[3] the share of the young population that is not in employment, education or training (NEET) is highest in Turkey among all OECD countries. For men aged 20–24, this rate is 20.5 percent; for women in the same age group, it is 51 percent. So, we are talking about a population group which has both a very low level of political representation in the National Assembly and has a very vulnerable socio-economic portrait, although its importance increases day by day.

Even though young voters are very important for the Turkish election results, they were specifically addressed only recently in political campaigns. Before the general election of 7 June 2015, the hash-tag 'my first vote, my first excitement' circulated on Twitter together with a video clip of the ruling AKP's election song, which specifically targeted young people. Although one in three Turkish voters is under 30, this was the first audio-visual electoral campaign aimed at Turkish youth. As this segment of the population gains power in terms of the effect of its votes, it is imaginable that their socio-economic situation will affect their voting preferences. Therefore, finding the factors that determine the voting behavior of the youth in Turkey is of crucial importance, both to understand and shed light on future electoral outcomes.

There are some survey studies after 1999 which specifically focus on the political participation of the youth in Turkey. The ARI Movement conducted three surveys in 1999, 2003, and 2008, which all aimed to understand both conventional and unconventional political participation of young people in

Turkey. Summary statistics of those surveys show that the percentage of young people who were voting in elections decreased from 1999 to 2008. It was 62 percent in 1999, 53 percent in 2003, and 48 percent in 2008. Another study conducted in 2009 also presented the descriptive findings of the data from 1203 individuals aged between 16 and 30, collected in 2007 in several city centers in Turkey. It finds that only 9 percent of young people in that survey reported having 'a very high interest' in conventional politics.[4] Around 60 percent of them, however, say that they are 'not at all interested' in politics. Another study[5] uses a 2014 survey of 2508 individuals aged between 18 and 25 to understand the role of socio-economic status of the young people in Turkey on their political participation and, presenting the descriptive statistics of the survey results, its authors argued that young people have more inclination towards conventional political participation than unconventional ones. Thus, the general conclusion of these descriptive studies about the political participation of the youth in Turkey is that young people have low levels of political participation, which is not surprising when we consider the general trend of political participation in general public in Turkey.

Although the above-mentioned studies are descriptive, there is some recent empirical analysis of the youth's political activism in Turkey. A recent study,[6] for example, analyzes a 2014 individual-level data of 2295 individuals across 18 provinces in Turkey to understand whether being young matters for the level of political participation. It argues that there is no effect of age on both conventional and unconventional political participation when it controls for gender, economic status, and residential type. Then, it discusses that the reason behind young people dominating the Gezi Part protests can be understood through politicized collective identities rather than demographic or socio-economic factors. In addition to those studies which directly focus on the young population in Turkey, there are also some micro-level studies of voting behavior that briefly mention young people's conventional political participation by looking at the impact of age on voting behavior. Aiming to understand the party preferences in Turkey using survey data, one study[7] argues that young male voters form the AKP's electoral base. Another study[8] employing micro-econometric analysis argues that young people are, on average, more inclined to vote for AKP when other control variables are held constant. Apart from emphasizing the differences and similarities between political participation of older and younger citizens in Turkey, there are also some studies that try to understand the reasons behind these changes in participation trends between different generations. One of those studies,[9] for instance, argues that low political participation of the young in Turkey can be attributed to the low trust levels of them towards the Turkish political system which can be linked to their personal economic uncertainties and military takeover experiences in Turkish political history.

Consequently, it seems that there is an interest in understanding the political participation of the young people in Turkey since 1999 but there are still many unanswered questions about the issue.

Empirically analyzing an individual vote intention function, this study aims to understand the voting behavior of young people by answering the following research questions in particular:

(1) What are the non-economic and economic factors that determine the voting behavior of young people in Turkey?
(2) Does ethnicity matter in the voting behavior of young people?
(3) Which factors determine the voting behavior of first-time voters?
(4) Are economic voting theories valid for the young population?
(5) How do non-conventional forms of civic/political activism affect the voting behavior; in other words, what is the impact of the Gezi protests on average on voting behavior?
(6) What are the explanatory factors for disillusioned young voters?
(7) Is there any persistence in abstaining?

The structure of this paper is as follows: Section 2 will briefly explain the data and methodology. Section 3 will present the results of the empirical analysis with eight subsections devoted to the research questions, and Section 4 is the conclusion.

2. Data and methodology

Pooled data of monthly *KONDA (Konda Research and Consultancy) Barometer* survey results from January 2013 to December 2014 are used for the empirical analysis. *KONDA Barometers* are collected in the first week of each month, and they aim to measure the political preferences of voters in Turkey. Monthly data are collected from a nationally representative sample in accordance with the election results.[10] Thus, the data collected from 12 regions in Turkey show similar coverage with each region's proportion of voters. The respondents are asked not only about their choice in the previous general elections but also about their voting behavior if there were a new election today. The data used for the analysis of this paper comprise only the data for young people whose ages are between 18 and 25. Detailed information about the sample and descriptive statistics of the variables in empirical models are provided in the Appendix.

We employed the Multinomial Logit (MNLM) when analyzing the determinants of voting behavior for various alternatives as it provides more information about the alternatives compared to a binary choice model, which only provides information about the incumbent party choice vs. the rest.[11] The Binary Logit Model was used to analyze the determinants of disillusioned youth where the dependent variable is a dummy variable. The likelihood-ratio tests for independent variables were carried out to decide about their inclusion in the final model specification. The Wald test for combining alternatives in MNLM was carried out and found that all the alternative outcome pairs (of voting choices) are distinguishable. This means there is no need to combine the alternatives of the dependent variables. In addition to providing marginal effects of each independent variable on each category, factor change coefficients are also presented, as marginal effects are only informative about the effect of discrete changes in a specific independent variable on the dependent variable, whereas odds ratios (factor change coefficients) inform us about the dynamics among different outcomes. For example, as explained in detail below, the marginal effect of the Gezi Park protests shows the percentage increase in the probability of voting for the opposition Republican Peoples' Party (*Cumhuriyet Halk Partisi*, CHP) and the Peace and Democracy Party (*Barış ve Demokrasi Partisi*, BDP[12]), but the effect of the Gezi Park protests on the voting behavior for the CHP relative to the BDP will be answered through factor change coefficients.

3. Empirical analysis

This section answers the research questions listed in Section 1 of the paper using the results of empirical analysis.

Factors that determine voting behavior of young people in Turkey

Table 1 provides the marginal effects of the multinomial logit model for all the alternative outcomes, namely voting decision choices if an election were held today. There are seven choices: AKP, CHP, MHP (*Milliyetçi Hareket Partisi*, Nationalist Action Party), BDP, indecisive, abstain, and others. The 'others' category comprises votes for independent nominees and political parties other than the AKP, the CHP, the MHP, and the BDP that receive a very small percentage of the votes. Marginal effects show that being a woman increases one's probability of voting for the CHP. Furthermore, the MHP and the BDP get more votes from males compared to females. It is also interesting that young females have a higher inclination to being indecisive or abstaining. The data consist of only young people aged 18–25, but the findings for the variable 'age' show that older young people have a higher probability of voting for the CHP and the BDP and a lower probability of voting for the MHP, when other variables are held constant. Gender and age do not seem to be important when the AKP is the choice. The results for what impact education levels have is interesting as they show that more educated young people are less inclined to vote for the AKP and the BDP when controlled for other variables. This, in fact, confirms a general claim especially with regard to AKP

Table 1. Marginal effects of multinomial logit model for alternative outcomes using total sample (dependent variable: vote choice today).

Variables	AKP	CHP	MHP	BDP	INDECISIVE	ABSTAINER
Female	.007	.039***	−.087***	−.015**	.047***	.017***
	(.012)	(.008)	(.009)	(.007)	(.01)	(.006)
Age	−.003	.008***	−.004**	.005***	−.003	−.004***
	(.002)	(.002)	(.002)	(.001)	(.002)	(.001)
Education level (scaled from 1 to 7)	−.030***	.022***	.004	−.017***	.012***	.010**
	(.006)	(.005)	(.005)	(.004)	(.006)	(.004)
Job status						
(Reference category: employed)						
Unemployed	.004	.019	−.008	−.001	.027	−.035***
	(.019)	(.015)	(.013)	(.011)	(.017)	(.009)
Student	−.068***	.038***	.005	−.001	.012	.002
	(.014)	(.010)	(.009)	(.008)	(.012)	(.007)
Housewife	.102***	−.026*	−.051***	−.005	.024	−.027***
	(.022)	(.015)	(.014)	(.011)	(.017)	(.010)
Lifestyle						
(Reference category: religious conservative)						
Modern	−.315***	.364***	−.003	−.022***	−.012	−.006
	(.014)	(.023)	(.012)	(.008)	(.013)	(.008)
Traditional conservative	−.169***	.176***	.039**	−.027***	.006	−.018**
	(.014)	(.024)	(.013)	(.008)	(.014)	(.009)
Economic voting						
Household income	−.001	.023***	.011***	−.022***	−.009***	−.005*
	(.005)	(.004)	(.003)	(.003)	(.004)	(.003)
Sociotropic-prospective	−.172***	.089***	.069***	.008	−.021***	.023***
	(.014)	(.010)	(.009)	(.007)	(.010)	(.007)
Egotropic-prospective	−.060***	.002	.021**	.009	.023***	.003
	(.012)	(.009)	(.009)	(.248)	(.010)	(.007)
Residential area						
(Reference category: rural)						
Urban	−.011	−.043***	−.021**	.001	.026*	.038***
	(.015)	(.010)	(.010)	(.009)	(.014)	(.011)
Metropol	.003	−.046***	−.042***	−.003	.039***	.040***
	(.014)	(.010)	(.010)	(.008)	(.012)	(.010)
Gezi Park Protests	−.046***	.033***	.021***	.032***	−.018*	−.026***
	(.012)	(.008)	(.008)	(.006)	(.010)	(.007)
Predicted Probability	.32	.16	.14	.09	.19	.08
# of obs	8864	8864	8864	8864	8864	8864

voters, as they are argued to be less educated. Moreover, a higher education increases the probability to vote for the CHP more than any other political party. More educated young people were also found to have a higher likelihood of being indecisive and abstaining.

When we look at the impact of job status, unemployed young people are found to be more likely to vote, and unemployment does not affect their party preference. Furthermore, students are around 7 percent less likely to vote for the AKP and 2.2 percent more likely to vote for the CHP. Another important but scarcely studied issue is the decisions of 'housegirls' – housewives below the age of 25. Being a housewife was found to increase the probability of voting for the AKP by 10 percent and had a negative impact on voting for the CHP and the MHP.

Compared with other variables in the model, lifestyle choice was found to be very important and powerful in explaining voting choices. Empirical analysis finds that people who define themselves as 'modern' are more inclined to vote for the CHP. Furthermore, being modern compared to being a religious conservative decreases the likelihood of voting for the AKP by 31.5 percent. Interestingly, a traditional conservative young person is also less inclined to vote for the AKP compared to a religious conservative. It is important to note that the effects of lifestyle choices are the same for the AKP and the BDP, but the magnitude is greater for the AKP.

Another general finding concerns the role of economics on voting choices. Economic voting theories suggest that the incumbent party will be punished if there is any deterioration in a voter's own economic well-being or in a country's economic situation. Table 1 shows that young people punish the AKP if they expect both national and personal economic well-being in the future to deteriorate. More interestingly, young people are more likely to punish the AKP when the national economy worsens; they seem to link the relationship between the deterioration in their personal income with government policies to a lesser extent. Moreover, we can say that the votes lost by the AKP due to a worsened national economy are distributed between the CHP and the MHP if they are cast.

When we look at the impact of the place of residence on voting behavior, we find no effect on the voting choice of the AKP, contrary to claim that the AKP receives more votes from rural areas. Another interesting finding is that young people in rural areas are more likely to vote for the CHP compared to those who live in urban areas and metropolises. Furthermore, young people in urban areas and metropolises are more likely to abstain. Last but not least, the Gezi Park protests in Turkey were found to increase the conventional political participation of young people. They decreased the probability of being indecisive and abstaining by around 2 percent and 3 percent, respectively. In terms of voting behavior, it seems that the Gezi Park protests decreased the probability of voting only for the AKP but increased the probability of voting for all of the opposition parties. The following subsections will analyze these generalized findings in detail, especially with regard to the voting movements from one political party to another.

Role of ethnicity in determining voting behavior

This subsection analyzes the role of ethnicity in party choice by estimating the empirical models using two different subsamples, one for Turkish youth and one for Kurdish youth. These two groups were chosen because they are the main ethnic groups in the country. Table 2 presents the marginal effects for young Turks, whereas Table 3 presents the marginal effect results for Kurdish youth.

Table 2. Marginal effects of multinomial logit model for alternative outcomes using sample of ONLY TURKISH YOUTH (dependent variable: vote choice today).

Variables	AKP	CHP	MHP	BDP	INDECISIVE	ABSTAINER
Female	−.002	.049***	−.113***	−.002	.058***	.023***
	(.014)	(.011)	(.011)	(.002)	(.011)	(.007)
Age	−.005*	.014***	−.003	.001***	−.003	−.005***
	(.003)	(.002)	(.002)	(.0003)	(.002)	(.002)
Education level (scaled from	−.041***	.018**	.007	−.001***	.020***	.012**
1 to 7)	(.008)	(.007)	(.007)	(.0008)	(.007)	(.005)
Job status						
(Reference category: employed)						
Unemployed	.002	.025	−.007	−.008	.018	−.041***
	(.022)	(.013)	(.017)	(.005)	(.020)	(.009)
Student	−.075***	.057***	.004	−.003	.005	−.007
	(.016)	(.013)	(.012)	(.002)	(.014)	(.009)
Housewife	.127***	−.045**	−.053***	−.002	.021	−.029***
	(.026)	(.015)	(.018)	(.002)	(.021)	(.010)
Lifestyle						
(Reference category: religious conservative)						
Modern	−.336***	.381***	−.025	.000	−.008	−.002
	(.014)	(.025)	(.015)	(.002)	(.005)	(.010)
Traditional conservative	−.171***	.161***	.027*	−.003	.006	−.010
	(.017)	(.029)	(.017)	(.002)	(.018)	(.011)
Economic voting						
Household income	−.006	.016***	.007	−.000	−.009***	−.006*
	(.006)	(.005)	(.005)	(.001)	(.004)	(.003)
Sociotropic-prospective	−.177***	.097***	.081***	.003*	−.025**	.016*
	(.014)	(.012)	(.012)	(.002)	(.012)	(.008)
Egotropic-prospective	−.060***	.005	.028**	−.000	.023*	.005
	(.014)	(.011)	(.012)	(.002)	(.012)	(.008)
Residential area						
(Reference category: rural)						
Urban	−.012	−.048***	−.022*	−.003	.025	.038***
	(.018)	(.014)	(.013)	(.002)	(.016)	(.011)
Metropol	.008	−.041***	−.048***	.000	.038***	.031**
	(.017)	(.014)	(.013)	(.002)	(.015)	(.013)
Gezi Park protests	−.046***	.049***	.036***	.002	−.016	−.027***
	(.012)	(.011)	(.011)	(.002)	(.012)	(.008)
Predicted probability	.31	.20	.18	.004	.20	.08
# of obs	6811	6811	6811	6811	6811	6811

Gender and age were found to not affect the voting behavior of Kurdish youth in Turkey. However, a higher education level seems to have a different effect on the likelihood to vote for the BDP. Although a higher level of education decreases the probability that a young Turk would vote for the BDP, it increases the probability of a Kurdish youth to vote for the BDP. Moreover, job status is not found to be statistically important for young Kurds but does appear to be important for young Turks. Turkish housegirls are found to be less inclined to vote for the CHP and MHP but are 12.7 percent more likely to vote for the AKP, when other variables are controlled for. Furthermore, lifestyle choices are more influential on the voting behavior of young Turks. For example, the likelihood of a young Turk voting for the AKP is almost 34 percent lower if the person in question defines him or herself as 'modern'; this figure is 18 percent lower for a young Kurd.

Table 3. Marginal effects of multinomial logit model for alternative outcomes using sample of ONLY KURDISH YOUTH (dependent variable: vote choice today).

Variables	AKP	CHP	MHP	BDP	ABSTAINER
Education level (scaled from 1 to 7)	−.047***	.006*	.006***	.032**	.018***
	(.012)	(.003)	(.002)	(.013)	(.007)
Economic voting					
Household income	.013	.008**	−.001	−.017	.003
	(.015)	(.003)	(.002)	(.017)	(.006)
Sociotropic-prospective	−.128***	.017**	−.0002	.097***	.034**
	(.034)	(.009)	(.004)	(.033)	(.017)
Egotropic-prospective	−.083***	−.004	.003	.068*	−.009
	(.030)	(.006)	(.005)	(.042)	(.015)
Lifestyle					
(Reference category: religious conservative)					
Modern	−.181***	.115**	−.001	.081	−.002
	(.034)	(.057)	(.005)	(.081)	(.018)
Traditional conservative	−.123***	.062*	−.005	.066*	−.010
	(.030)	(.029)	(.005)	(.040)	(.017)
Residential area					
(Reference category: rural)					
Urban	−.317	−.024	−.007	−.434	−.036
	(2.96)	(.108)	(.100)	(5.54)	(2.08)
Metropol	−.130	−.023	−.006	−.291	.037
	(9.78)	(.350)	(.210)	(12.93)	(4.31)
Gezi Park protests	−.030	−.004	−.013*	.094**	−.029*
	(.031)	(.007)	(.101)	(.038)	(.017)
Predicted probability	.31	.02	.008	.47	.07
# of obs	1493	1493	1493	1493	1493

Interestingly, both Turkish and Kurdish youth punish the AKP for the deterioration in the national economy; however, they reward different political parties instead. Worsened national economic conditions lead young Turks to vote more for the CHP and the MHP, while young Kurds divert their votes more to the BDP. In terms of egotropic-prospective behavior, we observe that young Kurds are harsher when it comes to that aspect with regard to the AKP; their likelihood of voting for the AKP decreases by 8.3 percent while the probability that they will vote for the BDP increases by around 7 percent when their personal economic situation is believed to have deteriorated. When we look at the effect of the Gezi Park protests, we see that for both ethnicities it increased political participation. The Gezi Park protests were found to decrease the likelihood of both groups abstaining. Furthermore, it appears the decreased votes for the AKP from young Turks shifted to the CHP and the MHP after the Gezi Park protests. However, for the Kurdish youth, they only increased the likelihood that they would vote for the BDP by 9.4 percent.

First-time voters

This subsection analyzes the voting decisions of young people who had never voted before as they were below the legal minimum age of 18 and, thus, if an election were held today, they would be first-time voters. A total of 2109 individuals out of 8864 in the data set are first-time voters. The marginal effects for the empirical model for this subpopulation are presented in Table 4. It appears being female increases the likelihood of voting for the CHP by 4.1 percent compared to males, while it decreases the likelihood of a vote for the MHP by 10.9 percent and for the BDP by 2.6 percent. Furthermore, females seem to be more indecisive and abstain compared to males. For first-time voters, a higher level of education was found to decrease the likelihood of a vote for the AKP by around 5 percent and for the BDP by around 2 percent while it increases the likelihood of a vote for the CHP by around 3 percent, which is higher compared to the effect of education for the general population. As is the case for the young population overall, first-time voters also act in line with what economic voting theories suggest. They punish the government for the economic downturn at both the national and individual level. When we look at the impact of lifestyle, we can see in Table 4 that first-time voters who define themselves as religious conservatives are more inclined to vote for the AKP and the BDP compared to modern and traditional conservatives, though the effect on the AKP vote is much larger.

Table 4. Marginal effects of multinomial logit model for alternative outcomes using sample of ONLY FIRST-TIME VOTERS (dependent variable: vote choice today).

Variables	AKP	CHP	MHP	BDP	INDECISIVE	ABSTAINER
Female	.018	.041***	−.109***	−.026***	.032*	.050***
	(.021)	(.015)	(.016)	(.010)	(.019)	(.014)
Age	.013	.006	−.002	.010***	−.005	−.017***
	(.009)	(.006)	(.007)	(.003)	(.008)	(.007)
Education level (scaled from	−.046***	.029**	.006	−.019***	.016	.018
1 to 7)	(.012)	(.012)	(.012)	(.006)	(.013)	(.010)
Economic voting						
Household income	−.009	.030***	.003	−.011**	−.008	−.008
	(.010)	(.007)	(.008)	(.005)	(.009)	(.007)
Sociotropic-prospective	−.140***	.080***	.062***	.028**	−.039*	.012
	(.028)	(.019)	(.020)	(.013)	(.021)	(.016)
Egotropic-prospective	−.058**	−.009	.018	−.004	.034	−.001
	(.025)	(.018)	(.02)	(.012)	(.022)	(.016)
Lifestyle						
(Reference category: religious conservative)						
Modern	−.253***	.298***	−.015	−.043***	.015	−.003
	(.028)	(.042)	(.024)	(.013)	(.029)	(.019)
Traditional conservative	−.150***	.170***	−.005	−.031***	.025	−.009
	(.029)	(.049)	(.026)	(.012)	(.031)	(.021)
Residential area						
(Reference category: rural)						
Urban	−.007	−.053***	.058**	.011	−.046*	−.001
	(0.31)	(.019)	(.028)	(.015)	(.025)	(.020)
Metropol	−.005	−.046**	.023	−.005	−.021	.010
	(.029)	(.020)	(.023)	(.016)	(.024)	(.019)
Gezi Park protests	−.095***	.052***	−.018	.037***	.003	−.023
	(.024)	(.015)	(.017)	(.010)	(.020)	(.015)
Predicted probability	.31	.14	.16	.06	.21	.10
# of obs	2109	2109	2109	2109	2109	2109

Last but not least, we can see the effect of the Gezi Park protests on the voting decisions of first-time voters. They were found to punish the AKP more than the general young voter. The likelihood that they would vote for the AKP decreased by around 10 percent after the Gezi Park protests, and first-time voters report they are more likely to vote for the CHP and the BDP.

Role of social and spatial factors

Although the impact of various socio-economic determinants on the voting behavior of young people is explained above, their role on voting for a specific political party compared to another will be explained in this subsection. Table 5 provides the factor change coefficients among alternatives by a unit increase in the level of education. As can be seen in Table 5, the odds of voting for the CHP relative to the AKP are 1.26 times greater for young people with a higher level of education, holding other control variables constant. This rate is especially high for young Kurds and first-time voters. Furthermore, when we compare the voting behavior of young Kurds between the BDP and the AKP, more educated Kurdish youth were found to be more inclined to vote for the BDP than the AKP. Moreover, as the level of education increases, Kurdish youth move from being indecisive to voting for their choice. However, it seems that a higher level of education leads the youth to abstain from voting. For young people on average, the odds of abstaining relative to voting for the AKP are 1.25 times greater for the more educated, holding other covariates constant.

As is explained above, lifestyle is one of the most powerful explanatory factors in understanding the voting behavior of young people. Table 6 provides the statistically significant odds comparisons for a modern lifestyle relative to religious conservatives. It seems that the effect of lifestyle choice is

Table 5. Factor change in the odds of voting choice today due to education level of respondents (scaled from 1 to 7).

Alternative 1 to Alternative 2	ALL	TURKISH YOUTH	KURDISH YOUTH	FIRST-TIME VOTERS
CHP–AKP	1.26***	1.25***	1.58***	1.42***
MHP–CHP	0.90**	0.87**	–	–
MHP–AKP	1.14***	1.09*	2.45***	1.20*
BDP–CHP	0.72***	0.66**	–	0.58***
BDP–MHP	0.80***	–	0.51**	0.69***
BDP–AKP	0.91**	–	1.25***	–
INDECISIVE–CHP	–	–	0.65**	–
INDECISIVE–MHP	–	1.15**	0.42***	–
INDECISIVE–BDP	1.29***	1.53**	0.82**	1.50***
INDECISIVE–AKP	1.17***	1.26***	–	1.25**
ABSTAINER–BDP	1.38***	1.60**	1.22*	1.55***
ABSTAINER–AKP	1.25***	1.32***	1.52***	1.29**
ABSTAINER–MHP	–	1.21**	–	–
ABSTAINER–INDECISIVE	–	–	1.47*	–

Table 6. Factor change in the odds of voting choice today due to modern lifestyle (reference category: religious conservative).

Alternative 1 to Alternative 2	ALL	TURKISH YOUTH	KURDISH YOUTH	FIRST-TIME VOTERS
CHP–AKP	22.68***	20.26***	36.98***	16.55***
MHP–CHP	0.13***	0.14***	0.05**	0.13***
MHP–AKP	3.07***	2.90***	–	2.20***
BDP–CHP	0.10***	0.19***	0.06***	0.07**
BDP–MHP	0.77*	–	–	0.49**
BDP–AKP	2.36***	3.81**	2.33***	–
INDECISIVE–CHP	0.13***	0.16***	0.05***	0.16***
INDECISIVE–AKP	2.92***	3.24***	1.75**	2.65***
INDECISIVE–BDP	–	–	–	2.43***
ABSTAINER–CHP	0.13***	0.16***	0.05***	0.15***
ABSTAINER–AKP	2.87***	3.32***	1.90**	2.52***
ABSTAINER–BDP	–	–	–	2.31***

especially strong with regard to a choice between the CHP and the AKP. Table 6 shows that, for all different subsamples, the odds of voting for the CHP relative to the AKP are 22.68 times greater for young people who define themselves as modern compared to religious conservatives. This rate is 20.26 times greater for Turkish youth, about 37 times greater for Kurdish youth and 16.55 times higher for first-time voters. When we analyze the odds of voting for the AKP relative to various other categories (voting for the MHP and the BDP or being indecisive and abstaining), we see that having a modern lifestyle decreases the likelihood of voting for the AKP compared with religious conservatives.

Other than education level and lifestyle, one's place of residence also seems to explain the preferences of young people among alternatives. Table 7 shows the factor changes in the odds of young people who live in metropolises compared to those from rural areas. As can be seen in Table 7, young people who live in metropolises are more inclined to vote for either the AKP or the BDP

Table 7. Factor change in the odds of voting choice today due to living in a metropolis (reference category: rural area).

Alternative 1 to Alternative 2	ALL	TURKISH YOUTH	KURDISH YOUTH	FIRST-TIME VOTERS
CHP–AKP	0.74***	0.79**	0.37***	0.71*
MHP–AKP	0.73***	0.74***	–	–
MHP–CHP	–	–	–	1.61**
BDP–CHP	1.29**	–	2.10**	–
BDP–MHP	1.30**	–	–	–
INDECISIVE–CHP	1.65***	1.48***	2.68**	–
INDECISIVE–MHP	1.66***	1.58***	–	–
INDECISIVE–BDP	1.27*	–	–	–
INDECISIVE–AKP	1.22**	–	–	–
ABSTAINER–CHP	2.17***	1.83***	10.05***	1.54*
ABSTAINER–MHP	2.18***	1.95***	5.61**	–
ABSTAINER–BDP	1.67***	–	4.79***	–
ABSTAINER–INDECISIVE	1.31*	–	3.75***	–
ABSTAINER–AKP	1.60***	1.45**	3.68***	–

relative to the CHP and the MHP. Furthermore, living in a metropolis was found to increase the likelihood of abstaining or being undecided. Kurdish youth are especially more likely to abstain or be undecided if they live in a metropolis as opposed to a rural area. For example, the odds of abstaining relative to voting for the CHP are ten times greater for young Kurds. When we compare the effect of living in urban areas relative to rural regions, the findings are similar and presented in Table 8. In terms of voting between the CHP and the AKP, it appears urban residents are more likely to be inde-cisive or abstain rather than vote for a political party when other explanatory variables are held constant.

Economic voting

In addition to analyzing various micro-level determinants of a young popu-lation's voting behavior, this paper will also test the economic voting hypoth-eses for the young people in Turkey. Economic voting hypotheses argue that incumbent parties will be punished or rewarded for changes in economic events, whether personal or nationwide. Thus, they argue that voters' reac-tions could be future- or past-oriented and that they may care more about their own economic well-being or the nation's economic situation. Those who care about their own economic situation and compare their current situ-ation with the past are said to exhibit 'egotropic-retrospective' behavior. Thus, one can argue that retrospective behavior shapes the voting choice through the economic performance of the incumbent party rather than economic pol-icies or promises.[13] If their voting decision is formulated using their future expectations, then this is called 'prospective' behavior. Thus, a voter who gives more importance to his or her country's economic situation in the future is said to exhibit 'sociotropic-prospective' behavior. In the micro-survey we analyzed, there are two specific questions that can be incorporated into the empirical model to test the economic voting hypotheses. One of the

Table 8. Factor change in the odds of voting choice today due to living in an urban area (reference category: rural area).

Alternative 1 to Alternative 2	ALL	TURKISH YOUTH	KURDISH YOUTH	FIRST-TIME VOTERS
CHP–AKP	0.74**	0.74***	0.49*	0.67*
MHP–CHP	–	–	–	2.14***
MHP–AKP	–	–	–	1.44*
BDP–CHP	1.35**	–	2.74**	1.81**
INDECISIVE–CHP	1.52***	1.45***	2.80**	–
INDECISIVE–MHP	1.34**	1.28***	–	0.56**
INDECISIVE–AKP	1.18*	–	–	–
ABSTAINER–CHP	2.03***	1.84***	10.20***	–
ABSTAINER–MHP	1.78***	1.62***	3.57*	–
ABSTAINER–BDP	1.51**	2.88*	3.72***	–
ABSTAINER–INDECISIVE	1.33*	–	3.64***	–
ABSTAINER–AKP	1.58***	1.37*	5.00***	–

questions asks 'Do you expect an economic crisis in Turkey in the coming months?'. Answers to this question are used to see if the 'sociotropic-prospective' hypothesis plays a role in the voting behavior of the young people. Another question in the survey asks 'Do you expect any economic hardship in your own life in the coming months?'. This question enables us to test whether the 'egotropic-prospective' hypothesis has any importance in the voting choices of young people in Turkey.

The majority of studies found that voters in Western countries are more sociotropic; however, they are argued to be egotropic if the country of analysis has a strong welfare state which may cause people to believe that their personal income is also directly affected by government policies.[14] As is the case in literature on voting behavior, the impact/role of economic voting on electoral choices is studied widely in the literature, although its micro-level analysis only started to appear in the Turkish case especially after the 2000s, once micro-level survey data on the subject became available.[15] Analyzing a survey result for 1807 individuals, one of those studies[16] concluded that sociotropic voting hypotheses were more important for the general Turkish voters.

Tables 9–11 present the factor change in odds stemming from the economic variables in the model. Table 9 shows that an increase in the household income increases the probability of voting for the CHP relative to the AKP. When it comes to the dynamics between the BDP and the AKP, a higher level of household income is found to decrease the likelihood of voting for the BDP compared to the AKP. Another interesting dynamic shows that the higher the level of income, the lower the likelihood of voting for the BDP relative to being undecided or abstaining. Moreover, it was found that the leading party in Parliament, the AKP, is punished if the personal and national economic situation is expected to deteriorate. The odds of voting for other political parties and being undecided or abstaining relative to voting for the AKP are greater for young people with an either egotropic-prospective or sociotropic-prospective behavior, holding other control variables

Table 9. Factor change in the odds of voting choice today due to household income.

Alternative 1 to Alternative 2	ALL	TURKISH YOUTH	KURDISH YOUTH	FIRST-TIME VOTERS
CHP–AKP	1.16***	1.11***	1.45***	1.27***
MHP–CHP	0.93*	–	0.62*	0.82**
MHP–AKP	1.08**	–	–	–
BDP–CHP	0.67***	–	0.64	0.66***
BDP–MHP	0.72***	–	–	0.81**
BDP–AKP	0.78***	–	–	0.84*
INDECISIVE–CHP	0.83***	0.86***	0.63***	0.77***
INDECISIVE–MHP	0.88***	0.90**	–	–
INDECISIVE–BDP	1.22***	–	–	–
ABSTAINER–CHP	0.81***	0.86***	0.69**	0.75***
ABSTAINER–MHP	0.87***	0.89**	–	–
ABSTAINER–BDP	1.21***	–	–	–

Table 10. Factor change in the odds of voting choice today due to egotropic-prospective behavior.

Alternative 1 to Alternative 2	ALL	TURKISH YOUTH	KURDISH YOUTH	FIRST-TIME VOTERS
CHP–AKP	1.23**	1.25**	–	–
MHP–AKP	1.41***	1.42***	–	1.35
BDP–AKP	1.34***	–	1.52***	–
INDECISIVE–AKP	1.37***	1.36***	1.58**	1.41**
ABSTAINER–AKP	1.26**	1.29**	–	–

Table 11. Factor change in the odds of voting choice today due to sociotropic-prospective.

Alternative 1 to Alternative 2	ALL	TURKISH YOUTH	KURDISH YOUTH	FIRST-TIME VOTERS
CHP–AKP	3.03***	2.95***	3.53***	2.76***
MHP–AKP	2.88***	2.86***	–	2.36***
BDP–CHP	0.65***	–	0.54*	–
BDP–MHP	0.68***	–	–	–
BDP–AKP	1.96***	3.85***	1.92***	2.53***
INDECISIVE–CHP	0.52***	0.55***	0.37***	0.48***
INDECISIVE–MHP	0.55***	0.56***	–	0.56***
INDECISIVE–BDP	0.81*	0.42**	0.69*	0.53***
INDECISIVE–AKP	1.59***	1.61***	–	1.33*
ABSTAINER–CHP	0.78**	0.76**	–	0.66**
ABSTAINER–MHP	0.82*	0.78*	–	–
ABSTAINER–INDECISIVE	1.48***	1.39***	1.88**	–
ABSTAINER–AKP	2.36***	2.24***	2.48***	1.81***

constant. It is notable that young people punish the incumbent political party more when they expect a downturn in the national economy.

Gezi Park protests

As is explained above, the empirical analysis found that the Gezi Park protests increased the conventional political participation of young people in Turkey. This subsection discusses the dynamics of this higher level of political engagement. The likelihood of voting for the AKP was found to decrease relative to other alternatives. This effect is especially strong for first-time voters. Table 12 shows that the odds of voting for the CHP relative to the AKP, for example, are two times greater for first-time voters, holding other variables constant. The Gezi Park protests were also found to divert undecided voters and those abstaining from voting for the CHP, the MHP, or the BDP. The migration of votes to the BDP was found to be the greatest.

Disillusioned young voters

This subsection addresses factors that explain the behavior of respondents who voted in the 2011 general election but plan 'not to vote' if an election

Table 12. Factor change in the odds of voting choice today due to Gezi protests.

Alternative 1 to Alternative 2	ALL	TURKISH YOUTH	KURDISH YOUTH	FIRST-TIME VOTERS
CHP–AKP	1.44***	1.51***	–	1.99***
MHP–AKP	1.35***	1.44***	0.35**	1.50***
BDP–MHP	1.27**	–	3.94***	1.82**
BDP–AKP	1.71***	–	1.36**	2.74***
INDECISIVE–CHP	0.72***	0.71***	–	0.68**
INDECISIVE–MHP	0.78***	0.75***	2.77**	–
INDECISIVE–BDP	0.61***	–	0.70*	0.50***
INDECISIVE–AKP	–	–	–	1.36**
ABSTAINER–CHP	0.59***	0.56***	–	0.54***
ABSTAINER–MHP	0.63***	0.59***	–	0.71*
ABSTAINER–BDP	0.50***	0.47*	0.55***	0.39***
ABSTAINER–INDECISIVE	0.82**	0.79**	–	–
ABSTAINER–AKP	0.85*	–	–	–

were held today. Those young people cannot be called 'purely apathetic' or 'purely alienated' because they had already voted at least in the 2011 General Elections. Youth in this category is named as 'disillusioned' to denote the fact that they had voted in the previous election but they are not anymore interested in democratic politics or they have turned against the act of voting for various reasons. It is, therefore, important to analyze the determinants of being disillusioned, as it will help us to understand why young people decide to abstain from voting although they had conventional political participation before. First, a dummy variable is created and assigned the value of 1 if the respondent voted in the 2011 election but declared they would abstain if an election were held today. Table 13 presents the marginal effects of the logit model for the total sample. The Gezi Park protests were found to have the strongest effect as they decreased the likelihood of being disillusioned on average by 2.1 percent, when other variables are held constant. Thus, one can argue that the Gezi Park protests, even if they are in themselves a form of non-conventional political participation, also energized conventional political participation of young people in Turkey. It was also found that being female, older and having a higher level of education increase the likelihood of being disillusioned. On the contrary, students, the unemployed, and housegirls are less inclined to be disillusioned relative to the employed. Interestingly, one's personal or national economic situation or lifestyle choice is not found to matter for being disillusioned, although they were significant determinants of voting behavior. Moreover, urban and metropolitan residents were more inclined to be disillusioned relative to residents of rural areas. However, it should be noted that the model is weak in predicting the probability of being disillusioned, and it seems there are other important factors that affect the dependent variable which do not exist, unfortunately, in our data set.

Table 13. Marginal effects after logit model (dependent variable: dummy variable for disillusioned voters).

Variables	ALL
Female	.008***
	(.003)
Age	.001**
	(.001)
Education Level (scaled from 1 to 7)	.005***
	(.002)
Job Status	
(Reference category: employed)	
Unemployed	−.008***
	(.003)
Student	−.003
	(.003)
Housewife	−.007**
	(.003)
Economic Voting	
Household Income	−.001
	(.001)
Sociotropic-Prospective	.001
	(.003)
Egotropic-Prospective	.001
	(.003)
Lifestyle	
(Reference category: religious conservative)	
Modern	.000
	(.004)
Traditional Conservative	.004
	(.004)
Residential Area	
(Reference category: Rural)	
Urban	.011*
	(.007)
Metropol	.016***
	(.005)
Gezi Park Protests	−.021***
	(.005)
Predicted Probability	.013
# of Obs	5843

Persistence in abstaining

The most important result in Table 14 is the persistence in abstaining; young people who did not vote in the 2011 election were found to have around an 18 percent higher likelihood of maintaining their decision to abstain again if an election were held today, keeping other variables constant. Other variables that increase the probability of abstaining are having a higher level of education, having a sociotropic-prospective attitude, and living in urban areas and metropolises. Furthermore, unemployed young people have a 3.6 percent lower probability of abstaining.

Table 15 shows the odds ratios for the alternatives bundles. It was found that young people who did not vote in the 2011 election have, for example, an 8.31 times greater likelihood of abstaining relative to voting for the

Table 14. Marginal effects after MNL model for being abstainer.

Variables	Abstainer today
Abstainer in 2011	.176***
	(.015)
Female	.003
	(.007)
Age	−.001
	(.001)
Education level (scaled from 1 to 7)	.008**
	(.004)
Job status	
(Reference category: employed)	
Unemployed	−.036***
	(.007)
Student	.004
	(.007)
Housewife	−.014
	(.010)
Economic voting	
Household income	−.001
	(.003)
Sociotropic-prospective	.027***
	(.007)
Egotropic-prospective	.003
	(.007)
Lifestyle	
(Reference category: religious conservative)	
Modern	−.008
	(.008)
Traditional conservative	−.018**
	(.009)
Residential area	
(Reference category: rural)	
Urban	.044***
	(.013)
Metropol	.045***
	(.010)
Gezi Park protests	−.006
	(.007)
Predicted probability	.06
# of obs	6626

AKP. Holding other variables constant, the odds of abstaining relative to voting for the CHP, the MHP and the BDP are, respectively, 7.7, 10, and 11 times greater for the youth who did not vote in the last general election.

4. Conclusion

This study analyzes the voting behavior of the Turkish youth using micro-level data. It is found that women, highly educated and urban area residents are more inclined to abstain from voting. Besides, 'housegirls' are more inclined to vote and, when they vote, they are more likely to vote for the ruling AKP compared to other alternatives. Interestingly, various socio-economic factors have a similar impact on the voting behavior of AKP and pro-

Table 15. Factor change in the odds of abstaining today due to abstaining in 2011 general elections.

Alternative 1 to Alternative 2	ALL
INDECISIVE–CHP	3.94***
INDECISIVE–MHP	5.12***
INDECISIVE–BDP	5.62***
INDECISIVE–AKP	4.26***
ABSTAINER–CHP	7.69***
ABSTAINER–MHP	9.99***
ABSTAINER–BDP	10.99***
ABSTAINER–INDECISIVE	1.95***
ABSTAINER–AKP	8.31***

Kurdish BDP voters. The educated young are more inclined to vote for the main opposition CHP. Lifestyle choice is found to be the most important factor behind voting behavior. One can argue that it reflects the importance of everyday life practices on conventional political participation.

Moreover, the Gezi protests decreased the young people's likelihood of voting for the AKP, being undecided and an abstainer. When we look at the importance of economic voting theories, we found that 'economic voting' exists for the young. The ruling party is punished for both personal- and country-level economic prospects. Furthermore, the comparison of different ethnicities shows that the place of residence is not at all important for voting behavior and that the 2013 Gezi protests only increased the likelihood of voting for the BDP for Kurdish youth. For first-time voters, lifestyle and the Gezi protests were found to determine voting behavior. Voters who define themselves as modern and those traditional conservatives are more inclined to vote for the CHP. Religious conservatives vote more for the AKP and the BDP.

Interestingly, there is persistence in abstaining from voting. Having abstained in the 2011 general election increases the likelihood of abstaining by 18 percent. The analysis of disillusioned youth shows that the Gezi protests increased the probability of conventional political participation of the young. Factor change analysis shows that abstained and indecisive young Kurds decided to vote for the BDP after the Gezi Park protests.

Notes

1. Young people's lack of interest in conventional politics is widely studied in established democracies. For example, Kimberlee ("Why Don't British Young People Vote") argues that 'young people's changing transition journeys to adult statuses' is the reason behind very low political participation rates of the youth in the UK. Dermody, Hanmer-Lloyd, and Scullion ("Young People and Voting Behavior") found that cynicism causes political alienation for the British youth. Wattenberg (*Where Have all the Voters Gone?*) shows that the 'generation gap' of voter turnout is above 30 percentage points in the US,

Japan and Switzerland, while it is smaller in Australia, the Netherlands and Spain. Last but not least, by providing a multilevel analysis for 22 European nations, Fieldhouse, Tranmer, and Russell ("Something about Young People") found that not only individual-level determinants but also election-specific information (such as the level of political interest and civic duty) affect the voting behavior of young people. There are also comparative studies which argues that young people are more active in unconventional politics than conventional one. Among others see, for example, Inglehart, *Modernization and Postmodernization*; Flanagan, "Developmental Roots"; Dalton, *The Good Citizen*; Goerres, *The Political Participation*; and Melo and Stockemer, "Age and Political Participation."

2. According to a report from the National Human Rights Institution of Turkey (TIHK), 3,611,208 people participated in 5532 events between May 28 and September 6, 2013. See TIHK, *Gezi Parkı Olayları Raporu*.
3. See https://data.oecd.org/youthinac/youth-not-in-employment-education-or-training-neet.htm.
4. Kılıç, "Kentsel Gençlik Araştırması Anketi," 31–68.
5. Yılmaz and Oy, "Türkiye'de gençlik ve siyasi katılım," 41.
6. Erdoğan and Uyan-Semerci, "Understanding Young Citizens' Political," 2.
7. Başlevent, Kirmanoğlu, and Şenatalar, "Empirical Investigation of Party Preferences," 547–62.
8. Çarkoğlu, "The Nature of Left–Right Ideological," 253–71.
9. Çarkoğlu, "Electoral Participation and Preferences."
10. Data are collected through face-to-face interviews on the first weekend of each month with 1800–3600 people representing the electorate of Turkey. To construct the sample, KONDA employs the electoral registers and results of 2011 General Parliamentary election. 'Firstly the regional information and election results of the 46,797 neighborhood and villages (the smallest administrative units) are stratified. The locations where interviews will be conducted are selected randomly according to the population size of the strata.' (KONDA, *Konda Barometer*, 17). In addition, a total of 12–18 individuals are interviewed in each location choice according to strict gender and age quotas determined to represent the electorate population.
11. As the data is not collected interviewing the same individuals, a panel data analysis is not possible. However, the data collection procedure and sampling is not changed each month, which makes a pooled data analysis plausible.
12. The Kurdish-oriented BDP existed from 2008 to 2014. In 2014, it was formally re-organized and subsumed into the Peoples' Democratic Party (*Halkların Demokratik Partisi*, HDP).
13. Başlevent, Kirmanoğlu, and Şenatalar, "Empirical Investigation of Party Preferences," 547–62.
14. See, for example, Kinder and Kiewiet, "Economic Discontent," for the US case, Sanders, "Conservative Incompetence," and "The Real Economy," for the UK case, and Nannestad and Paldam, "Into Pandora's Box," and "What Do Voters Know?" for the Danish case.
15. The impact of macroeconomic variables and, thus, the economic performance of incumbent parties began to be analyzed in the 1970s. Those studies employ macro data and address the importance of various economic factors on voting behavior. The main economic variables that affect the voting choice are argued to be inflation, unemployment and economic growth. Among others see, for

example, Bulutay, "Türk Toplumsal Hayatında İktisadi," Çarkoğlu, "Macro-economic Determinants," and Akarca and Tansel, "Economic Performance."
16. Başlevent, Kirmanoğlu, and Şenatalar, "Empirical Investigation of Party Preferences," 547–62.

Acknowledgements

I would like to thank KONDA Research and Consultancy for providing the data.

Disclosure statement

No potential conflict of interest was reported by the author.

ORCID

Ayşegül Kayaoğlu ⓘ http://orcid.org/0000-0003-1484-184X

References

Akarca, Ali T., and Tansel Aysit. "Economic Performance and Political Outcomes: An Analysis of the Turkish Parliamentary and Local Election Results Between 1950 and 2004." *Public Choice* 129, no. 1/2 (2006): 77–105.

Başlevent, Cem, Hasan Kirmanoğlu, and Burhan Şenatalar. "Empirical Investigation of Party Preferences and Economic Voting in Turkey." *European Journal of Political Research* 44 (2005): 547–562.

Bulutay, Tuncer. "Türk Toplumsal Hayatında İktisadi ve Siyasal Gelişmeler (Economic and Political Developments in Turkey's Social Life)." *SBF Dergisi* 25 (1970): 79–119.

Çarkoglu, Ali. "Macro-economic Determinants of Electoral Support for Incumbents in Turkey, 1950–1995." *New Perspectives on Turkey* 17 (1997): 75–96.

Çarkoğlu, Ali. "The Nature of Left–Right Ideological Self-placement in the Turkish Context." *Turkish Studies* 8, no. 2 (2007): 253–271.

Çarkoğlu, Ali. "Electoral Participation and Preferences among the Young Generations in Turkey." Unpublished paper presented in Youth and Participation Project Workshop, İstanbul Bilgi Üniversitesi, 21–22 June 2013, Istanbul. http://www.sebeke.org.tr/calistay-1-genclerin-siyasi-katilimi-21–22-haziran-2013/.

Dalton, R. J. *The Good Citizen: How a Younger Generation is Reshaping American Politics.* Washington, DC: CQ Press, 2009.

Dermody, Janine, Stuart Hanmer-Lloyd, and Richard Scullion. "Young People and Voting Behavior: Alienated Youth and (or) an Interested and Critical Citizenry?" *European Journal of Marketing* 44, no. 3/4 (2010): 421–435.

Erdoğan, Emre, and Pınar Uyan-Semerci. "Understanding Young Citizens' Political Participation in Turkey: Does 'Being Young' Matter?" *Southeast European and Black Sea Studies* (2010). doi:10.1080/14683857.2016.1235000.

Fieldhouse, Edward, Mark Tranmer, and Andrew Russell. "Something about Young People of Something about Elections? Electoral Participation of Young People in Europe: Evidence from a Multilevel Analysis of the European Social Survey." *European Journal of Political Research* 46 (2007): 797–822.

Flanagan, C. A. "Developmental Roots of Political Engagement." *Political Science and Politics* 36 (2003): 257–261.

Goerres, A. *The Political Participation of Older People in Europe.* New York: Palgrave Macmillan, 2009.

Inglehart, R. *Modernization and Postmodernization: Cultural, Economic, and Political Change in Societies.* Princeton, NJ: Princeton University Press, 1997.

Kılıç, Kemal. "Kentsel Gençlik Araştırması Anketi Bağlamında: Gençlerin Siyasal Eğilimlerini Etkileyen Faktörler." In *Gençler Tartışıyor: Siyasete Katılım, Sorunlar ve Çözüm Önerileri,* edited by C. Boyraz, 31–68. Istanbul: Türkiye Sosyal Ekonomik Siyasal Araştırmalar VakfıYayınları, 2009.

Kimberlee, Richard H. "Why Don't British Young People Vote at General Elections?" *Journal of Youth Studies* 5 (2002): 85–98.

Kinder, D. R., and D. R. Kiewiet. "Economic Discontent and Political Behavior: The Role of Personal Grievances and Collective Economic Judgement in Congressional Voting." *American Journal of Political Science* 3 (1979): 495–527.

KONDA. *Konda Barometer 2012: Political and Social Survey Series.* Istanbul: KONDA, 2012.

Melo, D.F., and D. Stockemer. "Age and Political Participation in Germany, France and the UK: A Comparative Analysis." *Comparative European Politics* 12 (2014): 33–53.

Nannestad, P., and M. Paldam. "Into Pandora's Box: What is Exogenous in VP-Models? A Study of the Danish macro VP-Function 1986–1997." *Electoral Studies* 19 (2000): 123–140.

Nannestad, P., and M. Paldam. "What Do Voters Know about the Economy? A Study of Danish Data, 1990–1993." *Electoral Studies* 19 (2000): 363–392.

Sanders, D. "Conservative Incompetence, Labour Responsibility and the Feelgood Factor: Why the Economy Failed to Serve the Conservatives in 1997." *Electoral Studies* 18 (1999): 251–270.

Sanders, D. "The Real Economy and the Perceived Economy in Popularity Functions: How Much Do Voters Need to Know?" *Electoral Studies* 19 (2000): 275–294.

Türkiye Insan Hakları Kurumu (TIHK, The National Human Rights Institution of Turkey) *Gezi Parkı Olayları Raporu* [The Report for the Gezi Park Protests], 2014. http://www.tihk.gov.tr/tr/raporlar-ve-kararlar.

Wattenberg, M. *Where Have all the Voters Gone?* Cambridge, MA: Harvard University Press, 2002.

Yılmaz, V., and Burcu Oy. "Türkiye'de gençlik ve siyasi katılım: Sosyo-ekonomik statü fark yaratıyor mu?" [Youth and political participation in Turkey: Does socioeconomic status matter?] In *Istanbul Bilgi Üniversitesi Sebeke Gençleri Katılımı Projesi Kitapları,* 5, (2014). http://www.sebeke.org.tr/wp-content/uploads/2014/04/sosya-ekonomikstatufaryaratiyormu.pdf.

Appendix

Table A1. Sample size per monthly KONDA barometer surveys (only for aged 18–25).

Survey period	Sample size
January 2013	494
February 2013	530
March 2013	461
April 2013	462
May 2013	517
June 2013	537
July 2013	550
September 2013	484
October 2013	493
November 2013	508
January 2014	456
February 2014	499
March 2014	465
April 2014	527
May 2014	501
June 2014	511
July 2014	434
August 2014	469
October 2014	514
November 2014	484
Total sample size	9896

Table A2. Percentage distributions of variables in the total sample[a].

Variables	Percentage share in the sample (%)
Female	45.56
Education level	
Illiterate	1.13
Literate but without a degree	0.86
Primary school Diploma	7.75
Secondary school diploma	19.46
High school diploma	54.09
University degree	15.88
Graduate diploma	0.82
Job status	
Employed	29.53
Unemployed	9.81
Student	45.07
Housewife	14.26
Economic voting	
Household income	
<300 YTL	1.70
301–700	6.77
701–1200	28.92
1201–2000	35.60
2001–3000	16.94
>3000	10.08
Sociotropic-prospective	38.54
Egotropic-prospective	41.96
Lifestyle	
Modern	43.56

(Continued)

Table A2. Continued.

Variables	Percentage share in the sample (%)
Traditional conservative	39.39
Religious conservative	17.05
Residential area	
Rural	19.42
Urban	30.40
Metropol	50.18
Vote choice today	
AKP	32.11
CHP	19.25
MHP	13.75
BDP	8.01
Others	2.28
Indecisive	16.60
Abstainer	7.99
Vote choice in 2011 general elections	
AKP	24.47
CHP	13.67
MHP	8.06
BDP	4.64
Others	1.25
Independent	1.33
Noneligible	32.26
No vote	14.31

[a]Percentage shares for each variable is calculated after excluding the missing variables.

Between Gezi Park and Kamp Armen: the intersectional activism of leftist Armenian youths in Istanbul

Hrag Papazian ⓘ

ABSTRACT

This paper uses theories of intersectionality to study Nor Zartonk, an activist group of Istanbulite youths which is mostly comprised of Armenians. Based on ethnographic research, it first explores and analyzes the youths' subjectivities, ideology, and activism, exposing their intersectional nature. Furthermore, through the study of this particular case the paper identifies some general potentials of intersectional positionality: first, that the politicization of one dimension of individuals' intersectional subjectivities could pave the way for the politicization of others; second, that intersectional activists could 'intersectionalize' the events in which they participate, thus potentially pluralizing the socio-political implications of those; and third, that different dimensions of intersectional activism could support each other in practice and essence.

Introduction

The resistance in and partial return of Kamp Armen, an orphanage originally belonging to the Gedikpaşa Armenian Protestant Church, but expropriated by the Turkish state in 1987,[1] was one of the most attention-grabbing events related to the Armenians of Istanbul in recent times. With its 'Let Kamp Armen be returned to the Armenian people' slogan, the movement was mainly led by Nor Zartonk, an activist group of Istanbulite youths, mostly comprised of Armenians. Throughout the six months of resistance during the summer of 2015, the group's visibility increased in both the Turkish political arena and in the Armenian diaspora. Since the movement for Kamp Armen was a defense of *Armenians*' rights more than anything else, it might have fostered a solely *Armenian* image of the group, especially for those who were formerly unaware of its existence. However, Nor Zartonk has also actively participated in First of May protests, in Feminist and LGBT marches and in the Gezi Park occupation, to cite just a few of its activities. A holistic approach to the group's politics reveals a much more complex portrait of it.

This paper aims to study Nor Zartonk through the theoretical framework of intersectionality. Theories of intersectionality emerged from the field of feminist studies. They invited attention to the fact that women face multiple, overlapping, and mutually reinforcing types of oppressions, which arise from the different facets of their identities; most importantly gender, race, and social class.[2] The term 'intersectionality' was first coined by Kimberlé Crenshaw, a legal scholar and specialist in racial and gender studies, who emphasized the 'multidimensionality' of the experiences of black women.[3] Some later studies have enriched the gender-race-class triplet by adding variables such as caste, nation and ethnicity to the equation.[4] In short, this framework acknowledges 'that identity is complex, that subjectivity is messy.'[5]

Academics have studied activist groups that simultaneously address multiple forms of oppression arising from the different dimensions of their intersectional identities.[6] This latter type of politics has been rightly termed 'intersectional activism' by Sharon Doetsch-Kidder.[7] The intersectional framework has also been used in some studies of Turkish civil society in particular, but as the notion has emerged from feminist literature, most of those studies have been limited to the very same field of feminism,[8] looking at Islamist and Kurdish women's movements in particular.[9] Thus, I agree with Özkaleli that 'there is a need for further studies on the treatment of the intersectionality of identities within political groups and movements [in Turkey],'[10] and believe that the framework of intersectionality could also be fruitfully used for analyzing forms of activism that are not, or not only, feministic in nature. Focusing particularly on the intersection between ethnic and other types of activisms could be especially fruitful in broadening our understanding of social movements and civil society in Turkey. The country's multi-ethnic character, along with the fact that demands based on ethnic belongings are becoming more visible in Turkish civil society since the 1990s,[11] suggest so.

This paper aims to take a step in that direction, accepting as its case study Nor Zartonk, which developed from a mailing list to an active political voice after the assassination of the famous Turkish-Armenian journalist Hrant Dink by an ultranationalist young Turk in 2007. After exploring the subjectivities of the activists and the ideology and activism of Nor Zartonk through the framework of intersectionality, the paper also deals with more universal and practical questions: Can the politicization of one dimension of an intersectional subjectivity pave the way for that of other dimensions?; What effect can intersectional activists have on the events in which they participate, and, potentially, on the socio-political implications of those?; and Can different dimensions of an intersectional activism support and enrich each other?

Research methods

In order to study Nor Zartonk's intersectionality and answer the questions above, I analyze ethnographic data collected during fieldwork in Istanbul throughout 2014 and 2015. As part of a previous research project I had already made contact and interviewed a few members of the group in the summer of 2014. Building on that initial network, I reached out to other members during my research for this paper and interviewed them with special emphasis on their activistic trajectories and ideological thoughts. As for the members already interviewed beforehand, I met, conversed and in some cases re-interviewed them in accordance with the particular objectives of this paper. As a result, interviews with ten Nor Zartonk activists are referred to and analyzed in this paper. This selection is representative enough of the group, since its active members numbered only around 15 at the time of my research, and have barely been more numerous at any time. Four of the interviewed are founding members, aged more or less 30 years old at the time of the interviews, whereas the others, aged between 18 and 26, have joined the group at later stages. All of them were born in Istanbul in lower or lower middle-class families. Only two out of the ten interviewees are female, but this imbalance is conditioned by the simple fact that the number of female Nor Zartonk activists was negligible compared to that of the male ones, not only at the time of my research, but also at least for the last few years. Although there are also a couple of non-Armenian members in the group, I have nevertheless left them out of this study because they represent not only a scant minority, but also different cases in terms of identity and subjectivity. Lastly, for supplementary purposes I have also recorded four interviews with other Istanbulite Armenian activists aged between 30 and 40 years old, who are not members of Nor Zartonk but have had similar activistic experiences and at least partly share the same worldview. The paper will only incidentally refer to the latter.

In order to understand the nuances of the activists' subjectivities and ideologies, I also had recourse to the ethnographic technique of (participant) observation, by visiting Nor Zartonk's center multiple times, participating in a few of their meetings, attending several of their events, volunteering for the online radio station affiliated to them, and simply spending leisure time with some of the activists. Finally, I also analyzed the content and discourse of the group's website[12] and important print and social media publications, which shed further light on its ideology and activities.

Intersectional subjectivities, ideology, and activism

We shall start by analyzing the activists' subjectivities, that is, their 'inner life processes and affective states,'[13] before looking at the ideological and practical aspects of Nor Zartonk's politics. A thematic analysis of my semi-structured interviews with the activists reveals how multidimensional their identities are and how, as a result, they are subjected to multiple oppressions. As Kevork,[14] an activist, put it: 'The system hits you in one way or another.'

The ethnic Armenian identity is of course a very important dimension of the subjectivities of these activists, who are in fact grouped under an Armenian name, as *Nor Zartonk* means 'new awakening' in Armenian. This identity engenders a special social suffering for its bearers in Istanbul. Social suffering, defined as the result of 'injuries that social force can inflict on human experience,'[15] has two dimensions in the case of Istanbulite Armenians. The first consists of an 'everyday ecology of fear, mistrust, and anxiety,'[16] which is partly nurtured by the heavy burden of the generationally transmitted memory of traumatic historical events, and partly by contemporary acts of violence – be those direct and physical as in the murders of Hrant Dink,[17] Sevag Balıkçı,[18] and Maritsa Küçük,[19] or subtle, that is, 'everyday violence,'[20] which acts through the 'soft knife of routine processes,'[21] in the form of insults, threats and discriminatory acts. The second dimension of Istanbulite Armenians' social suffering consists of feelings of humiliation and resentment caused by a systematic neglect of their historical presence and legacy in Turkey.[22] The Armenian activists being studied here naturally share, to varying extents, the two-dimensional social suffering outlined above. I now turn to four selected interviewees and let them speak on this matter.

Aren, one of the founders of the group, expressed himself as follows:

> There are of course difficulties stemming from being Armenian. The prejudices [against us], the pressures because of nationalism … I first felt those in the *dershane* [private tutoring school], where my classmates started labeling me *gavur*.[23] We're in such a country where even if we deny being Armenian they tell us 'no! You're Armenians! Get lost!' …

For Saro being an Armenian in Turkey means 'to belong and not belong at the same time. Our roots are in these lands, we're not outsiders in reality, but we are outed by the state, we are outsiders politically.'

Melisa recalled how the ethnically Turkish teacher of history in the Armenian school she used to attend would 'tell us that we could be Christians, but we were Turks nevertheless. Wait! You're coming to an Armenian school and telling us that we're Turks?' She remembered how she was affected by the series of attacks on elderly Armenian women in the Samatya district in 2012: 'I was afraid that they could also kill my grandmother simply for being Armenian.'

Finally, Vartan's experience, far more traumatic than the ones noted above, was relayed to me in his shaky voice:

> It was 2007, sometime after the killing of Dink ... I was 13–14 ... I didn't even know who Dink was. Our downstairs neighbor started threatening us by coming to our door after midnight, banging on it very hard and screaming: 'Leave this country! We're going to kill you all like Dink!' Almost every night ... I remember my parents sitting and hopelessly crying ... I started praying, and when even that did not help I gave up believing. For months, I kept looking behind me while walking in the street. I literally wet the bed a few times! We complained to the police who only arrived some weeks later to tell us that the man was angry because we were making too much noise ... So I glued cotton to the soles of my slippers! Finally, we moved out of the house. We got another place nearby. I was still afraid. Several times I came home from school, and after seeing unknown faces at the entrance of our building I went back and waited for my parents to come for me. Later, we heard that the man did the same with the other Armenian family in the building, and even with the one who took our place after we left. Both families also moved out ... That was when I first learned what being an Armenian in Turkey meant ...

Thus it is clear that 'being an Armenian in Turkey,' together with the social suffering directly related to it, is a main constituent of the identities of these youths. But importantly for our argument here, the members of Nor Zartonk recognize that there are also other facets to their identities and suffered oppressions. I return to the same interlocutors in the same order, to highlight the intersectional character of their subjectivities:

> Aren: I experience problems because of my class identity first of all. I have economic difficulties as a young man: How will my future be? What kind of work will I do? Will I be able to get married? If the ethnic identity problem gets solved for the Armenians in Turkey, if discriminatory practices stop, are we going to be free? We're not. Because we're at the same time youths, proletarians, women, etc.

> Saro: The Armenian problem is not your only problem. You live, earn money and pay your taxes here ... and you have to struggle in these directions too.

> Melisa: I don't feel at ease here ... not only as an Armenian, but also as a woman, a student, the daughter of a man who's not well-off, as a person deprived of many social rights.

> Vartan: You're living as an Armenian and as a worker at the same time and you're being oppressed as both. Your financial situation is difficult, and thus you are harmed in different fields of your life, such as education or health. It's not a democratic country and you don't have safety as a person, let alone as an Armenian. You have the constitutional right to organize protests but the state intervenes and puts some limits, and if you cross them, even by words, you can get into danger.

Thus we see subjectivities that are clearly intersectional. These activists are inhabited by multiple identities – Armenian, proletarian, youth, student, woman – and feel being multiply oppressed by the existing power structures.

Those multiple oppressions, in turn, are reflected in and challenged by the ideology and political program of the group, which are also intersectional. In fact, the manifesto of the group states that Nor Zartonk: ' ... is on the side of the labor against capital'; ' ... defends the right of nations to self-determination'; ' ... opposes racism, nationalism, militarism and any kind of discrimination'; ' ... opposes patriarchy and discrimination of sexual orientations and identities'; ' ... defends the ecological life and is against anthropocentrism'; ' ... opposes gerontocracy.'[24] In those lines, one can clearly see how the activists' multiple identities raise their voices against their oppressors. The members I interviewed used 'Marxist,' 'Socialist,' 'Leftist,' 'New-Leftist', 'Democratic,' and 'Revolutionary' interchangeably in order to identify their ideological orientations. But importantly, they did not perceive their Leftist identifications as being in contradiction with their Armenian identity. For the group, there is of course the 'mission of guaranteeing the survival and continuation of our [Armenian] culture and heritage,' as Axel put it. In Natan's words:

> Both the leftist struggle and the communal struggle – [for] the mother tongue, our church, all that we have received through our culture – have to go hand in hand. You can't consider one as superior to the other. If you see yourself only as a leftist, then you will have to forget the past and think only about the future ... then you'll feel something to be missing.

On the other hand, he underlines: 'The Republic of Armenia is not my homeland [as long as] it's a patriarchal, anti-democratic and oligarchic place. People like me cannot live there.'

Nor Zartonk members perceive capitalism to be the common oppressor of *all* of their identities, including, importantly, the ethnic one. 'The oppressor is one: The state, the system, capitalism,' explains Aren. As *The Program of Nor Zartonk* states, not only 'capitalist relations of production legitimized the exploitation of labor,'[25] but also 'Racism, Imperialism, the destruction of the environment, sexual discrimination, and similar problems are results of the capitalist system in which we live.'[26] Even the past atrocities against Armenians in the Republic of Turkey and the Ottoman Empire are interpreted in light of Marxist understandings: '[the Armenian genocide] was planned for the purpose of creating a nation-state, a national bourgeoisie and national capital. It was a problem of classes,' argued Aren. According to Axel's worldview: 'It's capitalism that is attacking cultural identities and trying to impose homogenization. That's why we could say that the Armenian mission and leftist mission are interrelated. We consider the ethnic minorities' issue to be one of the issues of the New Left.'[27] Aren concluded: 'If you're a *real* leftist, then the Armenian issue is automatically your issue … ' Clearly, then, the 'real leftism' professed by Nor Zartonk is intersectional.

An analysis of the symbolic choices of the activists is also helpful for revealing the intersectional nature of their ideology. Most of the historical figures they commemorate and uphold had been active neither solely as Armenians, nor solely as leftists, but as both. The famous Maoist militant Orhan Bakır (Armenag Bakırcıyan), an ethnically Armenian citizen of Turkey, is a recurring figure in the activists' social media posts. Nareg stressed on the fact that:

> Armenag was not only a leftist partisan fighting against and shot by the state [in 1980].[28] He also used to go down to the villages in Dersim, find the Armenians [who were forced to convert and hide their identities] and tell them about their identities, as I read.

Similarly, the name of Manouchian – the famous Armenian Communist who led anti-Nazi militant groups in France during the Second World War, but has also done Armenian cultural and intra-community activism[29] – appears on posters in the group's meeting rooms and in their graffiti. The twenty martyrs of the Hunchak Party, also both Marxist and Armenian, executed in Istanbul in 1915; Armenian-Feminist writer Zabel Yessayan; Armenian Bolshevik revolutionary Shahumian; and finally of course the late Hrant Dink, are exemplary individuals which the activists actively select from Armenian history in accordance with their intersectional ideology.

Finally, this ideology finds its application in the groups' activism. Sharon Doetsch-Kidder gives the following definition in her recently published book:

> By 'intersectional activism,' I mean activism that addresses more than one structure of oppression or form of discrimination (racism, classism, sexism, heterosexism, transphobia, ableism, nationalism, etc.) Intersectional activists are often marginalized in social movement histories because they don't work in organizations that focus solely on 'women's issues,' 'gay and lesbian issues,' or 'race issues,' for example.[30]

Nor Zartonk's activism fits the latter definition. Feeling multiple responsibilities, the activists act accordingly. As Aren put it: 'If we leave this country, then who will defend our churches? Our community? Simultaneously, who will defend this country from the fascists? Who will fight for democracy, human rights, workers' rights?' Throughout the nine years of its existence between 2007 and 2016, Nor Zartonk has organized and/or actively participated in: protests in commemoration of the assassination of Hrant Dink,[31] protests and trials for the murder of ethnic Armenian Sevag Balıkçı during his military service[32] and for that of elderly Armenian woman Maritsa Küçük,[33] Armenian Genocide protests,[34] the resistance of Kamp Armen,[35] but also International Workers' Days,[36] Environmental Protests such as the Gezi Park occupation,[37] LGBT Pride Parades,[38] Feminist Marches,[39] protests for the rights of other ethnic or religious minorities such as those in commemoration of the 1993 killings of Alevi intellectuals to cite only one example,[40] and the like. Last but not least, it should be mentioned that Nor Zartonk has a representative in the highest council of the leftist, democratic and pro-Kurdish Peoples' Democratic Party (HDP), and is a member of the Peoples' Democratic Congress, a platform of multiple leftist organizations from which HDP has originated. In these ways, Nor Zartonk's activists get directly mobilized against the plural forms of oppression.

Intersectionality and activistic trajectories

Having set Nor Zartonk in the intersectional framework in terms of the subjectivities of its members, its ideology, and activism, I now turn to study the practical implications of these intersectional conditions. First, I start with the youths' activistic trajectories and try to draw conclusions about the mechanisms of enrollment in intersectional political activism. I ask: What are the motivations and routes that brought the activists to their current political positions? What specific role do their intersectional subjectivities have in this matter?

As the activists told me, the most influential founding members of the group had already been active in leftist activist circles during their university years, before resorting to Armenian-oriented activism with the foundation of Nor Zartonk in 2007. What is interesting here is the role the initial non-Armenian leftist activism had in motivating the activists towards Armenian activism. As several of them explained, they would probably not rise against the injustices and discrimination to which they were subjected as Armenians if it was not for the techniques and most importantly culture and psychology of resistance they acquired during their leftist activism in the pre-Nor Zartonk years. As Aren explained:

> Before founding Nor Zartonk we were members of a Turkish leftist youth movement [Sosyalist Umut Derneği]. We did feel ourselves as Armenians back then, that identity did exist, but it wasn't something very important for us ... But becoming socialist made us realize and understand more clearly that we had problems deriving from our [Armenian] identity. If I were a right-wing Armenian, maybe I would just curse and do nothing. It was the leftist movement that gave me this stance, [that taught me] how to stand up collectively [against oppression].

It is true that the growing influence of Istanbulite Armenian *Agos* newspaper and especially the shocking murder of its editor Hrant Dink, which was based on ethnic grounds, had an essential moral-psychological role in motivating these activists towards Armenian-oriented activism. In fact, the founding members 'really set Nor Zartonk into motion a few hours after the assassination of Dink, for it to become our promise to him that we will continue his work,' as Aren explained. Comments by two other Armenian activists, though not members of Nor Zartonk, might also be useful here to understand the influence of Dink's murder on the politicization of Istanbulite Armenians: 'The death of Hrant made us more Armenian'; 'I was a much more internationalist person before, but I got a bit too much immersed in the problems related to Armenian identity after the death of Hrant.'[41] Nevertheless, the activists' leftist militancy remains the defining factor behind their daring to engage in the Armenian-oriented activism. Saro put it very clearly: 'We have emerged from within the Leftists. It's the leftists that raised us to struggle and militancy.'

On the other hand, my analysis of the interviews shows that in the case of most, if not all, of those members who joined the group *after* it was founded, the main reasons prompting their engagement in political activism have been the Armenian dimension of their identity and the related oppressions. These individuals, who, unlike the founding members, were not involved in any kind of activism before joining Nor Zartonk, have decided to join the group mainly for the purpose of Armenian-oriented activism.[42] They might have had some sympathy towards the other, that is, non-Armenian, orientations of Nor Zartonk, since the latter addressed the rather dormant constituents of their intersectional subjectivities, but nevertheless 'it was the *Armenian* in me that initially went there,' as Saro confessed. Vartan, who went through the traumatic experience with his hostile neighbor, explained that it was that very same incident which led him 'to struggle in order to assure that no other Armenian will experience the same. And one day we crossed paths with Nor Zartonk.' What interests me the most, though, lies in the continuation of his story: ' … Before being a member of Nor Zartonk, I knew only in very broad terms that there was an idea of socialism, of equality, etc. I really learned about those after joining the group.' For another example that makes the link from purely Armenian to a more encompassing leftist activism clearer, I turn to Kevork:

> I had started going to demonstrations for Dink, but I didn't know much back then. The knowledge I had about Marxism, for example, was not accurate. I didn't know anything about the struggle of the Kurds, for instance. Media, education and all the ideological weapons of the state had somehow limited my understanding of things. Then I joined Nor Zartonk, where my ideas began to evolve and I succeeded in completely stepping outside of the ideological field of the state.

Thus, one could argue that Nor Zartonk, initially set in motion thanks to its founders' militant characters and experiences acquired within non-Armenian leftist circles, has eventually become an organization channeling youths from almost purely Armenian-oriented political stances to a more intersectional activism that situates itself in the broader New Left, as they see it accurate to qualify. It might thus be correct to speak of a formation of a new consciousness in the younger members' case, and of an *intersectionalization* of their ideologies and activisms.

Therefore, in the cases of both the founding members of Nor Zartonk and those who have joined later, we see how the politicization of one dimension of their intersectional subjectivities has paved the way for the politicization of others.

Intersectionalization of activist events

A second practical implication of the activists' intersectional nature is related, as it will be illustrated in this section, to the fate of the events in which they participate. In fact, the intersectionality of Nor Zartonk's activism consists of infusing multidimensionality in almost each and every event which the group joins. In other words, the very events these activists organize or take part in are *intersectionalized* by and through them.

This fact appears, first of all, in the primarily Armenian-oriented events organized by Nor Zartonk. For instance, during last year's protest march in commemoration of the Armenian Genocide and the murder of Sevag Balıkçı,[43] the Nor Zartonk activists led the crowd with their chants, amongst which, in addition to 'We will not forget you Sevag' they shouted the same slogan by replacing 'Sevag' with the names of other leftist and non-Armenian activists who perished in confrontations with the police during the Gezi riots. They also shouted the 'fraternity, liberty, equality' slogan – widely used in leftist circles. Thus, they brought non-Armenian, particularly leftist dimensions into an event, which mainly addressed anti-Armenian oppression. Similarly, during the struggle of Kamp Armen, the main objective of which was the return of the land deed to the Armenian Protestant Church, the camp was transformed into a space where informative talks about Women's Rights, LGBT rights, the protection of the environment and issues of other ethnic/religious minorities were held. Thus, the events in question became, at least to a certain degree, points of intersection for multiple causes and activisms.

This process of *intersectionalization* appears also and mainly in events that do not directly concern the Armenians as such. In order to clarify this point, we shall first return to a dimension of Istanbulite Armenians' social suffering and the social response to it, studied in more detail elsewhere.[44]

Istanbulite Armenians, similar to other marginalized communities, suffer from the fact that their 'existence is discounted and excluded.'[45] This fact in itself is two-dimensional. On the one hand, their history is neglected and erased – mainly through the denial of their genocide, the destruction of Armenian historical monuments that would have otherwise acted as 'place[s] of memory,'[46] and through the alteration of history, since in some Turkish historical writings 'Armenians [have been] made to vanish from their homeland, as if they never existed.'[47] On the other hand, many Istanbulite Armenians are incensed at the fact that their contemporary presence too is excluded from the public sphere. That exclusion results from Armenians' own tendency towards invisibility – a reaction to their feelings of fear and insecurity – and from the fact that Armenianness and its signs are often intentionally erased by anti-Armenian nationalistic tendencies. During recent years, a growing minority within the community struggles to change this situation of non-recognition, exclusion, and invisibility. To do so, they try, first, to propagate a 'counter-memory to the canonical ideological narratives'[48] of the Turkish state that dismiss and deny Armenians' historical presence and legacy, and second, to return signs and symbols of Armenianness into public visibility, for the contemporary presence of the community members to be recognized and normalized.[49]

Nor Zartonk has also had its share in the attempts of bringing both Armenians' historical legacy and contemporary presence in Turkey to visibility. More importantly for our point here, it often does that by intersectionalizing venues of activism. Let us illustrate this with some examples. Nor Zartonk had its own tent in Gezi Park during the latter's occupation in the summer of 2013. As the activists explained, they had initially gone there as environmentalists, for the purpose of defending the park from destruction, and as leftists resisting the neo-liberal policies of the political regime. However, at a certain point, 'after the park became a commune and every group was starting to present something to the others, we had this idea … ' explained to me Axel. The idea to which he referred was the installation of a fake gravestone, on which it was written: 'You took our cemetery, you won't be able to take our park!'[50] By this performative act, also referred to by other academics,[51] Nor Zartonk brought to the attention of the events' followers – and also of the co-protesters, a phenomenon to which we return in my next section – the fact that an Armenian cemetery used to exist in the area of the park but was confiscated and destroyed by the state in the 1930s. A second similar example was relayed to me by Aren:

> I was once invited to a panel about the history of socialism in Turkey, organized by a socialist organization. I started my talk by mentioning that the first socialists on these lands were, unlike how Turkey's most socialists think, not Turks who got organized during the first years of the Republic, but rather, Armenian socialist parties at the end of the nineteenth Century.

In both of the mentioned cases, originally non-Armenian activistic spaces are infiltrated by Armenian-oriented activism, which consists of reclaiming an erased history. Another interesting strategy by Nor Zartonk is participating in almost all public events by using the Armenian language on their placards and in their slogans. This is particularly significant, since the usage of Armenian in those venues is deliberate and calculated. In fact, the language these activists use in ordinary circumstances of their lives is Turkish, not Armenian. An activist, for example, laughingly recalled how he would always check the spelling of Armenian words before writing them on the wall during the Gezi Park protests. Thus, writing 'LGBT,'[52] '1st of May,'[53] or 'Woman, Life, Freedom'[54] in Armenian letters on protest banners and street walls is more than demanding the rights of LGBT people, workers, and women simply in a different language. It is a deliberate act that aims to mark the presence of Armenians in these movements and thus in the life of the city. One of the activists recalled:

> We were holding a banner during the meeting organized to protest the killing of Alevi intellectuals in 1993, on which we had written both in Turkish and Armenian: 'Fraternity, Liberty, Equality.' I heard people saying 'Oh! Armenians have come too!' Others were asking, 'Where have you come from? From Russia?' and we were responding: 'No, we're Armenians.'

Thus, the activists are fighting for the visibility and normalization of the Armenian presence in Istanbul. They are, again, clearly doing Armenian activism. But as they are doing it in the framework of other – socialist, feminist, environmentalist, etc. – activist events, they are intersectionalizing the latter. This process is, no doubt, conditioned by Nor Zartonk activists' intersectional subjectivities, ideology, and activism. In this sense, we can argue that activist groups, organizations, or movements whose ideology and activism are intersectional, have an intrinsic capacity of pluralizing and mutating events that they join. Most importantly perhaps, they thus have the potential, at least, to diversify the social, political, and cultural implications of the given public political events, and perhaps even create effects beyond the initially declared titles, demands, and goals of those. The citizens who come to an Armenian-oriented protest, or follow it on media or social media, become also exposed to other leftist ideas and demands infused in it. Similarly, those following LGBT, first of May, or other events, would eventually get exposed to the Armenian-oriented activism infused in those by Nor Zartonk.

Mutually reinforcing constituents of the intersectional activism

Lastly, we can discuss how the different constituents of this intersectional activism reinforce each other. One can particularly note that while, on the one hand being situated in the leftist/democratic political arena amplifies the impact of the Armenian-oriented activism, on the other hand being active and politicized as an Armenian enriches one's leftist/democratic struggle and makes it more comprehensive.

Although Nor Zartonk activists' participation in the non-Armenian leftist events is 'truly sincere and with equal force and motivation as in the Armenian events' as one of them put it, the fact that their position in the broader leftist/democratic political arena helps them in their Armenian-oriented mission is a reality that they do not deny. In other words, the fact that Nor Zartonk is located in the 'subaltern counterpublic' of Turkey, to use Fraser's terminology, 'where members of subordinated social groups invent and circulate counterdiscourses, which [...] permit them to formulate oppositional interpretations of their identities, interests, and needs,'[55] gives these activists crucially important moral/practical support in their Armenian-oriented activism and amplifies their voice. For instance, as the members of the group claimed, the Peoples' Democratic Party in which Nor Zartonk is represented has recently adopted the latter's demands regarding the issue of the Armenian Genocide as its own, thus elevating those to the level of a party that is represented in the Parliament. Similarly, the public events and activities organized by the group, like the 'occupation' of Kamp Armen, often get crucial practical support by other leftist/democratic political groups. Therefore, if not for its leftist/democratic ideology and activism which channeled it into the corresponding political networks, Nor Zartonk would have probably remained lonely and relatively unheard of in its Armenian-oriented activism.

On the other hand, Nor Zartonk activists' Armenian identity and the related activism serve as factors making their non-Armenian leftist/democratic struggle more encompassing and productive. In order to illustrate this point, I turn to the explication given to me by an Armenian journalist, not a member of Nor Zartonk, but clearly situated in a similar political position:

> Our Armenian identity gives us the opportunity to see different realities, to understand Turkey's history and present in a different way, from a different point of view, and, departing from these unique understandings, to bring our contribution to Turkey's democratization. If we weren't Armenians, we wouldn't have noticed some things. [For instance,] I believe that the Armenian [Genocide] issue has a very important place in our endeavor for a democratic Turkey. Without a liberal and democratic solution for that issue which is historically and symbolically very important, Turkey cannot really become democratic. And I, as a Turkish-Armenian can play a particular role in this direction.

The usage of those 'different point of view[s]' and 'unique understandings,' which Armenian activists owe to their ethnic identity, can be seen in the case of Nor Zartonk too. Telling about his speech in the panel dedicated to socialism's history in Turkey, Aren noted: 'I argued that *we, as socialists,* cannot understand our history and roots well if we neglect the historical Armenian socialist movements on these lands.' Aren has clearly made use of his ethnic baggage of knowledge for the good of the broader leftist movement of which he is part. Thus Armenian activists contribute to the non-Armenian members of the broader leftist/democratic movements by enriching their knowledge and understanding of the past, but also of the present of Turkey what concerns nationalism, racism, and the situation of minorities. Their intersectional participation has the potential to enrich the very notion of the sought-after 'democratic Turkey,' through making its preachers more and more sensitive towards the issues of ethnic/religious minorities. These are all achieved not only by simple interaction between the Armenian and non-Armenian leftist/democratic circles, as argued elsewhere,[56] but also and particularly through the very process of intersectionalization of events, which was discussed in the previous section. In fact, that process not only affects the public, but also and primarily the activists present there, who are thus treated as both co-militants in the non-Armenian cause *and* targets of the Armenian-oriented activism, such as in the cases of Gezi with the fabricated grave, and of all those events in which the Armenian language is strategically used. In fact, Nor Zartonk activists assert having indeed seen a positive change in some of the non-Armenian activists' stances as a result of that process of intersectionalization. Speaking about the Gezi Park experience, a member has noted: 'Some people came across an Armenian organization for the first time (...) This was very important. Gezi created an awareness.'[57] The image of the fake gravestone had indeed a fair share of circulation on social media and the slogan about the destroyed Armenian graveyard was repeatedly cited by non-Armenian protesters.[58] The Nor Zartonk activists claim that through these actions they are not only defending the rights of Armenians, but also trying to inform the general leftist and democratic front about the pending issues of ethnic/religious minorities in the country and about the fact that the broader goals of equality, freedom and democracy will never be fully achieved as long as those issues remain unresolved.

Conclusion

This paper studied Nor Zartonk through the theoretical framework of intersectionality. It showed how the multidimensional nature of the activists' subjectivities has resulted in a multidirectional and indeed intersectional ideology and activism. Furthermore, the analysis revealed some peculiar potentials of intersectional positionality by answering three questions to which I now return in order to conclude.

Can the politicization of one dimension of an intersectional subjectivity pave the way for that of other dimensions? We saw how, some Nor Zartonk activists' Leftist-oriented activism, built on some of the constituents of their intersectional subjectivities, was eventually crucial in enabling them to politicize another of those constituents – the ethnic one. On the other hand, we saw a similar process in the opposite direction among other, usually younger, members. The latter, mostly motivated towards an ethnic activism at first, were led to further politicize some of the other dimensions of their identities – gender, student, proletarian, etc. – thanks to the already established intersectional ideology of Nor Zartonk. This tells us a lot about the complexities of political activists' motivations and trajectories, and about intersectional subjectivities' role on the politicization of youths. This paper does not contend, of course, that all multiply oppressed people necessarily get mobilized in multiple – or even any – orientations. Rather, the point is that in order to understand the reasons and motivations behind activists' particular actions, we might well need to look deeper into their subjectivities and activistic trajectories. Nor Zartonk's founding members' engagement in Armenian activism cannot be explained simply by their being Armenian, but also and essentially by the initial politicization of another, class-related, dimension of their identities. Similarly, the group's younger members' engagement in leftist activism cannot be explained simply by their class identity, but also and essentially by their joining Nor Zartonk, which was initially instigated by another dimension of their identities – the Armenian one.

What effect can intersectional activists have on the events in which they participate, and, potentially, on the socio-political implications of those? The case study of Nor Zartonk showed that intersectional activists can 'intersectionalize' any given event in which they participate. This, consequently, can potentially bring forward such socio-political and cultural implications that were not anticipated in the declared titles, demands, and goals of the events. The impact of a public political event on the general audience may thus potentially be pluralized through a process of intersectionalization.

Can different dimensions of an intersectional activism support and enrich each other? Yes, at least in some cases, such as that of Nor Zartonk. While on the one hand the fact of being situated in the leftist political arena secures practical and moral support for its Armenian mission, on the other hand the Armenian identity and activism themselves are used as tools for being more original in the leftist/democratic activism and for expanding the ideological limits of the latter's followers, once again thanks to the process of intersectionalizing their spaces.

Applying the same questions to other intersectional groups in Turkey (and elsewhere) could possibly engender interesting results, be those conforming to or challenging the conclusions driven by the analysis of the particular case studied here. At least the work of some, out of the 104,066 associations and 4893 foundations active in Turkish civil society as of 2014,[59] could be analyzed through the intersectional framework. The following groups or movements seem promising in this regard and have not been studied yet: Laz Environmentalists,[60] Socialist and Environmentalist Zazas with graffiti such as 'Protect the nature, love the animals, let the Zaza language live,'[61] Feminist Hemşin activists who also struggle for the preservation of their language,[62] Alevi Arab Feminists,[63] the Armenian-Feminist Hay Gin platform (1998–2003).[64] This list is certainly not exhaustive. These groups, like Nor Zartonk, may be relatively smaller in membership number compared to other mainstream movements and organizations. Nevertheless, they might have 'the capacity to bridge movements and highlight connections among

70

different people and groups.'[65] They might, as Nor Zartonk, serve as channels for initially one-dimensional activists towards more encompassing, intersectional activistic experiences. They might, similar to Nor Zartonk, interfere in and even pluralize the social, cultural, and political impact of events they participate in. They might, finally, not only make use of the broader 'counterpublic' in order to advance the goals that are unique to them, but also use their unique identities and positions to enrich that counterpublic and expand the limits of its political imagination.

Notes

1. http://www.hurriyetdailynews.com/land-title-of-armenian-orphanage-kamp-armen-in-istanbul-returned.aspx?pageID=238&nID=90417&NewsCatID=339.
2. Zinn and Dill, "Theorizing Difference"; Hill Collins, *The Black Feminist Thought*; Hill Collins, "Moving Beyond Gender"; Hooks, *Ain't I a Woman?* and Hooks, *Talking Back.*
3. Crenshaw, "Mapping the Margins," 1244.
4. Brewer, Conrad, and King, "The Complexities and Potential"; Adib and Guerrier, "The Interlocking of Gender."
5. Nash, "Re-thinking Intersectionality," 13.
6. Beckwith, "Feminism and Leftist Politics"; Gellner and Karki, "The Sociology of Activism in Nepal"; Mishra, "Fijian Women's Activism"; Marik, "Breaking Through a Double Invisibility."
7. Doetsch-Kidder, *Social Change and Intersectional Activism.*
8. For an exception in this regards, see Ignatow, "Globalizations and the Transformation," 441–4.
9. Diner and Toktaş, "Waves of Feminism in Turkey"; Çağlayan, "Exploring the Intersections"; Çaha, "The Kurdish Women's Movement"; Çelik, "A Holistic Approach to Violence"; Al-Rebholz, "Gendered Subjectivity."
10. Özkaleli, "State of the State," 98.
11. Içduygu and Keyman, "Globalization, Civil Society and Citizenship"; Selek, "Les Possibilités et les Effets."
12. http://www.norzartonk.org.
13. Biehl, Good, and Kleinman, "Introduction," 6.
14. All names of interviewees are pseudonyms.
15. Kleinman, Das, and Lock, "Introduction," ix.
16. Das and Kleinman, "Introduction," 6.
17. Hrant Dink, then editor-in-chief of *Agos* weekly in Istanbul, was murdered by an ultranationalist teenager on 19 January 2007. See http://www.hurriyet.com.tr/turkish-armenian-journalist-shot-dead-5805519.
18. Sevag Balıkçı, an ethnic Armenian, was murdered during his military service on 24 April 2011. See http://www.bloomberg.com/news/articles/2011-04-26/ethnic-armenian-soldier-shot-on-genocide-day-radikal-reports.
19. Maritsa Küçük was murdered as part of a series of attacks on old Armenian women in Istanbul. See http://humanrightsturkey.org/2013/01/04/a-dark-christmas-for-armenians-in-turkey/.
20. Scheper-Hughes, *Death without Weeping*; Das, *Critical Events*; Kleinman, "Violences of Everyday Life."

21. Kleinman, Das, and Lock, "Introduction," x.
22. For more details on this social suffering and its response, see Papazian, "Emerging from the Shadows?"
23. A derogatory term used for non-Muslims, meaning infidel.
24. "What Is Nor Zartonk?," 57.
25. "The Program of Nor Zartonk," 4.
26. Ibid.
27. The activists explain that whereas the Old Left's goal was traditionally limited to the liberation of the working class, the New Left's goals also include the emancipation of oppressed identities.
28. http://www.demokrathaber.net/yasam/hrant-dinkin-arkadasi-orhan-bakirin-annesi-yasama-veda-etti-h36533.html.
29. Taturyan, "Manushyan Misak," 255–6.
30. Doetsch-Kidder, *Social Change and Intersectional Activism*, 3.
31. http://www.amerikaninsesi.com/content/hrant-dink-istanbulda-anildi/2604823.html.
32. http://www.cumhuriyet.com.tr/haber/diger/380878/Sevag_icin_Beyoglu_nda_protesto.html.
33. http://www.norzartonk.org/11858/.
34. https://www.youtube.com/watch?v=raIk1PY7o-g.
35. http://armenianweekly.com/2015/05/22/istanbul-camp-armen-protest/.
36. http://www.cumhuriyet.com.tr/haber/diger/338862/Yarin_istanbul_da_bu_yollara_dikkat_.html.
37. https://www.facebook.com/norzartonk/photos/a.147990138603798.33701.147807681955377/485347111534764/?type=3&theater.
38. http://www.norzartonk.org/%D5%B0%D5%B8%D5%BD-%D5%A5%D5%B4-%D5%BD%D5%AB%D6%80%D5%A5%D5%AC%D5%AB%D5%BD-hos-em-sirelis-2/.
39. http://www.kizilbayrak1.net/ana-sayfa/kadin/haber/ankara-kadin-platformundan-miting/.
40. http://bianet.org/bianet/toplum/115614-sivas-katliami-mitinginde-gericilikle-mucaledele-cagrisi.
41. For more on the influence of Dink's murder and of the subsequent show of solidarity by members of the Turkish public, see Papazian, "Emerging from the Shadows?"
42. It should be noted that Nor Zartonk is currently the only Armenian political organization in Turkey.
43. The murder of Balıkçı ironically coincided with April 24, the day in which Armenians commemorate the genocide of 1915.
44. See note 22 above.
45. Chuengsatiansup, "Marginality, Suffering, and Community," 33.
46. Küchler, "The Place of Memory."
47. Foss, "The Turkish View," 250.
48. Feldman, "Violence and Vision," 71.
49. See note 22 above.
50. https://www.facebook.com/norzartonk/photos/a.147990138603798.33701.147807681955377/478625808873561/?type=3&theater.
51. Ahıska, "Counter-movement, Space and Politics"; Gambetti, "Occupy Gezi as Politics"; Parla and Özgül, "Property, Dispossession, and Citizenship"; Tataryan and Von Bieberstein, "The What of Occupation."

52. https://www.facebook.com/norzartonk/photos/a.628695353866605.
    1073741830.147807681955377/660150897387717/?type=3&theater.
53. https://www.facebook.com/norzartonk/photos/a.147990138603798.33701.
    147807681955377/631783946891079/?type=3&theater.
54. https://www.facebook.com/norzartonk/photos/a.628695353866605.
    1073741830.147807681955377/768920053177467/?type=3&theater.
55. Fraser, "Rethinking the Public Sphere," 67.
56. Selek, "Les Possibilités et les Effets."
57. Çelebi, "Gezi ve Nor Zartonk."
58. Parla and Özgül, "Property, Dispossession, and Citizenship," 621.
59. Balcıoğlu et al., *Sivil Toplum İzleme*.
60. http://www.lazuri.com/sadik_varer/s_v_ekolojik_mucadele.html.
61. https://www.facebook.com/1510180462572492/photos/a.1510184142572124.
    1073741827.1510180462572492/1660580794199124/?type=3&theater.
62. https://www.facebook.com/photo.php?fbid=484229108396839&set=gm.
    705355349573140&type=3&theater.
63. http://mamasyria.blogspot.com.tr/2016/01/antakyada-arap-alevi-kadn-
    hareketi.html.
64. http://www.radikal.com.tr/radikal2/sibil-istanbullu-mu-870570/.
65. See note 30 above.

Acknowledgements

The author wishes to extend his thanks to Melissa Bilal and Laure Astourian who read the paper and commented on it.

Disclosure statement

No potential conflict of interest was reported by the author.

ORCID

Hrag Papazian ⓘ http://orcid.org/0000-0002-1254-8140

Bibliography

Adib, Amel, and Yvonne Guerrier. "The Interlocking of Gender with Nationality, Race, Ethnicity and Class: The Narratives of Women in Hotel Work." *Gender, Work and Organization* 10, no. 4 (2003): 413–432. doi:10.1111/1468-0432.00204.

Ahıska, Meltem. "Counter-movement, Space and Politics: How the Saturday Mothers of Turkey Make Enforced Disappearances Visible." In *Space and the Memories of*

Violence: Landscapes of Erasure, Disappearance and Exception, edited by Estela Schindel and Pamela Colombo, 162–175. New York: Parlgrave Macmillan, 2014.

Al-rebholz, Anil. "Gendered Subjectivity and Intersectional Political Agency in Transnational Space: The Case of Turkish and Kurdish Women's NGO Activists." In *Situating Intersectionality: Politics, Policy and Power*, edited by Angelia R. Wilson, 107–129. New York: Palgrave Macmillan, 2013.

Balcıoğlu, Zeynep, Sezin Dereci, Ayşegül Ekmekci, Tevfik Başak Ersen, Hazal İnce, Semanur Karaman, Burcu Uzer, et al. *Sivil Toplum İzleme Raporu*. İstanbul: TÜSEV, 2015.

Beckwith, Karen. "Feminism and Leftist Politics in Italy: The Case of UDI-PCI Relations." *West European Politics* 8, no. 4 (1985): 19–37. doi:10.1080/01402388508424552.

Biehl, João G., Byron Good, and Arthur Kleinman. "Introduction: Rethinking Subjectivity." In *Subjectivity: Ethnographic Investigations*, edited by João G. Biehl, Byron Good and Arthur Kleinman, 1–23. Berkeley: University of California Press, 2007.

Brewer, R. M., C. A. Conrad, and M. C. King. "The Complexities and Potential of Theorizing Gender, Caste, Race and Class." *Feminist Economics* 8, no. 2 (2002): 3–17. doi:10.1080/1354570022000019038.

Chuengsatiansup, Komatra. "Marginality, Suffering, and Community: The Politics of Collective Experience and Empowerment in Thailand." In *Remaking a World: Violence, Social Suffering, and Recovery*, edited by Veena Das, Arthur Kleinman, Margaret Lock, Mamphela Ramphele, and Pamela Reynolds, 31–75. Berkeley: University of California Press, 2001.

Crenshaw, Kimberle. "Mapping the Margins: Intersectionality, Identity Politics, and Violence Against Women of Color." *Stanford Law Review* 43, no. 6 (1991): 1241–1299. doi:10.2307/1229039.

Çağlayan, Hülya. "Exploring the Intersections: Subordination and Resistance among Kurdish Women in Aydınlı, Tuzla." Diss., Sabancı University, 2011.

Çaha, Ömer. "The Kurdish Women's Movement: A Third-wave Feminism Within the Turkish Context." *Turkish Studies* 12, no. 3 (2011): 435–449. doi:10.1080/14683849.2011.604211.

Çelebi, M. Ali. 2013. "Gezi ve Nor Zartonk [Gezi and Nor Zartonk]." Özgür Gündem, June 23. http://ozgurgundem4.com/yazi/76215/gezi-ve-nor-zartonk?page = author.

Çelik, Ayşe Betül. "A Holistic Approach to Violence: Women Parliamentarians' Understanding of Violence Against Women and Violence in the Kurdish Issue in Turkey." *European Journal of Women's Studies* 23, no. 1 (2014): 1–17. doi:10.1177/1350506814554487.

Das, Veena. *Critical Events: An Anthropological Perspective on Contemporary India*. Delhi: Oxford University Press, 1995.

Das, Veena, and Arthur Kleinman. "Introduction." In *Violence and Subjectivity*, edited by Veena Das, Arthur Kleinman, Mamphela Ramphele, and Pamela Reynolds, 1–18. Berkeley: University of California Press, 2000.

Diner, Cagla, and Şule Toktaş. "Waves of Feminism in Turkey: Kemalist, Islamist and Kurdish Women's Movements in an Era of Globalization." *Journal of Balkan and Near Eastern Studies* 12, no. 1 (2010): 41–57. doi:10.1080/19448950903507388.

Doetsch-Kidder, Sharon. *Social Change and Intersectional Activism: The Spirit of Social Movement*. Basingstoke: Palgrave Macmillan, 2012.

Feldman, Allen. "Violence and Vision: The Prosthetics and Aesthetics of Terror." *Public Culture* 10, no. 1 (1997): 24–60. doi:10.1215/08992363-10-1-24.

Foss, Clive. "The Turkish View of Armenian History: A Vanishing Nation." In *The Armenian Genocide: History, Politics, Ethics*, edited by Richard G. Hovannisian, 250–279. London: Macmillan, 1992.

Fraser, Nancy. "Rethinking the Public Sphere: A Contribution to the Critique of Actually Existing Democracy." *Social Text* 25–26 (1990): 56–80. doi:10.2307/466240.

Gambetti, Zeynep. "Occupy Gezi as Politics of the Body." In *The Making of a Protest Movement in Turkey: #occupygezi*, edited by Umut Özkırımlı, 89–102. Basingstoke: Palgrave Macmillan, 2014.

Gellner, David N. and Mrigendra Bdr Karki. "The Sociology of Activism in Nepal: Some Preliminary Considerations." In *Political and Social Transformations in North India and Nepal*, edited by Hiroshi Ishii, David N. Gellner, and Katsuo Nawa, 361–397. Delhi: Manohar, 2007.

Hill Collins, Patricia. *The Black Feminist Thought: Knowledge, Consciousness, and the Politics of Empowerment*. Boston, MA: Unwin Hyman, 1990.

Hill Collins, Patricia. "Moving Beyond Gender: Intersectionality and Scientific Knowledge." In *Revisioning Gender*, edited by M. F. Ferree, 261–284. Thousand Oaks, CA: Sage, 1999.

Hooks, B. *Ain't I a Woman?* Cambridge, MA: South End, 1981.

Hooks, B. *Talking Back: Thinking Feminist, Thinking Black*. Cambridge, MA: South End, 1989.

İçduygu, Ahmet and E. Fuat Keyman. "Globalization, Civil Society and Citizenship in Turkey: Actors, Boundaries and Discourses." *Citizenship Studies* 7, no. 2 (2003): 219–234. doi:10.1080/1362102032000065982.

Ignatow, Gabriel. "Globalizations and the Transformation of Environmental Activism: Turkey since the 1980s." *Globalizations* 5, no. 3 (2008): 433–447. doi:10.1080/14747730802252602.

Kleinman, Arthur. "The Violences of Everyday Life: The Multiple Forms and Dynamics of Social Violence." In *Violence and Subjectivity*, edited by Veena Das, Arthur Kleinman, Mamphela Ramphele, and Pamela Reynolds, 226–241. Berkeley: University of California Press, 2000.

Kleinman, Arthur, Veena Das, and Margaret M. Lock. "Introduction." In *Social Suffering*, edited by Arthur Kleinman, Veena Das and Margaret M. Lock, ix–xxvii. Berkeley: University of California Press, 1991.

Küchler, Susanne. "The Place of Memory." In *The Art of Forgetting*, edited by Adrian Forty and Susanne Küchler, 53–72. Oxford: Berg, 1999.

Marik, Soma. "Breaking Through a Double Invisibility." *Critical Asian Studies* 45, no. 1 (2013): 79–118. doi:10.1080/14672715.2013.758822.

Mishra, Margaret. "A History of Fijian Women's Activism (1900–2010)." *Journal of Women's History* 24, no. 2 (2012): 115–143.

Nash, Jennifer C. "Re-thinking Intersectionality." *Feminist Review* 89 (2008): 1–15. doi:10.1057/fr.2008.4.

Nor Zartonk. "The Program of Nor Zartonk." *Nor Zartonk* 3 (2015): 2–7.

Nor Zartonk. "What Is Nor Zartonk?" *Nor Zartonk* 3 (2015): 57.

Özkaleli, Umut. "State of the State in Their Minds: Intersectional Framework for Women's Citizenship in Turkey." *Women's Studies International Forum* 48 (2015): 93–102. doi:10.1016/j.wsif.2014.11.012.

Papazian, Hrag. "Emerging from the Shadows? Social Suffering and the Politics of Visibility among the Armenians of Istanbul." MPhil diss., University of Oxford, 2015.

Parla, Ayşe and Ceren Özgül. "Property, Dispossession, and Citizenship in Turkey; or, The History of the Gezi Uprising Starts in the Surp Hagop Armenian Cemetery." *Public Culture* 28, no. 3 (2016): 617–653. doi:10.1215/08992363-3511574.

Scheper-Hughes, Nancy. *Death Without Weeping: The Violence of Everyday Life in Brazil*. Berkeley: University of California Press, 1992.

Selek, Pınar. "Les Possibilités et les Effets de Convergences des Mouvements Contestataires, sous la Répression: Les Mobilisations au Nom de Groupes Sociaux Opprimés sur la Base du Genre, de l'Orientation Sexuelle, ou de l'Appartenance Ethnique, en Turquie." PhD diss., Université de Strasbourg, 2014.

Tataryan, Nora and Alice Von Bieberstein. (2013) "The What of Occupation: "You Took our Cemetery, You Won't Have Our Park!" Fieldsights - Hot Spots, Cultural Anthropology Online. http://culanth.org/fieldsights/394-thewhatof-occupation-you-took-our-cemetery-you-won-t-have-our-park.

Taturyan, Sh. "Մանուշյան Միսաք [Manushyan Misak]." *Soviet Armenian Encyclopedia* 7 (1981): 255–256.

Zinn, M. B., and B. T. Dill. "Theorizing Difference from Multiracial Feminism." *Feminist Studies* 22, no. 2 (1996): 321–333. doi:10.2307/3178416.

Negotiating 'the political': a closer look at the components of young people's politics emerging from the Gezi Protests

Pınar Gümüş

ABSTRACT
Based on ethnographic fieldwork conducted in Istanbul with participants of the Gezi Park Protests, this article studies how young people relate to the political. One of the most important priorities of this article is to discover new ways of thinking about young people and politics from a cultural perspective, and thereby rethink the notion of participation in relation to the political. Everyday life, values, and cultural practices are presented as lenses through which young people define the political. 'Politics as doing' emerges as the greatest commonality in the diverse definitions of the political, underlining the real, practical, and daily roots and effects of political action. Analyzing the diversity and overlaps within the differing perceptions and practices of the political by young people, this article underlines the need, and also possible ways, for thinking about youth political participation through new lenses.

Introduction

In 2013, the Gezi Protests started at İstanbul's Gezi Park before quickly spreading across the country. The broad participation of youth in the protests was unexpected, since the 1990s generation in Turkey has long been thought to be disinterested in political issues. Young people's engagement and signifi-cant visibility through their distinct ways of expression such as humor, chants, graffiti, and performances led these protests to be publicly perceived as youth protests. Whether they were youth protests or not is a question that needs to be discussed in its own right; however, it is not the main concern of this article. Moreover, the emphasis on the unexpectedness of young people's par-ticipation in the protests is also open to critical discussion, since it points to the biased perception of younger people as politically incapable. Nevertheless, what the Gezi Protests made definitively clear is that the ways we use to understand young people's relation to politics are limited in terms of explaining the complex and various ways of their engagement with political action. Not only mass youth participation, but also young people's modes of being in the protests revealed the gap between the young participants' understandings of what political action is and the existing literature's way of dealing with the political and youth participation.

What motivates young people to engage in political action and protest? What are the causes of their dissent? How do they imagine change? In which ways do they express their dissent and demands, and what do these modes of expression tell us about their ways of relating to politics? Embedded in all of these questions is the question of how young people define the political. Following this question, this article focuses on the diverse ways young participants of the Gezi Protests describe and relate to the political. In accordance with the young people's descriptions of the political, this article works through a definition of the political as actualized in daily acts and performances, which have a strong basis in values. Therefore, the political is studied in its informal meaning, as embedded in micro-processes, and covering the complex relations and structures of daily life. Based on the descriptions of the political by young people, the possibility of a refocusing of the perspectives employed so far to understand youth political participation is discussed.

In order to achieve these aims, in the first part of the article, the current discussions about young people, politics, and participation are reviewed, with a special focus on the critical works in the field. Then, how young people's participation in the Gezi Protests has been viewed and contextualized so far in the literature is examined in detail. Some theoretical points are reflected upon regarding the conceptualizations of youth and the political. After providing the details of the methodology of the field research, the article continues with the discussion of the empirical data based on the in-depth ethnographic interviews conducted with the young participants of the Gezi Protests. This article analyzes young people's perceptions of the political and discusses the new characteristics of the political emerging from the Gezi Protests under the categories awareness, everyday life, values, and politics as doing.

Young people, participation, and politics

Young people's participation in politics, or rather their apathy and disinterest in conventional political processes has been discussed as a problem for a long time. The problematization of young people's political participation as a 'crisis of democracy' and policy perspectives aimed at increasing youth political participation have been critically discussed by drawing attention to the structural

problems that hinder young people's social, economic, and political participation.[1] Many studies that emphasized young people's perceptions in their
relation to formal politics found that young people do not participate in the
formal processes of politics because they do not think that these conventional
processes are open to them and their day-to-day concerns; moreover, they do
not trust politicians or the political system, seeing them as dirty, corrupt, and
dishonorable.[2]

Uncertainty during the transition to adulthood, mostly in the form of social
and economic insecurity, has been underlined as a factor in young people's
disinterest in political processes. Since they devote their energy to 'saving
themselves' by securing a successful education and a good job, young
people do not have the time or motivation for collective political processes.
Struggling with collectively experienced structural problems as individuals
is one effect of neoliberal and globalization processes. Therefore, focusing
on individualization in risk societies has been one approach to thinking
about youth political participation in recent decades.[3] Young people's participation in new social movements has been discussed as a disintegration of the
older forms of collective identity, the politicization of the 'personal,' and a
rejection of the politics rooted in the old social order, rather than a disinterest
in politics.[4]

Youth political participation literature has developed around the binary
opposition of engaged and active youth, on the one hand, and the disengaged
and apolitical youth, on the other hand. Departing from this binary, Rys
Farthing suggests a new conceptualization of 'radically unpolitical young
people,' based mainly on Beck's discussion of youthful antipolitics, and underlines the need for a deep understanding of how young people are radically
reshaping the political by rejecting both traditional parties as well as new electronic and consumer forms of political engagement.[5] Anita Harris, Johanna
Wyn, and Salem Younes focus on ordinary young people, that is, to say the
ones neither deeply apathetic nor unconventionally engaged. Looking more
closely at how these mainstream young people reflect and act upon social
and political issues, they underline unspectacular and everyday activities as
individualized forms of political participation which could open up new possibilities for a non-adult-centric redefining of politics.[6] Erik Amnå and Joakim
Ekman take the active/passive distinction as a critical point of departure and
argue that not all forms of political passivity are the same. They suggest three
forms of young citizens – unengaged, disillusioned, and stand-by – the latter
of points to a potential of political knowledge and perspective which can
reveal itself under certain conditions.[7]

Young people's presence and leading role in the Occupy movements,
the anti-austerity protests in Europe, and the revolutionary uprisings in
the MENA region all underlined the need to better understand young
people's relation to politics and the political. Nadine Sika, analyzing

young people's political participation in Egypt prior to the uprisings, argues that young people's non-participation in politics, that is, to say their abstention, was a result of their perceptions of the authoritarian state and corrupt politics as non-changeable. However, when the political opportunity arose, they participated actively in changing the politics of the country.[8] Phil Mizen, writing on youth participation in a local Occupy movement in the U.K., reveals the importance of emotional reasoning for young people in political processes.[9] In their edited volume, Linda Herrera and Rehab Sakr present a wide range of case studies on young people's activism in the Middle East, with a special focus on changing patterns and experiences of citizenship for young people through online spaces.[10] The Gezi Protests, too, have triggered discussions on youth political participation in Turkey.

In Turkey, young people's relation to politics is mostly discussed in terms of the apolitical youth discourse, which referred to the generation that grew up in the years after the 1980 coup, when society was depoliticized in all domains and neoliberal policies started to alter the economic and social dynamics. Quantitative studies have dealt with the apolitical youth discourse in Turkey by researching young people's engagement in political parties, interest in parliamentary politics, as well as political and civil society organizations, and mostly proved that youth political participation is limited in Turkey.[11]

On the other hand, in order to go beyond the insufficiency of evaluations of young people as apolitical or apathetic, researchers from the fields of sociology and cultural studies have pointed out the need to look more closely at the main concerns of young people. Lüküslü, after conducting extensive field research with young people, argued that the post-1980 youth in Turkey are aware of the political arena and are unhappy with it; for that reason, they consciously choose not to participate. Rather, they use coping tactics in everyday life that can be defined as necessary conformism, such as humor, making fun of serious things, or not paying attention at all, allowing them to continue in the midst of this seemingly passive, but in itself uneasy, social situation.[12] Analyzing the public discourse on youth in Turkey, Neyzi states that the post-1980 generation, in contrast to previous generations, attempts to construct their subject positions by expressing their identities, performing cultural practices, and participating in civil society. In that sense, the diverse, newly emerging youth cultures in Turkey grow in parallel to new political identities.[13] Therefore, the popular discourse that judges young people for being apolitical is not only incorrect, but also fails to see how people are active and motivated to make decisions about their everyday lives and to shape the society they are living in, even if this is not considered 'politics' or 'participation.'

Youth in the Gezi Protests

Young people's visibility in the Gezi Protests has once more made the super-ficiality of the apolitical youth discourse obvious. Moreover, the participation of youth from various socio-political backgrounds, but especially that of indi-vidual nonpolitical young people – often referred to as apolitical – revealed the need for a nuanced analysis of young people's relationship with the political in Turkey in its complexity and diversity, going beyond binary oppositions such as political-apolitical or engaged-unengaged. What sort of contact with the political prompted these young people, who seem to be disinterested in poli-tics, to go to the streets at that particular time in history, for that event, in that way?

Quantitative data give some clues regarding the level of youth participation and the profile of the young participants in the protests. According to the face-to-face survey research conducted by KONDA with 4411 participants in the park area over the course of the protests, 30.8 percent were aged between 21 and 25, while 20.3 percent were 26–30.[14] Moreover, 78.9 percent of the par-ticipants were not members of any political party, organization or association, foundation, or platform. In addition, 93.6 percent of the participants declared that they took part in the protests just 'as citizens,' that is, not as representa-tives of any group or entity.[15] This study therefore shows that the majority of protestors in the park were young people under the age of 30, who for the most part do not identify their participation in the protests with any political affiliation.[16]

The socio-political context in which the Gezi Protests emerged, along with the motives of the participants, have been discussed widely. Cihan Tuğal, con-necting the Gezi Protests with the global wave of uprisings between 2009 and 2014, compares them with protests in Greece, Spain, the U.S.A, Egypt, Tunisia, and Brazil. Tuğal examines these cases within the context of a hege-monic global capitalist order – in other words, neoliberal capitalism and American leadership – and describes the protests as anti-commodification and anti-authoritarian: 'As the hegemons turn from consent to coercion, anti-authoritarian and anti-war protests spread, and are likely to spread further. Depending on the national context and the timing, anti-commodifi-cation protests have been (again contingently) articulated to anti-authoritar-ian protests.'[17] In this way, Tuğal suggests a way of analyzing how a protest against the commodification of a park turned into a one against authority. Barış Mehmet Kuymulu, drawing upon the concept of the right to the city in reference to Henri Lefebvre, reads the protests as a resistance against an urbanism that prioritizes capital over the interests of the inhabitants, and points to the shift in the agenda of the protests to civil rights and individual and collective freedoms.[18] Tayfun Atay draws attention to the need to look more closely to the Gezi Protests through the notion of 'culture.' Underlining the policies of the ruling party since 2011, Atay suggests that the Gezi Park demonstrations are 'cultural and rooted in the worries of the "secular masses" about the shrinking ground of their lifestyle as a result of government pressures'.[19] Ayhan Kaya discusses how Turkish society and politics have undergone a drastic transformation under the influence of Islam and neoliberalism since 2002, and argues that the Gezi Protests were partly 'a social upheaval against the subtle Islamisation of Turkish society and politics.'[20] Demet Lüküslü states the emergence of a new myth of a pious generation through her analysis of education and youth policies, as well as governmental discourses from 2011 to 2014, and claims that the Gezi Protests were a sociopolitical challenge to this 'myth of pious youth and all it entails – from the project of Islamization and authoritarian control in general and gender segregation and alcohol restrictions in particular.'[21]

A middle-class background has been identified as the most common characteristic of the young participants in the Gezi Protests. Çağlar Keyder described the main actors of the protests as young members of a new middle-class formation, who 'work in relatively modern workplaces, with leisure time and consumption habits much like their global counterparts'. But they also look for new guarantees for their way of life, for their environment, of their right to the city; and they resent violations of their personal and social space.'[22] Similarly, Tuğal suggests that Gezi was mainly a middle-class movement, in which the professionals made up the core participant group. What caused this class to take to the streets was not economic exploitation or impoverishment, but the impoverishment of social life. Lacking a feeling of fulfillment in their lives, what participants experienced in the Gezi Protests provided them with a non-commodified, solidary form of life. It was for this that they stayed in the park.[23] Erdem Yörük and Murat Yüksel claim that class cannot explain the dynamics or the profile of the Gezi Protests. What distinguished the Gezi protesters was not their class position, but their political and cultural orientation; Yörük and Yüksel therefore approach the Gezi Protests as a people's movement based on political demands – rather than strictly class-based ones – in which members from all social classes participated.[24]

The diversity in the socio-political backgrounds of the participants was one of the most significant features of the Gezi Park Protests, especially when considering the unexpected coexistence and cooperation among such different groups as leftists; nationalists; Kurdish groups; activists of new social movements like feminism and Lesbian, Gay, Bisexual and Trans (LGBT) and environmental rights; Armenian, Alawite, and anti-capitalist Muslim young people; as well as football fan groups, individual participants, and many others. The need to adopt new perspectives, in other words 'spoiling memorization,'[25] to understand the politics emerging from this diversity and practiced as being together with differences, has been underlined by Yael Navaro-Yashin:

These protests have not allowed themselves to be placed in any known frame-works of analysis such as secularism versus Islam, modernists versus tradition-alists, liberals versus conservatives, the bourgeoisie versus the working classes, left versus right, cosmopolitans versus nationalists, feminists versus sexist men, gay-rights activists versus homophobes. The protesters in the square rep-resented all these inclinations, as well as none. Or rather, the way they expressed their sentiments and desires, spoke their minds and hearts, fitted with no predisposed lenses.[26]

In light of this, developing empirically informed, in-depth understandings of the motives and cultural and political tendencies of the protestors takes on crucial importance. Moreover, such a way of analyzing the components and the politics of the protests opens up the way to a sense of the 'Gezi spirit,' referring generally to the unique experiences and practices of the protestors in Gezi Park, and how it is 'produced as an interactive and shared definition that is, continually negotiated, tested, modified and reconfirmed by several individuals and groups.'[27]

İlay Romain Örs and Ömer Turan argue that an unwritten code of conduct, which they describe as the 'manner of contention,' realized in the ethos of col-lective work, a spirit of exchange and gift-giving, politeness and non-violence, provided the ground for peaceful cultural and political pluralism in Gezi Park.[28] Onur Bakıner emphasizes the processual nature of politics and under-lines that, even if the protestors did not start with the aim of transforming society, their rainbow of political agendas and willingness to expand the limits of these agendas through dialogue allowed them to perform the fulfill-ment of their demands.[29] In a similar vein, Buket Türkmen's work focuses on how feminists' experiences in the protests affected them, and analyzes the long-term transformative effects of the Gezi resistance for women partici-pants.[30] Funda Gençoğlu Onbaşı accentuates that the Gezi Protests triggered an inquiry into the definition of politics and the political, and points to other, unconventional ways of *doing politics*[31] and the importance of individual pol-itical action.[32] In her analysis, informed by radical democratic theory, Genço-ğlu Onbaşı criticizes essentialism, which discusses the political identities in the Gezi Protests as complete and fixed. Rather, she offers an understanding of political subjectivities as relational, continuously constituted through the pol-itical realm and open to new articulations.[33]

Qualitative studies with a theoretical focus on youth look at young people's perceptions to develop an understanding of the politics of the Gezi Protests. Emre Erdoğan looks at young people's political participation through the con-cepts of political psychology. His research shows that 'grievance,' 'anger,' 'feeling excluded,' and 'political cynicism' are some of the common themes that provide an understanding of the roots of young people's participation in the protests. Moreover, Erdoğan discusses the possibility of young protes-tors constructing a collective political identity based on these feelings, and points to the young participants' unwillingness to transform the Gezi movement into a long-term political movement as a significant obstacle to the construction of this collective identity.[34] Bahar Tanyaş investigates how young people in the Gezi Protests give meaning to the discourse of the nonpolitical youth generation and position themselves and their generation in relation to this notion. In her analysis, Tanyaş writes that young people tend to distance themselves from this nonpolitical youth discourse in one way or another, yet do not ignore or deny it; what is more, they talk within this discourse and are worried about the next generations being nonpolitical. The notion of political apathy, therefore, still has substantial power.[35] Yılmaz and I study the Gezi Protests by focusing on young participants from new social movements. Based on qualitative field research conducted with feminists, LGBT youth, and environmental activists, we argue that young people's interest in and struggle to influence public matters in the Gezi Protests was not unrelated to the youth participation that had already been developing in these movements.[36]

This article is also based on young people's perspectives on the Gezi Protests and develops an in-depth understanding of how these young participants relate to politics and the political. Being aware of their socio-economic and political backgrounds, but not limited by the inferences and predictions stemming from these differences, this article approaches young people's relation to the political as constructed in a relational, process-focused, dynamic, and pluralistic way. Through participants' descriptions of the political, the emergence of a new politics based on pluralism and 'the Gezi spirit' will be studied, as will the components of this politics. This article also aims to pave the way for breaking the apolitical vs. political duality by discovering different parts of the complex picture of youth political participation.

Theoretical reflections

Bourdieu offers a sociological description of youth as a power relationship based on age.[37] Society often grants power to older people while seeking to limit it among younger ones, thereby creating an age-based hierarchy. When it comes to young people's participation in politics, this young-old divide crystallizes. The positioning of young members in many political parties as 'interns' or 'prospective' members is just one of the common examples. Therefore, in order to start a discussion of young people's political participation, this notion of age hierarchy should be taken into consideration. Youth sociology has also taught us that the experience of youth is not homogenous, and can change depending on time, geography, cultural and ethnic identity, socio-economic situation, and gender, among other factors. All these various experiences of being young should undoubtedly be analyzed in the discussion of young people's participation, yet it is nevertheless significant that youth cuts across this broad range of experiences as an age-based social relationship. The nature of this relationship changes in different contexts, and the way it functions has the potential to inform us about the very dynamics and divisions within our society. In Alberto Melucci's words, youth is a mirror that makes the problems of a society visible.[38] Therefore, this article focuses on youth as a sociological category that opens up new perspectives through which to understand society. Moreover, discussing youth as a sociological concept based on power relationships necessitates a critical approach in both theory and methodology. Recreating concepts and revisiting theoretical discussions informed by young people's perspectives, rather than interpreting their accounts in limited, externally imposed categories, makes for a more suitable research strategy.

In their work on youth political participation, Therese O'Toole, Michael Lister, Dave Marsh, Su Jones, and Alex McDonag discuss how the mainstream literature's use of 'the political' imposes a conception of politics and political participation upon respondents and limits the political to particular types of participation, thereby creating the political participation/political apathy dichotomy. This approach overlooks how young people themselves see politics and therefore limits a coherent understanding of how and why young people participate or not. O'Toole et al. call for a broader conception of the political, putting the focus on how young individuals define the political in reference to their experiences:

> To move to a broader conception of 'the political,' we argue that it is important to allow individuals themselves to say how they conceive of politics, what it means to them and how they relate to it. In this sense, 'the political' is conceived of less as an arena or set of arenas, but rather as a lived experience ... [39]

Inspired by their approach, this article does not start by pre-defining the political, but rather keeps it as an open term to be filled by young people's accounts. In doing so, it aims to discover young people's ways and modes of approaching and recreating the meanings of the political, as well as performing politics in their complexity and multitude.

Ulrich Beck discusses the reinvention of politics in relation to the processes of individualization and globalization. In the transition from industrial to global risk society, '"individualization" means the disintegration of the certainties of industrial society as well as the compulsion to find and invent new categories for oneself and others without them.' In this way, Beck portrays individualization as a process and struggle of managing new and unexpectedly risky life situations, through which individuals are thought to be the *actors*, *designers*, *jugglers*, and *stage directors* of their own biographies, identities, social networks, commitments, and convictions.[40] This definition of the individual also invites a rethinking of the political aspect of individuality, and especially a contextualization of young people's growing tendency to define the political in individualistic terms.

As institutions go through the process of reflexive modernization, so does the political sphere. Moreover, similar to other institutions such as the family, economy, or education, the transformation in politics is subtle and difficult to analyze and understand through old categories. Beck writes on the changing meaning of the political as such:

> In other words, politics breaks open and erupts *beyond* the formal responsibilities and hierarchies, and this is misunderstood particularly by those who unambiguously equate politics with the state, the political system, formal responsibilities and full-time political careers. An ambivalent, multi-level, 'expressionistic concept of politics' (Jürgen Habermas), which permits us to posit the social form and politics as mutually variable, is being introduced here for a very simple reason. It opens a possibility in thought which we increasingly confront today: the political constellation of industrial society is becoming *un*political, while what was unpolitical in industrialism is becoming political. This is a category of transformation of politics with *unchanged* institutions, and with intact power elites that have not been replaced by the new ones.[41]

This understanding of the transformation in politics speaks to this article's question regarding where to look for politics. Looking to traditional institutions such as parliaments, political parties, trade unions, etc. in order to understand the change in the political sphere and the meaning of the political is not only limited, but also invalid and misleading. However, focusing on 'subpolitics' provides a way beyond these old categories to see what is political and how it is performed. Therefore, this article does not depart from a given categorization of the spaces of the political; rather, it looks more closely at all the areas of life seen by young people as political, driven by a curiosity to discover where politics is still 'ticking.' In his discussion on the conceptualization of subpolitics, Ulrich Beck writes:

> People expect to find politics in the arenas prescribed for it, and they expect it to be performed by the duly authorized agents; parliament, political parties, trade unions and so on. If the clock of politics stops there, then it seems that politics as a whole has stopped ticking. [...] Anyone who stares at politics from above and waits for the results is overlooking the self-organization of politics, which – potentially at least – can set many or even all fields of society into motion 'subpolitically.'[42]

This article studies the ways and the spaces in which the young participants of the Gezi Protests define, give meaning to, and act the political, without limiting itself to the institutional dimension. These new spaces, particularities of everyday life, and areas conventionally regarded as outside the political – such as relationships, values, and daily individual practices – will be discussed as at the heart of the politics of young people. The differences and commonalities in young people's perspectives will be highlighted in order to develop a nuanced understanding of the politics of the Gezi Protests.

Methodology

This article grounds its discussion in the qualitative field research conducted with young participants of the Gezi Protests in İstanbul.[43] An ethnographic approach has been selected as the main methodological guide in this study, since it provides the tools for the discovery and interpretation of how people give meaning to their experiences, as well as for investigating the complexity of people's culture and political world.[44] Moreover, as reflexivity is an inherent part of ethnographic methodology, it also provides an opportunity for the researcher to continuously reflect on her own role and effect in the process of the field work, as well as on the knowledge that results from it.

The main method of fieldwork was in-depth ethnographic interviews, of which the primary aim was to produce a deep and detailed knowledge of the young people's experiences. Even though the fieldwork did not include comprehensive participant observation during the protest period (since interviews were conducted after the protests took place), all of the fieldwork was conducted through an ethnographic gaze. Field data were therefore produced through a combination of the interviews and ethnographic fieldwork diaries. The fieldwork places a clear emphasis on the voices and concerns of young people; accordingly, open-ended interviews with minimum interventions were conducted, in order to enable the interviewees to say what they felt was relevant and important to them.[45]

In total, 40 in-depth interviews were conducted with young people between the ages of 18–33[46] who participated in the Gezi Protests. Participation is defined as having taken part in the demonstrations and/or the occupation of the park. Some interviewees were active members of local initiatives founded after the protests, in addition to having demonstrated and camped in Gezi Park.[47] Interviewee profiles were formed to reflect the variety of the social and political backgrounds of the participants, such as the environmental, feminist, LGBT, right-to-city, and anti-capitalist/anti-militarist movements; Kurdish, Armenian, and Alawite young people; oppositional Muslim groups; members of the nationalist and leftist organizations; independent activists, youth work volunteers, as well as young people who did not have any political affiliation. In terms of the age and gender distribution, 30 of the interviewees were between the ages of 18–24, while 8 were between 25 and 30; 2 participants were 33 years old. Twenty-three interviewees were female, 16 were male, and 1 was transgender. Twenty-two were students, while 18 worked in different sectors or were unemployed.

In September 2013, preliminary fieldwork was conducted in order to explore the possible connections between the analytical perspective of the research project and the field material. Fieldwork was then completed in two stages, between April–November 2014 and January–July 2015. Extending the fieldwork over time made continuous interaction between the data and the theoretical framework of the research possible. After each stage, the theoretical framework was revisited and revised. In that way, this investigation aimed a continuous interplay between data and ideas, which is inspired by grounded theorizing as a way of working with data. In this process, 'ideas are emergent from one's experience in the field, and from one's preliminary analytic reflections on the data. As this should make clear, emergence is a function of the analytic work one puts in: it does not "just happen."'[48] Thus, the analysis is the final product of constant work by the researcher on her field experiences. Accordingly, data analysis was already in progress from the beginning of the fieldwork, and did not have to wait until all of the data had been collected. As the fieldwork proceeded, the focus of the research progressively narrowed.[49]

The data consisting of full transcriptions of the interviews and field notes, were thematically analyzed. Following the preliminary fieldwork, protest, politics, and youth were defined as three of the investigation's main themes. Accordingly, the data were organized along these three themes in the initial phase of data analysis. After that, through repeated and close readings of the material, concepts were generated under each main theme, and the ways the young people described these concepts were studied. The interviewees' accounts were analyzed against the backdrop of their socio-economic and cultural conditions, as well as their political or group affiliations. Regarding 'the political,' the main concepts to emerge at the end of the analysis phase included awareness, action, and practice; everyday life, relations, consumption, locality; and values such as trust, ethics, and conscience.[50] This article grounds its discussion in this selected part of the data analysis, focusing on young participants' reflections on the notion of the political and their relationship with politics in the context of the Gezi Protests. Based on the extensive field material, developing a complex and detailed account of how young people attribute meanings and perceive processes regarding politics and the political is one of the primary aims of this work.

What is 'the political'? The characteristics of the new politics emerging from Gezi

Young participants in the protests mostly discussed the political as a positive concept, pointing to the possibilities of transformation and social change, and emphasizing the oppositional potential. While describing the notion of the political, the young people pointed to many different aspects of the social and political spheres, and emphasized their ways of relating to these various processes.

First of all, participants' accounts share a common point regarding the political as a general consciousness about the social and political events/issues around them, as well as an attempt to affect these events/issues. Secondly, young people referred to the concept of the political as an overarching one, whose manifestations and practices are found in many spheres of everyday life, such as consumption, personal relations, leisure time preferences, etc. The political is, therefore, far from being limited to any space or institution, but is in everything, everywhere. Thirdly, what was so significant is that the basis of the political is described in reference to values. Living ethically, having a conscience, and being humane were mentioned frequently. Lastly, what was highlighted in all the discussions is that the political is about doing; it is practice-based, and thus cannot be understood purely through theory or discussion.

Awareness: What is happening in society?

For some of the interviewees, being political refers to being conscious of one's socio-political environment. One interviewee, who has worked as an active member of a nationalist youth organization since she was a student, describes being political this way:

> One does not need to be organized in order to be political. If she has an idea about her country and the world, understands what is happening, as Nazım Hikmet said, for example, follows the current political developments – not only what the political leaders say but workers' deaths, occupational struggles, etc. – all the social events, thinks on them, presents ideas, and talks about them from time to time, then she is a political student for me. (Member of nationalist youth organization, 23)

While identifying an awareness of what is happening as the very foundation of being political, the interviewee also accentuates that one should be able to analyze, reflect on, and share ideas considering the processes around them. In this way, the interviewee frames being political as an active, conscious, and continuous type of engagement with society's issues and problems. Her account is meaningful, given her own experience as an active, organized student in a nationalist youth organization. However, since she also stresses that being political is not the same as being formally organized, the interviewee distances herself from the organized-political vs. unorganized-apolitical[51] duality, presenting instead a broad understanding of the political as a type of social behavior, a point of view, a way of positioning oneself in society. Another respondent, who is active in a leftist organization, expressed a similar idea, although she was more focused on issue-based political thinking and action. She states that:

> For me, being political corresponds to seeing an issue – it can be just a women's issue or a Kurdish one, minorities' issues, all the issues at stake in Turkey –

[and] to develop an approach and idea for an issue, trying to organize your idea, to reflect on it, that kind of thing … (Member of leftist organization, 25)

In reference to the two quotations above, it can be argued that young people who are involved with more conventional organizations, such as nationalist or leftist organizations, have a quite structured, process-based, and coherent understanding of being political. Both of the interviewees underlined the processes of, first, being aware of a social problem, analyzing it, producing their own ideas, and finally, developing a response.

Another participant sees being political as related to being aware of others in society, who may have different values and problems, and doing something for them. She says:

I can talk (about the political) on the basis of active citizenship. To protect, to do something about the environment we live in, about the people we live with and their values. I can make a definition based on being sensitive to these issues, to embracing the existence of others and their values, and to fight for them. (Youth work volunteer, 23)

The interviewee depicts being political as being active in reciprocal relations and a collective spirit in society, and as such, her way of describing the political seems to relate to her experience as a voluntary worker. That is, to say, being political is, in a sense, volunteering for the struggle to solve our collective problems. In addition to her previous volunteer experience, the interviewee reported that her understanding of the political deepened throughout the protests. Having an awareness of each other's needs and ideas, protecting each other, being kind to other, sharing – regardless of prejudices stemming from cultural and social differences – were the most important aspects of the way young people related to one another in the Gezi Protests. These experiences formed the basis of collective action, thinking, and political discussions, and accordingly, a redefinition of politics.[52]

Everyday life: relations, consumption, and the local

The participants define the scope of the political as encompassing all the particulars of everyday life. The basic daily practices of eating, relating to others – including to nature and animals – and consumption, along with holiday or leisure time preferences and neighborhood life, were all considered to belong within the arena of political thinking and action.

The environmental activists interviewed emphasized the way people construct their relationship to the natural environment as an important part of the political. One of the interviewees explains how 'natural' and 'small' things became political. What is more, being political emerges as a direct consequence of living in a context where one's ecological surroundings are under threat. Therefore, being political is defined as a necessity reflex to today's conditions. The interviewee is a member of an alternative farming group and spends a considerable amount of time every week in the garden. She states that:

> If you want to save the trees as we did in the Gezi Protests, or if you want to save your rivers, you are opposing the system, because these are the things imposed upon you by the system and when you oppose, as a matter of course you become political. The 90s generation is always referred to as apolitical, but we became political out of necessity. For example, I did not think that I was participating in food politics, I realized afterwards how valuable a seed is – okay, it's just a seed, normally it's like flowers or birds, and you may think, why do all these need to be political? However, our time is the one in which all these things became political. (Environmental activist, 24)

The interviewee's expression 'our time' is also worthy of attention. Pointing to the shifting spaces of oppression and threat under the system, she also refers to the changing meaning of the political resulting from wider socio-political change. Since power and oppression can be exercised through and on such small natural things as rivers and seeds – in the form of neoliberal policies, prioritization, and commodification – then these issues are at the heart of politics. Moreover, her account invites one to consider the limits of the categories apolitical-political when trying to understand young people's politics, since, in these new areas of struggle, the young people referred to as apolitical define themselves as political.

Emphasizing daily and basic activities when defining the political goes along with a focus on the individual. A feminist activist, who takes part in an anti-capitalist and anti-militarist group, presents her understanding of the political, stressing the individual's relationship with her environment:

> For me, it starts with relations. It's about how we relate and how we live … How do we share the place we live in, what we eat, how do we form trust-based relationships? If we cannot trust each other, we cannot change other things. These other things are also the ones that affect us. I do not differentiate between inside and outside. We can start a political transformation by practicing [this new politics] in our lives … We are severely alienated. Capitalism determines our relationships, too: If you don't have money, you can't go anywhere with your friends in a social environment. Finding out the things that can be done free of charge is therefore very political for me. (Feminist and activist in anti-capitalist and anti-militarist group, 33)

In this way, the interviewee defines the political as a bottom-up process that starts with an individual's daily acts, positions, and relations within the society; eventually, this process has the potential to create change. The interviewee's account highlights that day-to-day experience, affective relations, and the deep motivations of individual behavior become the battleground for social conflicts, where new powers and new forms of resistance and opposition confront each other.[53] As the political is defined as embedded in any relation one has, be it with the social environment or food, one's political stance is imprinted deep in the particulars of daily life. The interviewee also emphasizes how material conditions determine the content of one's life – how one spends leisure time with friends, for example. Therefore, opposition even in the tiny spaces of systemic oppression, such as finding activities free of charge, is an important part of being political. Consumption therefore also emerges as one of the main spaces for political acts. Another respondent, who had no political affiliation prior to the Gezi Protests but, as a result of the protests, recently started identifying as an environmental activist, reports how her relationship with consumption has changed:

> [The political] is life itself ... When you get political in some way, it spreads to every aspect of your life. The shoes and bag I buy, my holiday preferences ... For example, I do not think that I will be going on luxury holidays anymore. Consumption is in all fields, so when you get critical about consumption, you change many things. (Environmental activist, 24)

As consumption is an all-pervasive phenomenon in our daily lives, changing consumption practices is an important first step towards greater change. Throughout the Gezi Protests, several boycotts were organized: many brands, shops, and restaurants were boycotted as a response to their attitude or statements regarding the protests.[54] These examples show that the field of consumption bears significant potential for mass political action.

Local initiatives, and particularly neighborhood solidarity initiatives, in İstanbul and many other cities were a product of the post-Gezi process. After the period of communal life in Gezi Park ended in June 2013 (due to police intervention), protest participants started to gather in 'park forums' in their neighborhoods in order to discuss their local issues, a reference to the forum experience of Gezi Park. The inner dynamics, profiles of the participants, and the content of the discussions undoubtedly varied in each of the park forums. However, the interviewees who participated in the park forums expressed similar views on them. They felt that they had brought the transformative potential that emerged in the Gezi Protests to these forums, and that these spaces functioned as experimental schools of politics in which they were free to express themselves.[55] One interviewee, who had no political affiliation to any group prior to the Gezi Protests, started to attend the park forum in her neighborhood, and subsequently became an activist in the neighborhood solidarity initiative. Her story is telling in terms of thinking about the politicization of young people in today's world. She reported that she decided to become a member of the initiative at the very moment she could not find an apartment at an affordable price in her neighborhood, thanks skyrocketing prices related to the urban regeneration process. She describes what is political for her:

For me, anything that affects my life is political. For this reason, I find neighborhood solidarity very important. Whatever their problem is, people should try to solve it. Trying to do something about the course of one's own life is important. Very small things may be political; political attitudes are all the things about everyday life. (Activist in neighborhood solidarity initiative, 30)

Since politics is described as built into the fabric of everyday life, politics is practiced mostly in local arenas. Neighborhood solidarity initiatives, as an example of local initiatives, have been underscored as the places where people can find solutions to their problems, or in other words, do politics. Another activist from a neighborhood solidarity initiative, who has also been a member of right-to-city movements for a long time, underlines the limits of representative democracy and the people's right to express themselves and to participate in the decisions that affect them. He says:

[The political means] letting the people express themselves, giving them the authority … If you only allow people to express themselves once every five years, this is not representative democracy. I see the issue as one of rights. People should be able to make decisions about the place they live in, their education, and the taxes they pay … My understanding of the political is not about political ideologies, but about living humanely. (Activist in right-to-city movements, 23)

This quotation reveals the discrepancy between how representative democracy actually functions and young people's expectations concerning a political structure.[56] For young people, the local structures in which they struggle to affect the decision-making processes are more meaningful than political ideologies, or elections every five years.

Values: trust, ethics, and conscience

Young people often referred to values when discussing the notion of the political. Trust-based relationships were mentioned by one activist (in the quotation above) as an important requirement for change. Described in this way, the political is constructed as a direct contrast to the existing norms and practices of the formal political sphere: the political, as it is understood by young people, has a strong basis in real life and is built on trust and reliability.

In the context of the Gezi Protests, conscience was referred to as the basis for opposition to unjust treatment. Many young people's first motivation to take to the streets was the police violence against the initial protestors as it was witnessed through social media.[57] Therefore, many young people were spurred to collective opposition because of their conscience, and later, their descriptions of the political included conscience as a guiding principle. An environmental activist states that:

The solution is about conscience. If we have people with a conscience, wherever we are, we can solve our problems. It is an issue of conscience. Gezi was also an issue of conscience. You can solve this violence against people by following your conscience. (Environmental activist, 22)

The emphasis on conscience is also important in terms of explaining how many people from many different political backgrounds came together on the basis of common values. Moreover, it would not wrong to argue that, for young people who intentionally keep themselves at a remove from politics, conscience seems to function as a way to relate to the political beyond the constraints of ideologies and political organizations. One respondent, who became a member of a leftist organization after the Gezi Protests, highlights how empathy and conscience motivate young people into political action:

> We should look at the situation from a humanistic point of view. If we can offer something like this for youth, then a youth movement may appear. When it is political ideology, it ends after a while. They move when something is meaningful for their conscience, they can empathize. They did it at Gezi, [and] it needs to be done to continue this. (Member of leftist organization, 25)

An LGBT activist describes the political by referring to her relationship to life and herself. In this way, she presents a profound understanding of being political. To her, being ethical is the basis of the political, and it starts with freeing oneself from systemic impositions:

> I am trying to live a life, and politics means being ethical as far as possible in my relationship to life and myself. To the extent I can do this free from systemic impositions, I think that I will be that much more political. Resistance, etc., all these have that kind of a meaning for me, and this type of being political comes with some specific acts. (LGBT activist, 27)

Being ethical, in her account, mainly refers to being honest with herself and others, doing what she thinks is true regardless of the oppressions and norms – in essence, to maintain a consistency between one' beliefs, thoughts, and practices. As an LGBT activist, her description of the political is also telling. Her presence, sexual orientation, bodily expressions, lifestyle choices, and even emotions have the potential to be 'problems' for society. She therefore confronts 'systemic impositions' quite often, and resisting them turns into a struggle to be honest with herself, to live ethically, and, eventually, to be political.

Politics as doing: the political as practice

Interviewees' reflections on the political mostly point to a practice-based definition of the concept. They rarely mentioned theorizing, long discussions, developed action plans, etc.; rather, they emphasized a here-and-now approach – doing what one could do at the moment and thereby contributing to the transformation of social norms. One of the interviewees, who started identifying as an independent activist after the Gezi Protests, puts it clearly in his account:

> We do not need to talk over these things any more. Let's make it happen; action is important. (Independent activist, 23)

This action-based understanding of the political is undoubtedly related to the young people's perceptions of the conventional political sphere. They criticize politicians for just talking and doing nothing. The institutional political sphere is a distant realm for them, too far from their reality. Consequently, they opt for an understanding of the political that they practice and apply in every aspect of their lives:

> … They perceive politics as words, as making comments to each other. However, it is not like this. Life itself is political, what you wear, your style, your position in life, your way of communicating with a person … .(LGBT activist, 20)

Similarly, the practical in the political is pictured as the opposite of political ideologies. An environmental activist, based on the experience of his childhood years, emphasizes that practical things, such as solidarity-based relationships or subsistence farming, can change people's lives. Therefore, he believes in the power of the practical and describes change – the political – through practice:

> I have never defined myself as a communist, socialist, or anarchist. I have witnessed too many practical things, such as farming tomatoes in pots or people sharing things between them; I have never thought that there was a need for -isms. I have searched for something practical every time. The logic is that the practical is the political. (Environmental activist, 22)

All in all, political means practical. Action, doing, and practice represent the real side of the political and the only basis on which change can occur. This practice-based perspective also seems to be rooted in young people's experiences in the Gezi Protests, since their direct action succeeded in preventing the construction of the shopping mall in Gezi Park.

Conclusion

This article aimed to discover how the young participants of the Gezi Protests perceive the notion of the political. Some of the interviewees reported that their notions of the political were formed during their experience in the Gezi Protests, while others indicated that their understandings of the political were transformed, changed, and deepened during the course of the protests. Thus, the accounts of what is political reflect the politics of young people in the Gezi Protests, constructed by the exchange and blending of different ideas and experiences.

The interviewees defined the political with an emphasis on their everyday life experiences. Young people who are involved in conventional nationalist and leftist youth organizations emphasized political consciousness as the basis for the political, and described political acts in stages of analysis and action, followed by political consciousness. Moreover, collectivity, solidarity, and trust-based relationships were referred to as the crucial aspects through which the political is defined. Consumption was highlighted as a field bearing the potential of political protest, whether by altering one's everyday consumption preferences or by creating activities free of charge. Young participants identified their relationships with themselves, as well as with their social and ecological environments, as political relationships, guided by basic values such as trust, conscience, and ethical considerations. Young people also share a common understanding of the political as practice-based; they prefer action over dealing with ideologies and grand theories. What is more, the local is pointed to as the most important initial space where this action-based idea of the political is practiced.

What kind of clues can the Gezi Protests provide in terms of how to rethink young people's relation to politics? How can young people's perceptions and descriptions of the political inform our research on youth political participation? These accounts depict that young people do not lack a perception of the political. Indeed, they have extensive and well thought-out understandings of the political, which are embedded in the very details of their everyday lives, values, and practices. This picture proves that young people not only feel themselves disconnected from the current political systems, but have also developed their own notions of the political. It therefore seems that a reconsideration of the definition of the political, informed by young people's perspectives, would be of great value. Moreover, the characteristics of young people's notions of the political not only reveal their reasons for distancing themselves from traditional politics, but also inform us about the constituents of a new, more diverse, emerging politics. Young people speak of 'subpolitics' instead of the conventional institutional spaces and practices in which politics has long been thought to exist. The ways and concepts through which young people define politics also open up a new perspective to interpret their motivations for taking action and going to the streets in the Gezi Protests. What makes young people protest may indeed be a 'small' thing, such as the cutting down of trees; however, this 'smallness' does not reflect young people's limited relationship with politics. On the contrary, the views that politics about nature is not politics indicate an outdated understanding of politics.

The Gezi Protests provided social scientists with an extensive field for researching a variety questions among groups differing in age, class, gender, and ethnic and religious identities. This article focused on young people's politics within this broad field. The recent developments in Turkey – the attempted military coup and its aftermath – undoubtedly represents another period of great historical importance, and the need to puzzle out its societal effects is obvious. Therefore, how different groups in Turkish society are affected and relate to these recent events seems to be one of the most important future research topics for social scientists. These recent developments are also worth analyzing in terms of young people and politics. How do young people from different parts of the country and from different socio-economic and political backgrounds perceive these recent events? How did they relate to the political field throughout this period? How do they imagine change and the future of the country? Research on these initially formulated questions, along with many others, will obviously greatly contribute to our understanding of young people and their relation to politics and the political in Turkey.

Notes

1. Bessant, "Mixed Messages."
2. Furlong and Cartmel, "Young People and Social Change," 126–27.
3. Beck and Beck-Gernsheim, *Individualization.*
4. Furlong and Cartmel, "Young People and Social Change," 136.
5. Farthing, "The Politics of Youthful Antipolitics," 192.
6. Harris, Wyn, and Younes, "Beyond Apathetic or Activist Youth."
7. Amnå and Ekman, "Standby Citizens."
8. Sika, "Youth Political Engagement in Egypt."
9. Minzen, "The Madness That Is the World."
10. Herrera and Sakr, *Wired Citizenship.*
11. KONDA, "Türkiye'de Gençlerin Katılımı"; *Türk Gençliği 98*; "Türk Gençliği ve Katılım."
12. Lüküslü, *Türkiye'de "Gençlik Miti."* See also Lüküslü, "Necessary Conformism."
13. Neyzi, "Object or Subject?"
14. KONDA, "Gezi Report," 10.
15. KONDA, "Gezi Report," 14.
16. Undoubtedly, the quantitative data are limited in many aspects and far from being representative for the general population of young people in the Gezi Protests. For a critical discussion on the limitations and scientific credibility of quantitative data produced on the Gezi Protests, see Yavuz, "Kahrolsun Bağzı Veriler."
17. Tuğal, "Resistance Everywhere," 155.
18. Kuymulu, "Reclaiming the Right," 275–76.
19. Atay, "The Clash of 'Nations,'" 41.
20. Kaya, "Islamisation of Turkey," 64.
21. Lüküslü, "Creating a Pious Generation," 8.
22. Keyder, "Law of the Father."
23. Tuğal, "Resistance Everywhere," 157.
24. Yörük and Yüksel, "Gezi eylemlerinin toplumsal dinamikleri", 164.
25. As it is described by Yael Navaro Yashin in her article: "Spoiling memorization (*ezberi bozmak*) is a Turkish idiom. It refers to re-doing that which is taken-for-granted. It implies creativity, innovation ... " See Yael Navaro Yashin, "Editorial: Breaking Memory, Spoiling Memorization."

26. Ibid.
27. Özkırımlı, "Introduction," 4.
28. Örs and Turan, "The Manner of Contention."
29. Bakıner, "Can the Spirit of Gezi Transform?" 73.
30. Türkmen, "Gezi Direnişi ve Kadın Özneler."
31. Italics in original.
32. Gençoğlu Onbaşı, "Gezi Park Protests in Turkey," 279–80.
33. Ibid., 281–82.
34. Erdoğan, "Siyasal Psikoloji."
35. Tanyaş, "Gençler ve Politik Katılım," 43.
36. Gümüş and Yılmaz, "Where Did Gezi Come From?"
37. Bourdieu, "Youth Is Just a Word," 94.
38. Melucci, *Challenging Codes*, 127.
39. O'Toole et al., "Tuning Out or Left Out," 53.
40. Beck, *The Reinvention of Politics*, 95.
41. Ibid., 99.
42. Ibid., 98–99.
43. Doctoral project field research: "Youth in the Gezi Protests: Cultural Practices, Politics and Being Young in Turkey" conducted as a member of International Graduate Centre for the Study of Culture, University of Giessen.
44. Bray, "Ethnographic Approaches," 301.
45. Ibid, 310.
46. The initial age range defined for the participants was 18–30. However, in the course of the fieldwork, two interviewees aged 33 were included since their experiences were unique and important due to their political background.
47. Exceptions to this definition of participation took the form of two interviewees who were supporters in online spaces during the protests, but became active members of the local initiatives afterwards. Since the local initiatives have been taken as a part of the process of the Gezi Protests in this article, these two interviewees were included.
48. Hammersley and Atkinson, "The Process of Analysis," 159.
49. Ibid., 160.
50. I have discussed my field data on young people's protest experiences elsewhere. See Gümüş, "Emergency in Protest."
51. Young people's critical perceptions regarding political organizations, including both political parties and conventional leftist organizations, were a point of discussion in terms of their disinterest in politics. My field data validate that young people see political organizations as hierarchical bodies that function through strict procedures, rules, and ideologies, and therefore do not provide any space for the individual to make free choices. Young people do not want to be confined to such a structure, and therefore opt to distance themselves from these types of organizations, even if they agree with some of the organizations' positions. For a discussion on the relationship between young people's disinterest in politics and their critiques of the political organizations, see Lüküslü, *Türkiye'de Gençlik Miti*, 157–61.
52. See Gümüş, "Emergency in Protest."
53. Melucci, *Challenging Codes*, 106.
54. One of the biggest boycott campaigns was against Garanti Bank, a member of the Doğuş Group. Since the media branch of the group was thought to have censored the news about the protests, many customers canceled their credit

cards and withdrew their cash accounts: Accessed May 28, 2016. http://www.milliyet.com.tr/garanti-1500-kart-iptal-edildi/ekonomi/detay/1718470/default.htm.

55. See Gümüş, "Emergency in Protest," 14.

56. Young people's perceptions of the conventional political processes in Turkey have been discussed in relation to their disinterest in politics; see Lüküslü, *Türkiye'de Gençlik Miti*, 146–47.

57. See Erdoğan, "Siyasal Psikoloji"; Gümüş, "Emergency in Protest."

Acknowledgements

I would like to express my gratitude to my supervisor, Jörn Ahrens, as well as my second supervisor, Demet Lüküslü, for their support throughout my doctoral research, and for their comments on an early version of this article. My thanks also go out to two anonymous reviewers, and to Ayhan Kaya, Cristiano Bee, and the participants of the workshop for this special issue for their valuable contributions.

Disclosure statement

No potential conflict of interest was reported by the author.

Funding

I am grateful to the International Graduate Centre for the Study of Culture (GCSC) funded by the German Research Foundation in the context of the German Excellence Initiative for its financial support [grant id Doctoral scholarship].

Bibliography

Amnå, Erik, and Joakim Ekman. "Standby Citizens: Diverse Faces of Political Passivity." *European Political Science Review* 6, no. 2 (2014): 261–281.

Atay, Tayfun. "The Clash of 'Nations' in Turkey: Reflections on the Gezi Park Incident." *Insight Turkey* 15, no. 3 (2013): 39–44.

Bakıner, Onur. "Can the Spirit of Gezi Transform Progressive Politics in Turkey?" In *The Making of a Protest Movement in Turkey #occupygezi*, edited by Umut Özkırımlı, 65–76. New York: Palgrave Macmillan, 2014.

Beck, Ulrich. *The Reinvention of Politics: Rethinking Modernity in the Global Social Order*. Cambridge, MA: Blackwell, 1997.

Beck, Ulrich, and Elisabeth Beck-Gernsheim. *Individualization: Institutionalized Individualism and Its Social and Political Consequences.* London: Sage, 2002.

Bessant, Judith. "Mixed Messages: Youth Participation and Democratic Practice." *Australian Journal of Political Science* 39, no. 2 (2004): 387–0.

Bourdieu, Pierre. "Youth Is Just a Word." In *Sociology in Question*, edited by Pierre Bourdieu, 94–101. London, Sage, 1993.

Bray, Zoe. "Ethnographic Approaches." In *Approaches and Methodologies in Social Science: A Pluralist Perspective*, edited by Donatella della Porta and Michael Keating, 296–315. New York: Cambridge University Press, 2008.

Erdoğan, Emre. "Siyasal Psikoloji Siyasal Katılım Hakkında Ne Öğretebilir? Gezi Protestoları'na Katılanlar Üzerinden Bir Değerlendirme [What Can We Learn from Political Psychology about Political Participation? A Qualitative Fieldwork with GeziProtestors]." *Marmara Üniversitesi Siyasal Bilimler Dergisi* 3, no. 5 (2015): 31–58.

Farthing, Rys. "The Politics of Youthful Antipolitics: Representing the 'Issue' of Youth Participation in Politics." *Journal of Youth Studies* 13, no. 2 (2010): 181–195.

Furlong, Andy, and Fred Cartmel. *Young People and Social Change: New Perspectives.* Maidenhead: McGraw-Hill, 2007.

Gençoğlu Onbaşı, Funda. "Gezi Park Protests in Turkey: From 'Enough is Enough' to Counter-hegemony?" *Turkish Studies* 17, no. 2 (2016): 272–294.

Gümüş, Pınar. "Emergency in Protest: Young People's Politics in the Gezi Protests." *On_Culture: The Open Journal for the Study of Culture* 0, no. 1 (2016): http://geb. uni-gies- sen.de/geb/volltexte/2016/12069.

Gümüş, Pınar, and Yılmaz, Volkan. "Where Did Gezi Come From? Exploring the Links Between Youth Political Activism before and During the Gezi Protests." In *Everywhere Taksim: Sowing the Seeds for a New Turkey at Gezi*, edited by Isabel David and Kumru Toktamış, 185–200. Amsterdam: Amsterdam University Press, 2015.

Hammersley, Martyn, and Paul Atkinson. *Ethnography: Principles in Practice.* New York: Routledge, 2007.

Harris, Anitta, Johanna Wyn, and Salem Younes. "Beyond Apathetic or Activist Youth: 'Ordinary' Young People and Contemporary Forms of Participation." *Young: Nordic Journal of Youth Research* 18, no. 1 (2010): 9–32.

Herrera, Linda with Rehab Sahr. *Wired Citizenship: Youth Learning and Activism in the Middle East.* New York: Routledge, 2014.

Kaya, Ayhan. "Islamisation of Turkey under the AKP Rule: Empowering Family, Faith and Charity." *South European Society and Politics,* 20, no. 1 (2015): 47–69.

Keyder, Çağlar. "Law of the Father." *London Review of Books Blog*, June 19, 2013. http://www.lrb.co.uk/blog/2013/06/19/caglar-keyder/law-of-the-father/.

KONDA. "Gezi Report: Public Perception of the Protests, Who Were the People at Gezi Park?" June 5, 2014. http://konda.com.tr/en/raporlar/KONDA_Gezi_ Report.pdf.

KONDA. "Türkiye'de Gençlerin Katılımı [Participation of Young People in Turkey]." İstanbul Bilgi Üniversitesi Şebeke Gençlerin Katılımı Projesi Kitapları No:3 [Istanbul Bilgi University Network Participation of Young People Project Books No: 3]. İstanbul, 2014.

Kuymulu, Mehmet Barış. "Reclaiming the Right to the City: Reflections on the Urban Uprisings in Turkey." *City* 17, no. 3 (2013): 274–278.

Lüküslü, Demet. *Türkiye'de "Gençlik Miti": 1980 Sonrası Türkiye Gençliği* [The "Myth of Youth" in Turkey: The Post-1980 Generation]. İstanbul: İletişim Yayınları, 2009.

Lüküslü, Demet. "Necessary Conformism: An Art of Living for Young People in Turkey." *New Perspectives on Turkey* 48 (2013): 79–100.

Lüküslü, Demet. "Creating a Pious Generation: Youth and Education Policies of the AKP in Turkey." *Southeast European and Black Sea Studies* 16, no. 4 (2016): 637–649.

Melucci, Alberto. *Challenging Codes: Collective Action in the Information Age.* Cambridge: Cambridge University Press, 1999.

Minzen, Phil. "The Madness That Is the World: Young Activists' Emotional Reasoning and Their Participation in a Local Occupy Movement." *The Sociological Review* 63, no. 2 (2015): 167–182.

Neyzi, Leyla. "Object or Subject? The Paradox of 'Youth' in Turkey." *International Journal of Middle East Studies* 33, no. 3 (2001): 411–32.

Örs, İlay Romain, and Ömer Turan. "The Manner of Contention: Pluralism at Gezi." *Philosophy and Social Criticism* 41, no. 4–5 (2015): 453–463.

O'Toole, Therese, Michael Lister, Dave Marsh, Su Jones, and Alex McDonag. "Tuning Out or Left Out? Participation and Non-participation among Young People." *Contemporary Politics* 9, no. 1 (2003): 45–61.

Özkırımlı, Umut. "Introduction." In *The Making of a Protest Movement in Turkey #occupygezi,* edited by Umut Özkırımlı, 1–6. Houndmills: Palgrave Macmillan, 2014.

Sika, Nadine. "Youth Political Engagement in Egypt: From Abstention to Uprising." *British Journal of Middle Eastern Studies* 39, no. 2 (2012): 181–199.

Tanyaş, Bahar. "Gençler ve Politik Katılım: Gezi Parkı Eylemleri'nde 'Apolitik' Nesil [Young People and Political Participation: The 'Apolitical' Generation in the Gezi Park Protests]." *Eleştirel Psikoloji Bülteni* [Critical Psychology Bulletin] 6 (2015): 25–50.

Tuğal, Cihan. "'Resistance Everywhere': The Gezi Revolt in the Global Perspective." *New Perspectives on Turkey* 49 (2013): 147–162.

Türk Gençliği 98: Suskun Kitle Büyüteç Altında [Turkish Youth 98: The Silent Majority Highlighted]. Ankara: Konrad Adenauer Vakfı, 1999.

"Türk Gençliği ve Katılım." [Turkish Youth and Participation]. ARI Düşünce ve Toplumsal Gelişim Derneği, 2001.

Türkmen, Buket. "Gezi Direnişi ve Kadın Özneler" [Gezi Resistance and Women Subjects], in *Kültür ve İletişim* [Culture and Communication] 34 (2014): 11–35.

Yavuz, Onur. "Kahrolsun Bağzı Veriler." In *Gezi ve Sosyoloji: Nesneyle Yüzleşmek, Nesneyi Kurmak,* edited by Vefa Saygın Öğütle and Emrah Göker, 99–123. İstanbul: Ayrıntı Yayınları, 2014.

Yörük, Erdem, and Murat Yüksel. "Gezi eylemlerinin toplumsal dinamikleri [Social Dynamics of the Gezi Protests]." *Toplum ve Bilim* 133 (2015): 132–165.

The weakest link or the magic stick?: Turkish activists' perceptions on the scope and strength of digital activism

Şenay Yavuz Görkem

ABSTRACT
This article summarizes the first part of the findings of a larger study which gathers data on Turkish activists' perceptions on the scope, strength and limitations of digital activism. Specifically, the study explores what strength Turkish activists attribute to digital activism in achieving certain objectives, whether Turkish activists are optimistic, pessimistic or persistent in their attributions related to digital activism, and whether they believe in the possibility of an e-revolution. Both quantitative and qualitative data were collected via a web-based survey of 302 activists. The survey employed a Likert Scale to measure the efficacy that Turkish activists attribute to digital activism in achieving different objectives as well as six open-ended questions that provide in-depth qualitative data.

Introduction

Digital activism can be defined as the utilization of digital technologies by individuals with the aim of causing social or political change.[1] It covers a large array of activities. Because of this inclusiveness, discussions on the use of the term 'digital activism' continue, and alternative terms that embrace or question the content and effect of digital activism have emerged. Some of these terms are cyber activism, internet activism, online activism, e-activism, e-revolution, clicktivism, one click activism, armchair activism, slacktivism, hacktivism and electronic civil disobedience. It could be noted here that different attitudes to the concept are reflected in the array of terms developed for digital activism.

Some scholars have questioned the effects that individuals produce via digital activism.[2] They claim that digital activism creates 'weaker links' when compared to traditional activism, involves low-risk actions which do not break existing laws, and therefore does not lead to changes in political dynamics. These scholars argue that the only benefit digital activism offers is that it serves to increase the activists' 'feel good factor.' That is why digital activism is at times named 'slacktivism' by those who argue that it is not possible to create an impact by digital activism unless online collective action is transferred to the offline world.[3]

This article summarizes the first part of the findings of a larger study which gathers data on Turkish activists' perceptions on the scope, strength and limitations of digital activism. To be more specific, it explores what strength Turkish activists attribute to digital activism in achieving certain objectives, whether Turkish activists are optimistic, pessimistic or persistent in their attributions related to digital activism, and whether they believe in the possibility of an e-revolution. Additional research questions of the study focus on what purposes social networking sites such as Facebook or Twitter served for digital activism, situational factors that activists perceived as obstacles to their work, and activists' perceptions of the interaction between digital activism and offline activism. Due to space constraints, this article summarizes results relating only to the first three research questions.

It should be noted here that our knowledge on the perspectives of activists on the scope and strength of digital activism is limited. This article aims to fill this void and gather data to find out what strength Turkish activists attribute to digital activism in achieving certain objectives and to explore whether Turkish activists are optimistic, pessimistic or persistent in their attributions related to digital activism. The following section summarizes the related literature. The first part focuses on activism and digital activism and elaborates on in what aspects these two forms of activism interact with and support each other. The review of literature continues with a summary of different perspectives on the scope and strength of digital activism. The final subsection summarizes digital activism profile of Turkey.

Literature review

Activism and digital activism

Activism is a term denoting the abilities or practices of individuals with an effort to make a change on social, political, economic or another dimension of an existing situation.[4] The term emerged in the 1970s and is closely associated with the concepts of social movement, advocacy, resistance and protest. The term is also closely related with internal and external political efficacy, meaning the extent to which people believe they can initiate social and political change and the extent to which they believe they can urge government authorities to respond to their demands.[5] Activism can be used for reactionary or progressive purposes. Likewise, goals of activists can vary from hyper-local issues to global phenomena.[6]

Activists are defined as two or more individuals who come together to influence another public or other publics via tactics of training, negotiation, persuasion or power.[7] Digital activists, on the other hand, can be defined as people who support, oppose or resist change as part of an online collective action.[8] Digital technologies have changed the nature of activism. Unlike the past, a revolution can be declared on the internet with statements like 'Revolution starts on … .'[9]

Digital technologies are used with the aim of encouraging participation of larger numbers of people in activism. They are also used for mobilizing, activating and organizing.[10] When the term 'Twitter Revolution' was used for the informational activities of a group of activists organizing anti-government protests in Moldova on Twitter during 2009 elections, the concept 'digital activism' took its place in the related literature. In the same year, Twitter users in Iran mobilized through Twitter and commented on the victory of Mahmoud Ahmadinejad in the 12 June election. Their exposure of alleged electoral irregularities led to street protests and civil disobedience.[11] Anti-government protests that took place in Tunisia, Egypt, Libya, Yemen and Syria in 2011 and the way both online and offline forms of activism were combined during these protests boosted the upsurge of interest on the issue. Digital activism supported traditional activism, enhanced communication and coordination and even contributed to toppling dictatorships in these countries.[12]

Jurgenson[13] states that digital activism augments the reality of offline events. Information, visuals and videos about activism in the streets are shared and offline activism is commented online. In other words, social media leads to a snowball effect and what takes place offline becomes augmented online as more people share and comment on material related to the offline activism efforts. On the other hand, online activism is rooted in offline activism. Activism carried out online only would be limited in effect as offline reality is where the power of online activism lies. As Peña-López, Congosto and Aragón[14] state 'there is a strong bond between the online and offline worlds of activism … growth of activity is parallel in both worlds, backed by political marketing and communication techniques.'

Different perspectives on digital activism

There are three main perspectives on the value of digital activism: the optimistic perspective, the pessimistic perspective and the persistent perspective.[15] According to the optimistic perspective, nonviolent protest will be replaced by digital activism in the future. As activists will become computerized and computer hackers will be more politicized, traditional activism tactics will take a more digital form; for instance, trespasses or blockages will be

carried online. Electronic and communication infrastructures, not the physical infrastructures, will be the target of attack as many interactions that
change power relations in today's world are taking place online.[16] For this
reason, Wray asserts that activism, carried out against capitalism, for
example, has to be carried online since 'capitalism has become increasingly
nomadic, mobile, liquid, dispersed and electronic.'[17]

Optimistic scholars believe that digital technologies generate new forms of
collective action that can be used to voice dissident opinions. They emphasize
the transformative power of the internet and claim that digital activism not
only supports traditional activism but also breaks power relations in societies
and open new channels for political participation.[18] Optimists put forward
that digital activism will disrupt political hierarchy and empower citizens as
power relations in digital technologies become more integrated into our
real lives.[19]

The role that digital technologies play in activism efforts of individuals
ruled under oppressive regimes in which activists have many difficulties in
contacting each other offline, supports the optimistic perspective. Individuals
in these countries can get organized and coordinated with the help of online
anonymous discussion board and encryption software.[20] Another point put
forward by optimistic scholars is that whereas one's potential audience
during a protest in the offline world is limited and people can feel that
their effect is lost in large physical spaces, digital activism provides people
with the opportunity to follow the effects they create in the online community.
They can follow how many people view, like and share their online contributions. They can also follow the comments on their contributions. This
opportunity acts as an advantage in keeping the ' ... ambition, motivation
and a sense of hope that each individual is making a sense ... ' alive, which
is a must for individuals to keep on with their activism efforts.[21]

On the other hand, pessimistic scholars emphasize the power of the digital
technologies and assert that digital technologies are not good in nature. They
point to the examples of civil and military cyberattacks which resulted in large
explosions and significant damage[22] and claim that digital technologies serve
opportunities to individuals and groups with 'destructive' purposes opportunities to achieve goals that would previously have been beyond their reach.
Pessimistic scholars also assert that oppressive governments utilize the internet as a tool for propaganda, surveillance and censorship. They claim that the
internet not only empowers and liberates individuals living under oppressive
regimes but also enhances oppressive governments' ability to control and per-
secute dissidents, which is a sign that it is not the inherent nature of the internet to favor the oppressed over the oppressor.[23] As Ghannam[24] states it is not
unusual for governments to call for emergency, cybercrime, anti-terrorism
and press and publication laws and arrest and fine individuals for online
activities. Şener[25] names the ability of the governments to monitor and

control citizens' online activities as 'global digital panopticon.' By monitoring online activities of citizens, governments can identify, locate and target activists.[26]

The fact that digital activism is carried out under the limitations of many different factors also supports the pessimistic perspective. To start with, activists' communication and technical skills act as a pre-requisite for their activism efforts. As Gerbaudo[27] states 'No Android or iPhone App, no mapping software, no instant messaging or social networking service, no arrest alerting system, no online voting platform will ever solve technically the question of collective action, of how to mobilize and organize participants.' Activists' technical knowledge and skills have a very important role in this respect as it has to be the activists who use digital technologies effectively to achieve their goals.[28] There is no doubt that in order to contribute to digital activism efforts, one has to be digitally literate. Individuals' social and educational capital also plays a very important role in this respect.[29]

In order to use digital technologies effectively, one needs to access digital technologies. Economic limitations come into prominence within this framework; digital activism is more likely to be operational in countries where individuals can afford to buy digital technologies and access to the internet.[30] Technological infrastructure in a country is also influential on digital activism. Whether a country provides its citizens modern cable infrastructure for greater and faster internet connectivity and what percent of the population is connected to the internet are potential areas that pose technical limitations.[31] It is more probable that digital activism is carried out on a larger and more efficient basis in countries which have modern technological infrastructures and serve faster internet connection for reasonable prices.[32] In some countries, cost of internet access is high. The political system as well as the economic system of a country determines the cost of internet access. In many developing countries, internet service providers are monopolized by governments which results in higher prices for internet access. The term 'slacktivism' is also a reflection of pessimistic perspective. Pessimistic scholars put forward the idea that digital activism serves to increase the activists' 'feel good factor' without getting involved in any kind of physical action and as it is the physical action that can cause real social or political change, digital activism acts as a barrier for activism according to them. According to the pessimistic perspective, digital activism pacifies a great potential by giving activists a fake feeling that they did something of value.[33]

The last perspective, the persistent perspective, reflects the viewpoints of scholars who neither perceive digital activism as a new form of activism practice which disrupts power relations in contemporary societies and empowers citizens nor as a dangerous tool which offers opportunities to individuals, groups or governments with malevolent aims. Persistent scholars believe that digital activism enhances traditional activism by making it easier and faster to complete tasks such as message dissemination, organization and mobilization. However, they do not believe that digital technologies lead to fundamental changes in power relations in societies or produce new and more effective activism forms. They claim that the cumulative digital effect of bigger, cheaper, faster and further can only give birth to better versions of current activism tactics, but not create fundamentally different forms of activism.[34]

Digital activism in Turkey

A number of social and political factors accelerated the growth of digital activism in Turkey. It would not be wrong to claim that Gezi Park protests that took place between May 2013 and June 2013 were a catalyst for digital activism in Turkey. Online information and opinion sharing about the social and political issues that led to Gezi Park protests soared during the protests and still continue. When a handful of protestors who were trying to protect trees in the Gezi Park were attacked by the police with water cannons and tear gas before dawn,[35] the dissent that could not be expressed through representative participation was triggered.[36] The dissent already deep rooted due to the policies of the government was fueled by framing efforts of protestors on social media as well. Protestors aimed to sway the public that their definition of the situation and their claims were right and reasonable.[37] Frames created by the protestors addressed common grievances related to the authoritarian governing style of the prime minister, social policies of the government that do not respect individual life choices and neo-liberal urban development projects.[38] Frames worked well on potential protestors, many people empathized with the protestors and supported the protests, especially after the framing of disproportionate violence practiced by police forces. Emotions played an important part in framing efforts as well; people were united by solidarity, loyalty and love for each other and by anger, outrage and fear for the opposing parties as in many other protests.[39]

The fact that even the Gezi protests could not create solid social or political changes which would satisfy the protestors and supporters generated disappointment and affected people's perceptions on the potential of digital activism. This disappointment could be observed in two separate statements of a traditional activist. For ethical reasons, the identity of the activist will not be disclosed in this research study. During Gezi protests he said 'I told all my friends that I would be ashamed to organize one more protest after having seen how quickly and efficiently the youth could get organized within hours. I have been the chair of organization in my confederation and have not achieved such a success within all those years. I will resign right away.' However, what he said about the strength of digital activism two years later was 'Digital technologies are only good for fast correspondence and tapping the youth's creativity. But activism on digital technologies cannot lead to social or political change; we saw this during Gezi protests.'[40]

These comments indicate a risk for digital activism as research has shown moderate but significant links between perceived effectiveness and intentions to engage in collective action.[41] During the Gezi protests, individuals made personal sacrifices with the hope of causing social and political change. After having seen that even all those efforts could not lead to desired action on behalf of those in power, it would not be wrong to expect that these individuals might eventually sink into a state of passivity. The present study moves in this direction and the aims to find Turkish activists' perceptions on the scope and strength of digital activism in Turkey. As aforementioned, this article summarizes the findings related to the first three research questions of a larger study.

Research questions

To advance our understanding on the Turkish activists' perceptions on the scope and strength of activism, this study examines the following research questions:

> *RQ1*: What strength do Turkish activists attribute to digital activism in realizing different objectives?

> *RQ2a*: Are Turkish activists optimistic, pessimistic or persistent about the scope and strength of digital activism?

> *RQ2b*: Do Turkish activists believe in the possibility of an e-revolution?

Methods

A web-based survey was prepared and used for the purposes of this study. The survey had three parts. The first part focused on the socio-demographic profile of the respondents and asked them about their gender, age, marital status, their education and their perceptions on their competency in following and using digital technologies in a closed-ended format. This part of the survey aimed to gather data to be able to profile the respondents. The second part consisted of 25 statements each of which summarized a specific objective that digital activism could serve to achieve. The literature review on digital activism provided the basis of the items in this part of the survey. Respondents were expected to indicate their ideas about how efficient digital activism is in achieving each objective on a five point Likert Scale (1 – Very Inefficient, 5 – Very Efficient). The final part consisted of six open-ended questions. The questions asked were: (1) Do you think that it is right to use the term 'Twitter Revolution' for the revolutions that took place in Egypt and Tunisia; Do you believe in the possibility of an e-revolution? (2) What do you think are the contributions of digital technologies to the culture of activism? (3) Why are the social networking sites such as Facebook, Twitter and YouTube used for activism purposes according to you? (4) Do you think that there are factors that impede digital activism in Turkey according to you? If yes, please list the impeding factors. (5) Do you think that activism efforts initiated on digital mediums can make a difference when there is no corresponding activism in the streets? (6) Do you think that digital activism can make a difference even when it is not united with traditional activism?

The survey was prepared in Turkish as it aimed to gather data from Turkish citizens and data were collected between 1 April and 31 May 2015. The answers were than translated into English by the researcher, who has an MA degree in applied linguistics. As the survey was on digital activism and the aim was to reach people engaged in digital activism, online data collection method was preferred.

Sample

Given the scope of the research and the type of the respondents needed to answer the survey, purposeful sampling method was utilized to reach respondents which can provide in-depth information.[42] Large online communities with activism backgrounds were chosen with this purpose. These online groups on Facebook and Twitter were included in the sample as they comprised potential digital activists. The researcher did not have a pre-determined list of activists; members of these groups were approached as potential respondents. Among the online groups chosen were RedHack, Taksim Solidarity, OccupyGezi, Spirit of Gezi, Çarşı, Middle East Technical University and followers of Fuat Avni. Representatives of traditional activism were also included in the sample of the study. It should be stated here that many of these online communities have hundreds of thousands of members. Members of Confederation of Progressive Trade Unions of Turkey (DISK), Confederation of Public Worker's Union (KESK) and Education and Science Workers' Union (Eğitim-Sen) were invited to participate in the study in two different ways. First, the link to the online survey was shared on their Facebook and Twitter accounts. Second, they were invited to participate in the study through an e-mail, in which there was the link to the survey, by the union administration. The caricaturists of a famous humor magazine contributed to the study as well. Respondents were asked to forward the survey to other people they thought might be relevant for the study for a snowball effect and to increase the sample size in an efficient way.

Pro-government digital activists were not included in the sample of the present study for many reasons. It is quite easy to identify and reach anti-government activists on social media as Gezi protests led to the creation and popularity of these online communities. However, identifying pro-government activist groups has its own challenges. There are the official pages of Justice and Development Party (JDP) politicians, officials and JDP youth and women auxiliaries on Facebook and Twitter, however, these accounts do not reflect an informal organizational structure in which 'a collective identity is created, an identity that quickly overshadows more or less relevant individuals who could initially be identified'[43] as in many digital activism efforts but a formal one that follows JDP politics. That's why it was impossible to identify large groups of pro-government activists and balance anti-government and pro-government activists in the sample. Moreover, what pro-government social media accounts are mainly involved in is the propagation of the government policies.[44] Another reason was that pro-government digital activism is supported and even claimed to be organized by the government and these activists do not fear any consequences and express themselves freely in accordance with the policies of the government. They are protected and encouraged, and they can express their political ideas with confidence,[45] which could bias their perceptions on the strength and limitations of digital activism.

It should be noted here that purposeful sampling is not without its limitations. The selection criterion was subjective by nature[46] and as this sampling method was combined with online data collection method and the snowball technique, the selection process became more arbitrary. The researcher could not confirm that the activists reached were representative of the sample as the survey was online and as participants could forward the survey to others. Another drawback was the fact that data that was gathered depended on the self-reporting of activists. However, the high number of respondents and the in depth-data reached indicated that the sample reflected the selection criterion and the sample was representative. A total of 302 activists responded to the survey. Demographics of the sample are summarized below.

As can be seen in Table 1, majority of the activists that responded to the survey were young. Over 62 percent were between 18 and 39 years old. Almost 23 percent of the sample was between 40 and 49. Percentage of the activists who were 50 or above was below 14. The percentage of single people was slightly higher than the percentage of married people. Majority of the respondents (73.2 percent) had a BA or a higher degree. Almost 70 percent of the respondents felt competent in using digital technologies and 25.5 percent reported their competency as moderate.

Analysis

In order to calculate what strength Turkish activists attribute to digital activism in achieving different objectives, the scores that were assigned to each

Table 1. Demographics of the sample ($N = 302$).

Variable	Group	f	Percent
Age	18–29	76	25.2
	30–39	113	37.4
	40–49	69	22.8
	50 and above	41	13.6
	Missing	3	1.0
Gender	Women	172	57.0
	Men	128	42.4
	Missing	2	0.7
Marital status	Single	155	51.3
	Married	141	46.7
	Missing	6	2.0
Educational background	Primary education	0	0
	Secondary education	1	0.3
	High school Education	26	8.6
	Associate degree	24	7.9
	Bachelor's degree	145	48.0
	Master's degree	76	25.2
	Doctorate degree	26	8.6
Digital competency	Very incompetent	1	0.3
	Incompetent	11	3.6
	Moderate	77	25.5
	Competent	149	49.3
	Very competent	61	20.2
	Missing	3	1.0

different objective on the Likert scale were utilized. Descriptive statistics for each different objective were calculated by using Statistical Package for Social Sciences (SPSS) 20.

To develop an understanding on whether Turkish activists are optimistic, pessimistic or persistent about the scope and strength of digital activism and what their underlying assumptions are, respondents' answers to all six open-ended questions were analyzed holistically in content and each activist was grouped into one of the three categories: optimistic, pessimistic or persistent. Activists who emphasized their trust in the strength of digital activism and claimed that they will replace offline forms of activism in the future were coded as optimists; activists who voiced concerns about digital technologies and portrayed them as threats were categorized as pessimists; and activists who stated that digital technologies could only enhance offline activism but could never substitute for it were coded as persistents. Respondents that could not be grouped into any of these categories because of partial or inconsistent comments and respondents that did not provide any comments were grouped accordingly. An inter-coder reliability of 0.993 were calculated for this analysis.

With an attempt to investigate whether Turkish activists believe in the possibility of an e-revolution, participants' answers to the first open-ended question (Do you think that it is right to use the term 'Twitter Revolution' for the revolutions that took place in Egypt and Tunisia; Do you believe in the possibility of an e-revolution?) were analyzed in content. The written comments of the respondents were classified into categories of similar content.[47] The researcher did not have any pre-determined categories; the categories were developed inductively as data was processed.

Results

The first step of the analysis comprised the calculation of efficacy scores assigned to digital activism by Turkish activists for realizing specific objectives. Table 2 illustrates the average efficacy scores that Turkish activists assigned to digital activism as a tool for achieving each objective. The objectives are listed from the one with the highest efficacy mean score to the one with lowest.

> RQ1: What strength do Turkish activists attribute to digital activism in realizing different objectives?

As is seen, Turkish activists in the present sample assigned higher efficacy scores to digital activism for realizing objectives that require activists as an active agent mainly and thus are under activists' control to a great extent.

Table 2. Efficacy scores of digital activism for realizing different objectives.

Objective	$\bar{X}$	SD
Drawing attention to a problem.	4.3741	0.75912
Enabling the activists inform each other.	4.339	0.77832
Revealing information that is kept as secret by the power elites.	4.2678	0.74652
Supporting the protests in the streets.	4.101	0.93174
Showing the events that take place during the protests to the world.	4.0986	0.90907
Enabling dissident people living in oppressive regimes to communicate with each other	4.098	0.9282
Improving the morale and motivation of protestors.	3.9694	0.88353
Coordinating the protests.	3.9692	0.93559
Disrupting power relations in societies; empowering the individual.	3.9561	0.88763
Uniting people with similar opinions.	3.9527	1.01737
Creating pressure and forcing the media to cover events that it ignores.	3.9426	0.93885
Announcing the support of national or international individuals or institutions to the protests.	3.9426	0.92429
Drawing attention to the protests on a national basis.	3.9317	0.91156
Drawing attention to the protests on an international basis.	3.9178	0.97746
Mobilizing the dissident people.	3.8068	0.94758
Initiating dissent on an issue.	3.7483	0.96239
Ensuring that the protests will be covered in the media.	3.6826	0.96777
Persuading people that the protests are organized for justifiable reasons.	3.6633	0.91225
Gaining international support for the protests.	3.6339	1.06978
Gaining national support for the protests.	3.6094	1.07599
Accelerating dissent.	3.5952	1.00991
Establishing reputation for protestors in the public eye.	3.5051	0.9614
Expressing dissident opinions.	3.4646	0.96891
Initiating social or political change.	3.278	1.10535
Discrediting opposite groups.	3.1824	1.05469

For objectives related to awareness raising, communication and organization among activists, providing support to street protests, increasing the morale of the activists, increasing the visibility of protests and seeking support, digital activism received high efficacy scores from the activists. Activists also acknowledged the role of digital activism in disrupting power relations and empowering the individual with an efficacy score close to 4 (efficient). However, efficacy scores assigned to digital activism were lower when the objectives required other people's physical or mental involvement. For objectives such as mobilizing, persuading and gaining the support of other people, digital activism received lower efficacy scores. Digital activism received even lower efficacy scores for expressing dissident opinions and initiating social or political change. The lowest efficacy score was calculated for the utilization of digital activism for discrediting opposite groups.

RQ2a: Are Turkish activists optimistic, pessimistic or persistent about the scope and strength of digital activism?

The next step of the analysis aimed to shed light to from what perspective Turkish activists perceived digital activism. As aforementioned, respondents' answers to all six open-ended questions were analyzed holistically in content and their answers were categorized. The results are summarized in Table 3.

The results showed that almost half of the sample was persistent. In other words, they acknowledged the strategic role that digital activism plays in supporting traditional activism; however, they argued that digital activism can only initiate or support traditional activism, not act as a substitute to cause social or political change. In their point of view, nothing can be achieved without real action. Almost one fourth of the population was optimistic about digital activism. They highlighted the role technology plays in the contemporary world. The comments of the optimistic and persistent activists will be discussed in detail by including their comments on the notion 'e-revolution.'

Only nine activists were pessimistic about digital activism and argued that digital activism made people lazier, provided them with a fake clear

Table 3. Perspectives of activists on digital activism.

	Frequency	Percent	Valid percent	Cumulative percent
Pessimists	9	3.0	3.0	3.0
Persistents	147	48.7	48.7	51.7
Optimistics	73	24.2	24.2	75.8
Partial responses	12	4.0	4.0	100.0
Inconsistent responses	9	3.0	3.0	78.8
Missing responses	52	17.2	17.2	96.0
Total	302	100.0	100.0	

conscience and pacified their motivation to initiate change. They perceived digital activism as an obstacle for traditional activism. The following comments by Turkish activists illustrate this point:

> It makes people feel that they are activists although they actually are not. It provides self-satisfaction but it might be impeding medium term developments. Instead of cursing the dark, tweet a message. Have I tweeted a message? Yes … I feel relieved now. Next?

> It is a major obstacle for street protests. When people do not go out to the streets but express their opinions online, I believe their ideas become insignificant, even to themselves.

> I don't think it is possible to subvert or change a system via electronic tools. I even think that social media detracts people from real activism. The fact that digital activism provides people a fake 'clear conscience' when they sign online petitions or state their dissident opinions online for example can be a disadvantage in some circumstances

> It is a pacifier. Sharing things online makes people feel good and therefore the idea phase does not move to the action phase properly. People are overcome by languor and cannot put up a transformative fight.

> Most is idle talk I believe. Furthermore, I believe activism carried out without any action is nothing but an oxymoron.

Some activists even argued that digital activism was encouraged by the creation of a fake sense that activists were being prevented so that activists will not go into action. According to these activists, the government makes digital activism more appealing by blocking access to social networking sites and thus makes sure that dissent will be kept online and will not lead to physical action. The comments of an activist reveal this point.

> I think digital activism is encouraged in order to keep dissent in the digital sphere. Blocking of Twitter and the others do not avoid digital activism but encourage it.

RQ2b: Do Turkish activists believe in the possibility of an e-revolution?

As to the perceptions of Turkish activists regarding the notion of an e-revolution, 73 activists stated that it is right to use the term and that they believed in the possibility of an e-revolution. These activists highlighted the significance of technology in today's world, the capabilities of hackers and the 'keyboard empire' and opportunities that digital tools offer people to achieve activism purposes. The Arab Spring and Gezi Protests were given as examples consistently. Example statements include:

> E-revolution is possible. With internet 2.0 and the blogs, the first step to e-revolution has been taken. With Google and Facebook, revolution has already started.

… I think it is harder to revolutionize digitally now as the content and structure of the Internet, as well as the regulation on it are changing. I think such a revolution can only be possible with the help of 'hacktivism,' for example by taking over unmanned aerial vehicles …

E-revolution is possible as the whole economic system of the world is virtual. Most of the cash stock in the world is not even issued. E-revolution is possible at this point. The way to take control of the economic system and banks is an e-revolution.

Some activists acknowledged the role that digital technologies played but underlined the significance of physical action. In other words, 39 activists warned that digital activism can only turn into an e-revolution if it leads to, supports, or is supported and accompanied by physical action. Persistent comments below point to this argument:

Protests nowadays are initiated on digital mediums, and then they spread and are put into action. If an effort leads to a revolution, then I call it a digital revolution.

Life is out in the streets, if it manages to take people out, then yes.

E is a tool for communication. If the grassroots for a revolution is ready, it can be used to activate this in a fast and easy way. It is not sufficient by itself though.

Considering the Arab Spring, it looks possible. But it is certain that it is not sufficient by itself. Although social media is vital for organization, it is not possible to revolutionize without action.

Digital activism only unites people with similar ideas and empowers their ideologies. However, in order to transform it into an e-revolution, it needs pre-formed dissident grassroots that will realize it.

Some activists were even sarcastic in their comments about the term 'e-revolution.' They pointed to the fact that digital technologies are only tools and it is people's actions that lead to revolutions. One such comment is given below:

What is e-revolution for God's sake? Is it something like invading a radio station with ones and zeros? Is it something like pouring into streets through the internet? Internet is a medium … E doesn't revolutionize, people do.

A group of 42 activists pointed to situational factors and indicated that an e-revolution might be possible in other countries but not in Turkey because of these factors. Out of these activists, seven made general comments like 'Nothing is possible in Turkey nowadays.' or 'No kind of revolution is possible in this country.' Some activists pointed to the regime and oppression by the government. These 14 activists expressed concern about lack of democracy, claimed that the country has not completed its political evolution and prohibitions and oppression by the government made it impossible for Turkish activists to revolutionize. Example statements are given below:

… although I use internet as an 'opposition and freedom of speech tool' very much, e-revolution is not possible in Turkey. Above I couldn't fill in the Number 5, 'very efficient' blanks because in Turkey this would mean internet and freedom of speech is free and safe and every individual is safe when s/he expresses his/her opinion. It is not true; in Turkey e-revolution is not possible, when we cannot even speak of expressing an opposing idea on the net, without making sure our VPN cannot be tracked or our account won't be found and we will be tried in the most inhuman and unjust ways and courts just because of speaking our minds.

Yes, it can make a difference in the world but not in Turkey because of the oppressive regime.

We have seen that it is not possible at least in countries like Turkey where there is a lack of democracy.

Could be possible but not in Turkey because media and other apparatuses are sold and the government has all the control.

Ten activists put forward that an e-revolution is not possible due to national and international powers, low internet access rate in Turkey and because Turkey has not completed its social evolution. Eleven activists criticized the educational level of Turkish citizens and indicated that they do not believe in the possibility of an e-revolution in Turkey because the majority of people are not educated and aware. Their major argument was 'Nothing can change in Turkey unless Turkish people change.' They also expressed a concern about the ignorance of the society to social and political matters. Statements of participants are as follows:

… Turkish people believe what they read for the first time and do not feel the need to resort to other resources. Some do not even read, they believe what they listen to. That's why a revolution, even if it happens one day, will be questionable. However, I really want to say yes. Because our country is ruled in a regressive mode at the moment and I expect that the youth will unite and create an awareness platform and initiate an e-revolution but there might be huge electric cut-out problems.

Not probable as long as the media is biased because whatever is done or discussed are shown in a different way. In our country level of education is low; half of the population is not familiar with YouTube or Twitter. They believe in what they hear in the news that is squeezed in between TV series or what they read on the newspaper. That's why I think we need some more time for an e-revolution.

If we answer for Turkey, the answer is no. The majority of the people who use digital tools are informed anyway, but the rest still lives in the middle ages. A digital revolution is not possible unless the latter group change themselves.

Possible when people do not learn from a single and biased source, exploitation of religion is over and people know their rights and responsibilities.

Not for Turkey. Because opposing parties in Turkey do not have equal internet access, even the conflicts of individuals with equal internet access and use are not grounded rationally. In other words, problems cannot be solved in discussion platforms (For example, you cannot be a citizen of this country if you are not a Muslim; if you wear a scarf, you cannot understand why I advocate secularism.

Possible if the societies which use digital technologies are not ignorant.

No, although I want it to happen a lot it is not as easy as it looks to change people's dogmatized ideas as people seem to have buried their sense organs.

A group of 20 activists responded to the question asking if they believed in the possibility of an e-revolution with answers ranging from 'Maybe' to 'Not very probable.' Almost one fifth of the sample ($N = 58$) did not answer the question. Seventy-two activists expressed their disbelief in the notion 'e-revolution.' Example statements are given below:

No, nothing can be achieved without getting organized. Digital medium is good for correspondence but not for getting organized. An organized large group with the same cause is needed for a revolution. Digital technologies cannot unite people around a cause.

No, it is just that people who want to revolutionize want to use digital tools but not notice that the other party can use the digital tools against the revolution. In addition to this, the people, who are exposed to different and shady information, lose their faith in the credibility of information after a while.

E-revolution is not possible because whatever is written on digital media is destined to be forgotten in five minutes.

Discussion

As the name suggests, an activist is a person who strives to cause change, be it social, political or economic. The sample of this research can thus be positioned as people who are not satisfied with the policies of the JDP, which has been ruling Turkey since 2002. It is not surprising that Gezi Park protests were given as examples by the activists in their comments consistently. As Gürcan and Peker[48] note 'No specialist on Turkey could envisage a collective mobilization of such magnitude and versatility until the very moment it erupted.' The Gezi Park protests lasted more than a month and had both national and international support. The solidarity, festiveness and the sense of 'power' reached such a level that the activists and a great percentage of the public that supported them started to anticipate real social and political change. However, to the activists' and their supporters' disappointment, 30March 2014 local elections and the presidential election held on 10 August 2014 showed that Gezi protests could not trigger political change and the majority of Turkish people still preferred to live under the rule of

JDP and see Recep Tayyip Erdoğan, who was the main target of activists, as their president. The fact that the presidential election, in which Erdoğan was selected as the president was the first in which the public itself voted for the president, made it more obvious that the protests that attempted to degrade Erdoğan's reputation and his influence on the public did not produce the desired outcome. It should be noted here that the efficacy of the protests cannot be equated with electoral outcomes as there are many factors that interact and affect the voting behavior of publics. However, it would not be wrong to claim that the results of the elections led to a disappointment and weakened activists' perceived efficacy of the protests. It is this disappointment and perception of the activists that must shed light to how the findings of this study should be interpreted.

The differences found between the efficacy scores that were assigned to digital activism for achieving objectives that require activists as an active agent mainly and the ones that require other people's physical or mental involvement can be explained within this framework. The activists knew that the only way to cause political change was persuading the voters of Justice and the Development Party, which was around half of the Turkish population. Recep Tayyip Erdoğan was the most influential person within the government and had the power of shaping the opinions, attitudes and even actions of voters of the government. That's why activists criticized the government practices and targeted Erdoğan's credibility during Gezi protests.

During the protests many slogans used connoted a self-criticism, expressing that the public was suffering the consequences of its decisions; that the public in Turkey voted for a government, which in turn punished them for using their democratic right to protest. However, considering the fact that most protestors were not supporters of the government, there is no doubt that these slogans were a subtle invitation to JDP voters to act wisely and punish the party at the ballot box.

The results of the local and presidential elections however showed that the activists could not achieve these objectives. The JDP still got the highest percentage of votes and Erdoğan was elected president. The comments of an activist in this study calling JDP voters a herd of sheep that follow a leader was a reflection of the disappointment with the voters of the JDP. Eleven activists in the sample criticized Turkish people and society as the main reasons why an e-revolution is not possible in Turkey. Moreover, as part of the larger study, it was found out that more than 21 percent of the activists voiced criticism of Turkish people and Turkish culture in response to the open-ended question inquiring the limitations of digital activism in Turkey. Turkish people were condemned to be indifferent, ignorant, apolitical and inactive by the activists.

Activists assigned lower efficacy scores to objectives such as mobilizing, persuading and gaining the support of other people or discrediting opposite groups as one would expect since they have experienced a failure in this respect very recently. This failure can be explained with empirical data that supports that people tend to read and believe what reinforces their own value systems.[49] For example, Lawrence, Sides and Farrell[50] found that blog readers in the US gravitate toward blogs that are in line with their political beliefs; left-wing blogs are mainly read by leftists and right-wing blogs are read by rightists. This study also revealed that readers of the political blogs were more polarized than non-blog readers; they were almost as polarized as US senators. Being exposed to ideas that reinforce one's own ideas repeatedly and not confronting content that may lead one into critical thinking on notions that are taken for granted may polarize people. This tendency is prevalent in social media as well. People tend to follow others with similar profiles and viewpoints. There is a risk of homophily as people decide whom to follow and what topics to focus on.[51] That is why, it is claimed that digital activism helps to engage like-minded people. However, as Sunstein[52] has noted, the Internet also provokes group polarization; like-minded people communicate through the Internet, confirm and reinforce one another's ideas and sometimes move toward extreme ends. It would not be wrong to argue that this polarization is further nurtured when people know that there is another large group of people with exactly the opposite ideas. Expecting these polarized groups to follow each other on social media, to engage in true dialogue, to understand and respond in an unbiased way would be faulty, especially taking into consideration the polarizing discourse of public figures during the protests.

For example, Erdoğan warned the protestors by stating that they cannot keep the other 50 percent of the society at home, referring to JDP voters and asked his voters to denounce their neighbors who were making noise with pots at a certain time every day to show their support for the protests, which reproduced polarization.[53] However, it should be stated here that Erdoğan and the other JDP executives were not the only politicians who used polarizing discourse. Research showed that top political party executives of the Republican People's Party as well as the JDP used marginalizing and polarizing discourse in their Twitter accounts.[54]

The activists assigned high efficacy scores to digital activism for realizing objectives related to awareness raising, communication and organization among activists, providing support to street protests, increasing the morale of the activists, increasing the visibility of the protests and seeking support as they succeeded in achieving these goals. Perspectives of activists were also shaped by the relative success and failure of the Gezi Park protests. Almost half of the activists in the sample were persistent in their perceptions of digital activism, acknowledged the role digital technologies played in activism efforts but warned that they have to be supported or accompanied by the streets. The comments related to the notion of 'e-revolution' showed that almost one third of the sample believed in the notion of 'e-revolution' and another one third were convinced that digital activism can lead to or assist a revolution if political and social limitations were overcome. Having experienced Gezi and the following events, it is no surprise that the activists point to the political environment and the government, which they portray as oppressive and prohibitive as one of the main factors that weaken digital activism efforts.

This oppressive and prohibitive environment does not only weaken digital activism efforts but weakens all democratic attempts to voice dissident opinions. The Turkish media is lost in a spiral of silence since the government exerts different kinds of neoliberal pressures on media conglomerates when they become critical of the government and controls them via taking economic measures.[55] The number of jailed journalists in Turkey is quite high and this fact consequently led to a tendency in journalists to self-censor themselves.[56] This is reflected as the criticism of the mass media by the activists in the findings of this study as well as other studies. For example, Baruh and Watson[57] found that Twitter was used actively during the Gezi protests due to mistrust in mass media and in order to access and spread up to date information. The same oppression can be felt online as well due to Law No. 5651, which envisages harsh measures against freedom of expression on the internet with the justification of prevention of crime and protection of national security, public order, public health, life, property, and the esteem and honor of individuals against defamation on the internet. Amendments to Law 5651 were passed in 2014 after the Gezi protests, and the related measures became even harsher.[58] The fact that the control of the government on the judicial system has increased in the past decade has also added to oppressive and prohibitive atmosphere.[59] All these factors lower activists' perceived external political efficacy. The activists experienced that the government did not respond to their demands; on the contrary, it responded with harsher measures.

Notes

1. Amin, "The Empire Strikes Back," 64.
2. Putnam, *Bowling Alone*; Schulman, "Case Against Mass e-Mails"; and Morozov, "The Brave New World."
3. Micó and Ripollés, "Political Activism Online," 861.
4. Harp, Bachmann, and Guo, "The Whole Online World," 300–1.
5. Kenski and Stroud, "Connections Between Internet Use."
6. Harp, Bachmann and Guo, "The Whole Online World," 300–1.
7. Swann, *Cases in Public Relations*, 226.
8. Yang, *Power of the Internet*, 3.
9. Ibid., 3.
10. Shah, "Citizen Action," 666.
11. Burns and Eltham, "Twitter Free Iran," 299.
12. Baraković, "Facebook Revolutions," 195.

13. Jurgenson, "When Atom Meet Bits," 83.
14. Peña-López, Congosto and Aragón, "Spanish Indignados and Evolution," 212.
15. Sivitanides and Shah, "Era of Digital Activism," 4–5.
16. Wray, "On Electronic Civil Obedience," 108–9.
17. Ibid., 109.
18. Micó and Ripollés, "Political Activism Online," 860.
19. Sivitanides and Shah, "Era of Digital Activism," 4.
20. Murdoch, "Destructive Activism," 139.
21. Jurgenson, "When Atom Meet Bits," 87.
22. Murdoch, "Destructive Activism." 146.
23. Micó and Ripollés, "Political Activism Online," 862.
24. Ghannam, "Social Media, 2011 Uprisings," 7.
25. Şener, "Social Media, Social Struggle," 194.
26. Watson et al., "Citizen (In)Security?" 300.
27. Gerbaudo, *Tweets and the Streets*, 162.
28. Ghannam, "Social Media, 2011 Uprisings," 16.
29. Harp, Bachmann and Guo, "The Whole Online World," 299.
30. Sivitanides and Shah, "Era of Digital Activism," 3.
31. Ghannam, "Social Media, 2011 Uprisings," 5, 7.
32. Sivitanides and Shah, "Era of Digital Activism," 2.
33. Putnam, *Bowling Alone*; Schulman, "Case Against Mass e-Mails"; and Morozov, "The Brave New World."
34. Micó and Ripollés, "Political Activism Online," 860, and Sivitanides and Shah, "Era of Digital Activism," 5.
35. Bölükbaşı, *Devrim Taksim'de Göz Kırptı [Revolution Winked in Taksim]*, 18.
36. Peña-López, Congosto and Aragón, "Spanish Indignados and Evolution," 213.
37. Benford, "Social Movement Framing Perspective," 412.
38. Taştan, "Gezi Park Protests," 33, and Sarfati, "Dynamics of Mobilization," 26.
39. Goodwin, Jasper and Polletta, "Return of the Repressed."
40. Personal communication, May 29, 2013; May 12, 2015.
41. Hornsey et al., "Why Collective Action," 4.
42. Yin, *Case Study Research*.
43. Peña-López, Congosto and Aragón, "Spanish Indignados and Evolution," 212.
44. Costa, *Social Media in Turkey*, 152, 155.
45. Ibid., 138.
46. Black, *Doing Quantitative Research*.
47. Cho and Lee, "Grounded Theory and Qualitative."
48. Gürcan and Peker. "Turkey's Gezi Park Demonstrations."
49. Bickford et al, "Science Communication."
50. Lawrence, Sides and Farrell, "Self-Segregation or Deliberation?"
51. Peña-López, Congosto and Aragón, "Spanish Indignados and Evolution," 192.
52. Sunstein, *Republic.com,* 199.
53. Deniz, "Gezi Park," 107.
54. Karkın, et al. "Twitter Use by Politicians."
55. Akser and Baybars-Hawks, "Media and Democracy in Turkey," 307–8.
56. May, "Twelve Sycamore Trees," 300.
57. Baruh and Watson, "Using Twitter for What?"
58. Akgül and Kırlıdoğ, "Internet Censorship in Turkey," 11.
59. Ahn, "Turkey's Unraveling Democracy," 30, 31, 34.

Disclosure statement

No potential conflict of interest was reported by the author.

Bibliography

Ahn, J. S. J. "Turkey's Unraveling Democracy: Reversing Course from Democratic Consolidation to Democratic Backsliding." CMC senior diss., Claremont McKenna College, USA, 2014.

Akgül, M., and M. Kırlıdoğ. "Internet Censorship in Turkey." *Internet Policy Review* 4, no. 2 (2015): 1–22.

Akser, M., and B. Baybars-Hawks. "Media and Democracy in Turkey: Toward a Model of Neoliberal Media Autocracy." *Middle East Journal of Culture and Communication* 5 (2012): 302–321.

Amin, R. "The Empire Strikes Back: Social Media Uprisings and the Future of Cyber Activism." *Harvard Kennedy School Review* 10 (2009–2010): 64–66.

Baraković, V. "Facebook Revolutions: The Case of Bosnia and Herzegovina." *ActaUniversitatis Sapientiae. Social Analysis* 1, no. 2 (2011): 194–205.

Baruh, L., and H. Watson. "Using Twitter for What? A Segmentation Study of Twitter Usage during Gezi Protests." Proceedings of the European Conference on Social Media 33–41, 2014.

Benford, R. D. "An Insider's Critique of the Social Movement Framing Perspective." *Sociological Inquiry* 67, no. 4 (1997): 409–430.

Bickford, David, Mary Rose Posa, Lan Qie, Ahimsa Campos-Arceiz, and Enoka P. Kudavidanage. "Science Communication for Biodiversity Conservation." *Biological Conservation* 151, no. 1 (2012): 74–76.

Black, T. R. *Doing Quantitative Research in the Social Sciences: An Integrated Approach to Research Design, Measurement, and Statistics.* Thousand Oaks, CA: Sage, 1999.

Bölükbaşı, M. D. *Devrim Taksim'de Göz Kırptı [Revolution Winked in Taksim].* İstanbul: Kaldıraç Yayınevi, 2013.

Burns, A., and B. Eltham. "Twitter Free Iran: An Evaluation of Twitter's Role in Public Diplomacy and Information Operations in Iran's 2009 Election Crisis." In *Record of the Communications Policy & Research Forum,* edited by Franco Papandrea and Mark Armstrong, 298–310. Sydney: Network Insight Institute, 2009.

Cho, J. Y., and E. H. Lee. "Reducing Confusion about Grounded Theory and Qualitative Content Analysis: Similarities and Differences." *The Qualitative Report* 19, no. 64 (2014): 1–20.

Costa, E. *Social Media in Southeast Turkey.* London: UCL Press, 2016.

Deniz, E. "Gezi Park as a Place of Encounter for the Recent Local Struggles in Turkey." *Anuari Del Conflicte Social* 1, no. 4 (2013): 102–116.

Gerbaudo, P. *Tweets and the Streets: Social Media and Contemporary Activism.* London: Pluto Press, 2012.

Ghannam, J. "Social Media in the Arab World: Leading up to the Uprisings of 2011." Center for International Media Assistance. Accessed September 23, 2014. http://cima.ned.org/sites/default/files/CIMA-Arab_Social_Media-Report-10-25-11.pdf.

Goodwin, J., J. M. Jasper, and F. Polletta. "The Return of the Repressed: The Fall and Rise of Emotions in Social Movement Theory." *Mobilization: An International Journal* 5, no. 1 (2000): 65–83.

Gürcan, E. C., and E. Peker. "Turkey's Gezi Park Demonstrations of 2013: A Marxian Analysis of the Political Moment." *Socialism and Democracy* 28, no. 1 (2014): 70–89.

Harp, D., I. Bachmann, and L. Guo. "The Whole Online World is Watching: Profiling Social Networking Sites and Activists in China, Latin America, and the United States." *International Journal of Communication* 6, no. 1 (2012): 298–321.

Hornsey, Matthew J., Leda Blackwood, Winnifred Louis, Kelly Fielding, Ken Mavor, Thomas Morton, Anne O'Brien, Karl-Erik Paasonen, Joanne Smith, and Katherine M. White. "Why Do People Engage in Collective Action? Revisiting the Role of Perceived Effectiveness." *Journal of Applied Social Psychology* 36, no. 7 (2006): 1701–1722.

Jurgenson, N. "When Atom Meet Bits: Social Media, the Mobile Web and Augmented Revolution." *Future Internet* 4, no. 1 (2012): 83–91.

Karkın, N., Nilay Yavuz, İsmet Parlak, and Özlem Özdeşim İkiz. "Twitter Use by Politicians During Social Uprisings: An Analysis of Gezi Park Protests in Turkey." Proceedings of the 16th Annual International Conference on Digital Governance, 20–28, 2015.

Kenski, K., and N. J. Stroud. "Connections Between Internet Use and Political Efficacy, Knowledge, and Participation." *Journal of Broadcasting & Electronic Media* 50, no. 2 (2006): 173–192.

Lawrence, E., J. Sides, and H. Farrell. "Self-Segregation or Deliberation? Blog Readership, Participation, and Polarization in American Politics." *Perspectives on Politics* 8, no. 1 (2010): 141–157.

May, A. "Twelve Sycamore Trees Have Set the Limits on Turkish PM Erdoğan's Power." *American Foreign Policy Interests* 35, no. 5 (2013): 298–302.

Micó, J. L., and A. C. Ripollés. "Political Activism Online: Organization and Media Relations in the Case of 15M in Spain." *Information, Communication & Society* 17, no. 7 (2014): 858–871.

Morozov, E. "The Brave New World of Slacktivism." *Foreign Policy.* Accessed May 19, 2014. http://neteffect.foreignpolicy.com/posts/2009/05/19/the brave new world of slacktivism.

Muhammad, E. "Hactivisim." *Techno Fem* 74 (2001): 75–76.

Murdoch, S. "Destructive Activism: The Double-Edged Sword of Digital Tactics." In *Digital Activism Decoded*, edited by M. Joyce, 137–148. New York: iDebate Press, 2010.

Peña-López, I., M. Congosto, and P. Aragón. "Spanish Indignados and the Evolution of the 15M Movement on Twitter: Towards Networked Para-Institutions." *Journal of Spanish Cultural Studies* 15, nos 1–2 (2014): 189–216.

Putnam, R. D. *Bowling Alone: The Collapse and Revival of American Community.* New York: Simon & Schuster, 2000.

Sarfati, Y. "Dynamics of Mobilization During Gezi Park Protests in Turkey." In *The Whole World is Texting*, edited by I. Epstein, 25–43. Pittsburgh: Sense, 2015.

Schulman, S. W. "The Case Against Mass e-Mails: Perverse Incentives and Low Quality Public Participation in US Federal Rulemaking." *Policy & Internet* 1, no. 1 (2009): 23–53.

Şener, G. "Social Media as a Field of Social Struggle." *Journal of Media Critiques 2, Special Issue on Social Media and Network Society*, no. 2 (2014): 185–198.

Shah, N. "Citizen Action in the Time of the Network." *Development and Change* 44, no. 3 (2013): 665–681.

Sivitanides, M., and V. Shah. "The Era of Digital Activism." Education Special Interest Group of the AITP, CONISAR Proceedings, 2011. Accessed November 2, 2014. http://proc.conisar.org/2011/pdf/1842.pdf.

Sunstein, C. *Republic.com*. Princeton, NJ: Princeton University Press, 2001.

Swann, P. *Cases in Public Relations Management. The Rise of Social Media and Activism*. New York: Routledge, 2014.

Taştan, C. "The Gezi Park Protests in Turkey: A Qualitative Field Research." *Insight Turkey* 15, no. 3 (2013): 27–38.

Watson, Hayley, Lemi Baruh, Rachel L. Finn, and Salvatore Scifo. "Citizen (In)Security?: Social Media, Citizen Journalism and Crisis Response." Proceedings of the 11th International ISCRAM Conference, 299–303. University Park, PA, 2014.

Wray, S. "On Electronic Civil Obedience." *Peace Review* 11, no. 1 (1999): 107–111.

Yang, G. *The Power of the Internet in China. Citizen Activism Online*. New York: Columbia University Press, 2011.

Yavuz Görkem, Ş. "By the Power of the SNS We Can … And Yet … Potential and Limitations in Turkey." *The Turkish Online Journal of Design, Art and Communication* 6, no. 2 (2016): 230–243.

Yin, R. *Case Study Research: Design and Methods*. Thousand Oaks, CA: Sage, 2009.

Europeanization of civil society in Turkey: legacy of the #Occupygezi movement

Ayhan Kaya

ABSTRACT

As a clear depiction of unconventional forms of civic and political participation, the Occupygezi movement has revealed that a more comprehensive approach is needed to understand the deep socio-political drives underpinning the Turkish bid for EU membership. Focusing on three different framings, namely Euro-enthusiastic, Euro-sceptic and critical Europeanist frames, developed by civil society organizations in Turkey since the 1999 Helsinki Summit, this article will analyze the transformative effect of the Occupygezi movement on various civil society groups which had previously been Euro-sceptic. Subsequently, the article will claim that the critical Europeanist frame has recently become stronger. Methodologically, the article will be based on a literature survey on the civil society actors, as well as discourse analysis of some particular associations, trade unions and the media organizations in relation to their changing perception of the EU before and after the Occupygezi movement.

Introduction

The aim of this article is to examine the relationship between the European Union (EU) and Turkey from the specific angle of the process of Europeanization, a process which has facilitated the mobilization of Turkish civil society actors during and after the #Occupygezi movement in the summer of 2013. The author assumes that a more comprehensive approach needs to be taken in order to understand the deep socio-political drives underpinning the Turkish bid for EU membership as economic or geopolitical arguments do not exhaust the debate on Turkey's EU accession. From this perspective, understanding the broader process of Europeanisation in political and social terms is crucial in order to capture the real drives of the European integration process in its entirety.

This article focuses specifically on three different framings developed by civil society organizations (CSOs) in Turkey with respect to the European integration process, which is believed to have deepened since the 1999 EU Helsinki Summit. These three main frames are *Euro-enthusiastic*, *Euro-sceptic* and *critical Europeanist* attitudes generated by different civil society actors as a response to the changing political, social, economic and cultural climate between Turkey and the EU, as well as within Turkey itself. Theoretically speaking, the *Euro-enthusiastic* frame proposes a positive assessment of European development and detects some problems in the implementation of the project, which are believed to be resulting from EU institutions. The *Euro-sceptic* frame, on the other hand, tends to read the regional integration process as a set of detrimental dynamics that threaten the communitarian bases necessary for the sustainability of local and national political projects. This frame sustains a more local and nationalist interpretation of European integration, which is perceived as direct intervention into the sovereignty of the nation-states. The *critical Europeanist* frame, for its part, searches for a more social and democratic Europe rather than a market-based Europe. As will be further delineated, this last frame has been developed during and after the *Gezi* movement, which spilled over into the entire country in June 2013 as a popular form of resistance against the authoritarian rule of the Justice and Development Party (JDP), which has governed the country since 2002. It will be argued that it was this last form of framing that has made at least some Turkish civil society actors embrace the European integration process as an anchor for the democratization of the country.[1] Focusing on three different framings developed by CSOs in Turkey since the 1999 EU Helsinki Summit, this article will reveal the transformative effect of the *#Occupygezi* movement on the mind-sets of laicist/secular groups, who had previously been Euro-sceptic.

Methodologically, the article is based on a literature survey, as well as discourse analysis of civil society actors (associations, trade unions and the media) in relation to their changing perception of the EU. Discourse analysis deals with the relationship between language, socio-political processes and the power relations associated with them. It is based on earlier studies by Michel Foucault, Mikhail Bakhtin and Antonio Gramsci, and seeks to combine linguistics and sociological approaches within the analysis of the discourse in order to examine the complex interactions between discourse and society. In this article, I will use some extracts and quotations from speeches, declarations and media statements of relevant CSO, as well as make use of the online media archives of two Kemalist newspapers, *Cumhuriyet* and *Sözcü*, with regard to their perception of the *Gezi* Park protests and perspective towards the European integration process of Turkey.[2] Due to the fact that this work does not only concentrate on the discourse analysis of relevant civil society actors, but also aims to offer a framework to better understand different perceptions of the EU in Turkey, the discourse analysis section will be not be as widespread as originally intended.

Competing discourse frames on Europe in Turkey

In this section, different types of frames on Europe generated by Turkish CSOs will be delineated to see to which extent Turkish civil society has internalized and/or externalized the wider Europeanization trend. In this regard, three different forms of framing will be introduced: (a) *Euro-enthusiastic attitudes*; (b) *Euro-sceptic attitudes* and (c) *critical Europeanist attitudes*. However, the focus will be on the last frame, as the first two frames have so far been extensively discussed in the European Studies literature, and elsewhere. Kaya and Marchetti have already stated that there are three main frames which could be distinguished in the current debate among European civil society actors[3]: The predominant frame, at least before the eruption of the 2008 financial crisis, for the political action of many civil society actors is the *Euro-enthusiastic* attitude. Despite entailing different degrees of support for the European project, the Euro-enthusiastic frame proposes a positive assessment of the European process so far and, more importantly, detects the actual origin of current problems of EU institutions. *Euro-scepticism* as a frame suggests a reading of the regional integration process as a set of detrimental dynamics that threaten the communitarian bases necessary for the sustainability of local and national political projects. This frame has recently become very popular among private European citizens, who suffer from the devastating effects of neoliberal governance leading to the isolation and alienation of rural, less-educated, unemployed and elderly individuals. Finally, a third frame of growing importance is represented by the *critical Europeanists*. According to this, a social Europe should be strengthened in opposition to a Europe of markets. A more political Europe, it holds, is needed to counter an apolitical and elite-driven Europe, which we have known so far. The process of Europeanization is seen from this angle as developing also by contestation: a contested public debate is the surest path towards supranational legitimacy.

The EU perspective offered in Helsinki in December 1999 has radically transformed the political establishment in Turkey, opening up new prospects for various ethnic, religious, social and political groups in Turkish civil society. Kurds, Alevis, Islamists, Circassians, Armenians and a number of religious and ethnic groups in Turkey have become true advocates of the European Union in a way that has affirmed the pillars of a political union as a project for peace and integration. The normative and transformative power of the EU revealed immediately after 1999 was a great incentive and motivation for numerous groups in Turkey to reinforce their willingness to coexist in harmony. What lies beneath this willingness no longer seems to be the *glorious retrospective past*, which has lately been perceived to be full of ideological and political disagreements among various groups, but rather the *prospective future*, in which ethnic, religious and cultural differences are expected to be embraced in a democratic way.[4] The EU has thus appeared to be the major catalyst in accelerating the process of democratization in Turkey or, in other words, a lighthouse illuminating Turkey's road to modernization and liberalization.[5] However, this kind of Euro-Enthusiastic frame was later challenged by different groups on various grounds.

In the Turkish debate on Europe, there have also been moments and dimensions that have been critical of the EU. From 17th December 2004 to 3rd October 2005, when EU state and national government leaders decided to open accession negotiations with Turkey, tensions began to rise between nationalist, patriotic, statist, pro-status-quo groups on the one hand, and pro-EU groups on the other hand. This was the time when the *virtuous cycle* of the period between 1999 and 2005 was replaced by the *vicious cycle* starting in late 2005. A new nationalist and religious wave has embraced the country, especially among middle-class and upper middle-class groups. The actual start of the accession negotiations in 2005 has been a turning point towards Euro-scepticism. This was also observed in several previous cases during the accession negotiations of the 2004/2007 entrants. The political elite and the government had come to realize that accession negotiations are not in fact 'negotiations' but rather a unilateral imposition of policy changes on the part of the EU.[6] Furthermore, this reality of actual accession negotiations has often been abused by politicians to unfoundedly blame any governmental actions on the EU. Whether the 'blaming of Brussels' is honest or not, the overall impact on public support has almost surely been negative. The electoral cycle of presidential and general elections witnessed militarist, nationalist and Euro-sceptic aspirations coupled with rising violence and terror in the country prior to the elections in 2007. The fight between the JDP and other statist political parties, backed by the military establishment, became crystallized during the presidential elections of May 2007. The JDP gained an absolute majority of parliamentary seats in the 2002, 2007, 2011 and 2015 general elections, as well as in the 2004, 2009 and 2014 local elections. It became the first party, since 1987, to win the majority of seats in the Turkish parliament.[7]

Euro-scepticism, nationalism and parochialism in Turkey were triggered by sentiments of disapproval towards the American occupation of Iraq, the limitations on national sovereignty posed by EU integration, the high tide of the 90th anniversary in 2005 of the Armenian 'deportation'/'genocide' among the Armenian diaspora, the 'risk of recognition' of southern Cyprus by Turkey for the sake of EU integration, anti-Turkey public opinion in EU countries framed by conservative powers (e.g. France and Austria) and Israel's attacks on Lebanon in 2006. Against such a background, the state elite became also very skeptical of the Europeanization process. The best way to explain the sources of such skepticism among the state elite is to refer to the 'Sèvres Syndrome,' which is referring to a fear deriving from the post-World War I era, and characterized by popular belief, regarding the risk of a break-up of the Turkish state.[8] The JDP immediately stepped back after 2005 from its pro-European position, as it was perceived by the party elite that European integration no longer paid off. Actually, it was not the nationalist climax in the country that turned the JDP into a Euro-sceptic party, but rather the ruling of the European Court of Human Rights on the headscarf case *Leyla Şahin v. Turkey*, which challenged a Turkish law banning wearing the Islamic head-scarf at universities and other educational and state institutions.[9] The JDP apparently did not appreciate the decision taken by a European judiciary body with regard to the headscarf ban.

Public frustration about the European stance on Turkey's membership and associated Euro-scepticism reached its peak. The Transatlantic Trend survey by the German Marshall Fund undertaken in 2010 reveals this negative mood within civil society.[10] When asked about the relation between Turkey and the European Union, 35 percent of the Turkish public indicated a negative relation, 28 percent a mixed relation and only 22 percent a positive relation. When asked about countries that Turkey should act in closest cooperation with on international affairs, the EU scored a substantial decline from 22 percent down to 13 percent, and countries from the Middle East increased sig-nificantly between 2009 and 2010 from 10 percent to 20 percent. In the mean-time, 34 percent argued that Turkey should act alone. Additionally, when asked for a general assessment of Turkish membership in the EU, while 73 percent of the Turkish public had considered EU membership a *good thing* in 2004, the rate had declined to 38 percent in 2010. Furthermore, while in 2004 only 9 percent considered EU membership a *bad thing*, 31 percent viewed it as undesirable in 2010. However, after the *Occupygezi* movement, which will be discussed in the following section, the support for European Union membership went up to 43 percent.[11] The #Occupygezi movement has become the trigger for the emergence of a form of critical Europeanism.

Public support for the EU prior to the #*Occupygezi* movement dropped down to 34 percent primarily due to the Euro-sceptic political discourse of the Turkish government as well as due to the growing impact of the global financial crisis on EU countries, especially on neighboring Greece. However, there appeared a sharp increase in public support for Turkey's membership to the EU following the Gezi movement reaching up to 61 percent in 2015. The main driving force behind this support was the increas-ing longing of the majority of the Turkish society for democracy, accountabil-ity, transparency, freedom of speech and the rule of law, the values of which the EU is strongly believed to have. Recently, public support for the EU has become even higher, reaching up to 75 percent due to the probability of the

EU liberalizing the visa-regime for Turkish citizens.[12] The right to travel without any visa restrictions has always been the main source of inspiration for the Turkish public to generate a stronger European identity. However, one needs to scrutinize further to understand the motivations of Turkish citizens in becoming strongly pro-European. Data gathered by the Istanbul Development Association (IKV, *Istanbul Kalkınma Vakfı*), the foremost Turkish research foundation on economic and development-related issues, in May 2016 reveal that the JDP electorate have also become more pro-European during the intensification of the debates on visa liberalization, while critical Europeanists and pro-Europeanists seemed to be less inspired by these discussions as many of them were reportedly discontented by the content of the refugee agreement signed between Turkey and the EU in March 2016. Many critical Europeanists have blamed EU leaders, as well as the EU Commission, for not having shown any reaction to President Erdoğan's disputable moves on the freedom of speech, academics and journalists, as well as several other oppositional voices in the country criticizing his political maneuvers to monopolize power.

Emerging critical Europeanism in the aftermath of #Occupygezi

Occupygezi is one of the new global social movements bearing resemblance to its predecessors such as Tahrir Square, Occupy Wall Street and the European Indignados movement. The *Gezi* movement has become very instrumental in the sense that Turkish civil society actors have reframed European integration. Following the *Gezi* Movement, Turkish civil society has become much more pro-European, and European Union circles have also apparently changed their perceptions of Turkish society by positively acknowledging an active civil society. In the meantime, the main oppositional party, Republican People's Party (CHP), has also become much more pro-European after the *Gezi* movement. The leader of the CHP, Kemal Kilicdaroglu, even wrote a letter to German Chancellor Angela Merkel urging her not to block Turkey's EU accession talks in the face of the brutality of police forces against the protestors during the #Occupygezi movement. Following this correspondence, EU leaders, including Angela Merkel, heavily criticized Erdoğan's JDP for being so intolerant of peaceful civilian protests, and even threatened to cut off Turkey from accession negotiation talks.[13]

On 2 June 2013, the High Representative of the Union for Foreign Affairs and Security Policy, Catherine Ashton, expressed her deep concerns about the course of protests and police brutality underlining the necessity for a positive dialogue that was never pronounced by PM Erdoğan between all sides involved in these demonstrations.[14] Using social media, another quick response came from Martin Schulz, President of the European Parliament, who stressed that the police response was quite disproportionate. On 12

June, the European Parliament discussed in Strasbourg the situation in Turkey, and several MPs pointed out that the *Gezi Park* protests went beyond environmental issues and presented an opportunity where wider and restrained concerns for many years were being expressed.[15] In a way, *Gezi Park* protests were an eye opener for the European Union to see clearly the authroritarian direction that the Turkish leadership was taking. The explicit change in the discourse of European Union circles has also changed the perception of different segments of Turkish society with regard to their perception of European integration. In a way, *Gezi* protests have led to a substantial transformation of Turkish public opinion towards the EU: groups being both pro-JDP and Europeanists turned into being Euro-sceptic, and groups who were formerly Euro-sceptic turned into being more Europeanist.

After almost ten years of social polarization and the alienation of Kemalist groups, as well as other oppositional groups, domestic dissatisfaction could no longer be covered up. The *Gezi Park* demonstrations highlightened the deep polarization of the domestic environment, the contradiction between the Turkish government's rhetoric and reality. It was very remarkable that the *Gezi* movement actually made the CHP, as well as some previously Euro-sceptic CSOs like labor unions (e.g. the Confederation of Progressive Trade Unions, *DISK;* and Confederation of Public Labourer's Unions, *KESK*) and oppositional Kemalist newspapers such as *Cumhuriyet* and *Sözcü*, become pro-European, or rather critical Europeanist.[16] In a way, they have generated a more critical stance on Turkey–EU relations as they have become more in favor of a socially, democratically and politically prosperous European Union.

Brief summary of the #*Occupygezi* movement: right to the city!

The *Occupygezi* movement bears various characteristics of its predecessors such as Tahrir Square, Occupy Wall Street and the *Indignados* protests. Alain Badiou argued that Tahrir Square, and all the activities which took place there, such as fighting, barricading, camping, debating, cooking, bartering and caring for the wounded, constituted a 'communism of movement' in a way that it presented an alternative to the neoliberal Democratic and authoritarian state.[17] Similarly, Slavoj Žižek claimed that only these totally new political and social movements without hegemonic organizations and charismatic leaderships could create what he called the 'magic of Tahrir.'[18] And, Hardt and Negri also joined them in arguing that the Arab Spring, Europe's *indignados* protests and Occupy Wall Street expressed the longing of the multitude for a 'real democracy' against corporate capitalism.[19] The *Occupygezi* movement is similar to the others in the sense that it has brought about a *prefigurative form of politics*, as it symbolized the rejection in all walks of life of Erdogan's vanguardism and engineering of the life-worlds of Turkish citizens: raising 'religious and conservative youth,' his call to mothers to have at least three children, his direct intervention in the content of Turkish soap operas, his direct order banning alcohol on university campuses, his intention to build mosques in Taksim Square and Camlica Hill, his condescending say over the lives of individuals and his increasing authoritarian discourse, which is based in Islamic references.[20]

As Marina Sitrin put it in the context of the Occupy Wall Street protests, the purpose of the *Gezi* movement was 'not to determine the path the country should take, but to create the space for a conversation in which all can participate and determine together what the future should look like.'[21] Rejecting all kinds of hierarchies and embracing prefigurative politics, citizens of all kinds (youngsters, socialists, Muslims, nationalists, Kemalists, Kurds, Alevis, gays/lesbians, ecologists, football fans, hackers, artists, activists, academics, anarchists, anti-war activists, women's groups and others) gathered in *Gezi Park* in Taksim. *Gezi Park* has in the past been a site for left-wing working-class demonstrations, to create a multiplicity of spaces such as social centers, graffiti walls, libraries, collective kitchens, music venues, conference venues, day care corners, book fairs, barter tables, utopic streets and squares[22] and democratic fora which provided room for experimentation, creativity, innovation and dissent. These civil utopias brought about a form of solidarity which was cross-cultural, cross-religion, cross-ethnicity, cross-class and cross-gender. Respecting difference was also embedded in these civil utopias, where practicing Muslims respected atheists, atheists respected practicing Muslims, and all respected homosexuals, Kemalists respected Kurdish activists, Kurds respected Kemalists, Beşiktaş football fans respected Fenerbahçe fans and the elderly respected youngsters. In the spaces of communication created by the demonstrators, individual civil society actors coming from different ideological grounds had the chance to experience a form of deliberative democracy. In one of her works on current social movements, Donatella Della Porta draws our attention to the critical trust generated by demonstrators in such deliberative settings:

> By relating with each other, recognising the others and being by them recognised, citizens would have the chance to understand the reasons of the others, assessing them against emerging standards of fairness. Communication not only allows for the development of better solutions, by allowing for carriers of different knowledge and expertise to interact, but it also changes the perception of one's own preferences, making participants less concerned with individual, material interests and more with collective goods. Critical trust would develop from encounter with the other in deliberative settings.[23]

The *Gezi* movement also provided its participants with an experience of direct democracy by which the holders of different points of view interacted and reciprocally transformed each other's views.[24]

As in Tahrir Square and Zucotti Park, the demonstrators of Gezi Park also made a point of keeping the park clean throughout the demonstrations to show the capacity of 'the people' to govern themselves.[25] The *Occupygezi* movement was also meant to be an attempt to reassemble the social sphere, which had been polarized in different spheres of life between the so-called secularists and Islamists. It was revealed that most of the demonstrators had not been involved in any organized demonstrations before.[26] *Gezi Park* provided youngsters, who usually only communicate online, with a meeting ground where they experienced communication face to face. Against the segregation and isolation of everyday life, *Occupy* offered participatory structures and open communication. It invited passive citizens to experience an active sense of what James Hoslton calls 'insurgent citizenship,' by which they could see what an inclusive and egalitarian society might look like.[27] The *Gezi* movement was about creating alternative pathways for political organization and communication to prefigure real democracy and active citizenry to come. The movement introduced millions of citizens all around the country to the experience of direct democracy. It radicalized an entire generation of previously discouraged and apathetic youth, and it built test zones for imagining and living out a post-capitalist utopia organized outside profit, competition and the corporate world.

Henri Lefebvre's path-breaking notion of 'the right to the city' is probably the most meaningful theoretical intervention to be used to explain what the *Occupygezi* movement actually refers to. Lefebvre defines the city as 'an oeuvre, a work in which all citizens participate.'[28] Lefebvre does not accept the monopoly of the state in constructing the urban space. The city is a public space of interaction and exchange, and the right to the city enfranchises dwellers to participate in the use and reproduction of urban space. The right to the city is the right to 'urban life, to renewed centrality, to places of encounter and exchange, to life rhythms and time uses, enabling the full and complete *usage* of … moments and places.'[29] Similarly, David Harvey defines the right to the city as being

> far more than a right of individual or group access to the resources that the city embodies: it is a right to change and reinvent the city more after our hearts' desire. It is, moreover, a collective rather than an individual right, since reinventing the city inevitably depends upon the exercise of a collective power over the processes of urbanisation. The freedom to make and remake ourselves and our cities is one of the most precious yet most neglected of our human rights.[30]

What happened in *Gezi* Park was a revolt of the masses against the everlasting authority of the state in shaping the public space as well as the city. A handful of environmentalist protestors were staying in tents at *Gezi* Park to protest the Istanbul Greater Municipality and the JDP, who were keen on building a shopping-mall replacing the Park. Towards the morning of the 28th of May, the police forces put the tents into fire and brutally attacked the environmentalists who were accompanied by their children and spouses. The brutal act of the police immediately provoked thousands of individuals who went to the Park to express their solidarity with their environmentalist peers. The revolt was spontaneously organized by youngsters of every kind, who were mobilized through new social media like Twitter and Facebook. The choice of *Gezi Park*, which is located at the very center of the city next to Taksim Square, was also symbolically important, as it was meant to be the space restored from the hands of the corporate world collaborating with the neoliberal state. Lefebvre finds the use of the city center by the dwellers of that city to be very important with regard to the materialization of the right to the city:

> The right to the city, complemented by the right to difference and the right to information, should modify, concretize and make more practical the rights of the citizen as an urban dweller (*citadin*) and user of multiple services. It would affirm, on the one hand, the right of users to make known their ideas on the space and time of their activities in the urban area; it would also cover the right to the use of the centre, a privileged place, instead of being dispersed and stuck into ghettos for workers, immigrants, the 'marginal' and even for the 'privileged.'[31]

Hence, the *Occupygezi* movement has become a civil-political venue in which youngsters of every kind have communicated with each other in a deliberative form and have become active agents of civil society in a way that has proved the merits of the ongoing Europeanization processes. One should also not forget about the symbolic importance of Taksim Square, in the center of the city next to the *Gezi Park*, which is very meaningful to secular segments of Turkish civil society. The historical Republican Monument (*Cumhuriyet Anıti*) symbolizing the War of Independence and the foundation of the Turkish Republic, the Atatürk Cultural Centre (*Atatürk Kültür Merkezi*) symbolizing Kemalist modernity, modern arts and music and Taksim Square symbolizing the history of working-class movements and May Day celebrations are all very important symbols of modernity, Westernization, secularization and Europeanization, terms which are likely to be used interchangeably by Turkish citizens.[32]

The actors in the Turkish public debate on Europe

Europe and Europeanization are perceived very differently by various actors, depending on the ways in which these two entities have been operationalized by the actors in question. Europe has been an important anchor for the democratization process of Turkey in the last two decades. Particularly in the aftermath of the EU Helsinki Summit of 1999, EU harmonization efforts to align

Turkey's policies occupied the political agenda and led to various constitutional amendment packages.[33] However, while 1999–2005 marks the rapid reformation of the Turkish legal framework, 2005 marks the loss of momentum for said reformation process along the lines of the Copenhagen criteria. The EU anchor, which was considered to be at its strongest in the 1999–2005 period, hence it is being considered a 'virtuous cycle,' yielded to the 'vicious cycle,' where the EU anchor weakened and the reformation process almost came to a halt. There are several different social and political actors shaping the Europeanization process of Turkey: CSOs, trade unions and the media. Based on the discourse analysis of a limited number of civil society actors due to the space limitations, this section will elaborate on the perspectives of these actors on the EU before and after the Occupygezi movement.

Civil society organizations

Regarding the nature of civil organizations in Turkey, an important argument was made by Keyman and İçduygu, namely that the direction of Turkish modernization since the 1980s and the increasing participation of civil society actors in the policy-making process is a result of four processes: (1) the changing meaning of modernity or, in other words, the emergence of alternative modernities, which refers to, first, the emergence of a critique of the status of secular-rational thinking as the exclusive source of modernity in Turkey; and second, the increasing strength of Islamic discourse both as a 'political actor' and as a 'symbolic foundation' for identity formation; (2) the legitimacy crisis of a strong state tradition, which occurred as a result of the shift towards civil society and culture as new reference points in the language and terms of politics; (3) the process of European integration, referring to the assertion that reforms also indicate that the sources of democratization in Turkey are no longer only national but also global and, therefore, that the EU plays an important role in the changing nature of state–society relations in Turkey and functions as a powerful actor generating a transformative power in Turkish politics; and (4) the process of globalization, in which Turkish politics functions, as a significant external variable for understanding the current state of the political process in Turkey.[34]

Although Turkish CSOs have been deemed weak policy actors due to the assertion that respect for authority is stressed over citizen empowerment and participation, while democracy has been shallow, imposed from above by Westernizing elites on a largely peasant, passive society, in the 1980s and, particularly, in the 1990s, CSOs began to proliferate.[35] While it is agreed upon that this proliferation was highly contingent on economic liberalization, Keyman and İçduygu argue that this increase can also be associated with political parties, in a way that:

the centre-Right and centre-Left political parties have continuously been declining in terms of their popular support and their ability to produce effective and convincing policies, while at the same time both the resurgence of identity politics and civil society have become strong and influential actors of social and political change.[36]

Ersin Kalaycıoğlu agrees that although the visible statist orientation (*étatism*) in Turkey stresses community over the individual, uniformity over diversity and an understanding of law that privileges collective reason, the reasons for this phenomenon are founded on critical relations between the center and the periphery.[37]

Perhaps as a part of this dynamic, namely the association of the center with the state, Kalaycıoğlu argues that, among others, TÜSIAD (*Türk Sanayicileri ve İşadamları Derneği,* Turkish Industrialists' and Businessmen's Association), Türk-İş (*Türkiye İşçi Sendikaları Konfederasyonu,* Confederation of Turkish Trade Unions), TOBB (*Türkiye Odalar ve Borsalar Birliği,* The Turkish Union of Chambers and Stock Exchanges), MÜSIAD (*Müstakil Sanayici ve İşadamları Derneği*, Independent Industrialists and Businessmen's Association), and TUSKON (Turkey's Businessman and Industrialists Confederation) often benefit from their cooperation with the state, rather than from cooperation with other voluntary associations to pressure the state. As a rule, voluntary associations do not seem to consider the state as an adversary, but rather as an ally to be mobilized against their competitors.[38] The corporatist path-dependent stance of the aforementioned associations has also recently continued upon the rule of the President Erdoğan. On the other hand, protest movements and advocacy associations which confront the Turkish state and advocate change in the political system are not received well by the state, though they receive media attention.[39] In contrast, Atan argues that certain CSOs do not necessarily cooperate with the state and that

> ... while Turkish civil society is traditionally weak *vis-à-vis* the state, Turkish PBOs [Peak Business Organisations] appear as significant actors to challenge the government's policy agenda. Familiarisation with the EU-level governance system had provided them with additional resources to act upon the domestic agenda-setting process.[40]

To that effect, it should be noted that TÜSIAD, an association including big business, has been one of the most-discussed civil society actors in the literature. In terms of EU membership, Atan argues that TÜSIAD played an important role in the aftermath of 1997 by strengthening their ties with their European counterparts through EU institutions and governments in order to encourage Turkey's EU membership.[41] Additionally, TÜSIAD prompted domestic policy changes in Turkey in favor of harmonization with the EU member states through the 1997 report entitled 'The Perspectives on Democratisation in Turkey.'[42] These reports have been discussed and cited by many scholars as a reflection of growing civil society participation in the domestic policy-making process.

MÜSIAD (*Müstakil Sanayici ve İşadamları Derneği*, Independent Industrialists and Businessmen's Association) is another business association, which mainly consists of JDP supporters. MÜSIAD appears to be an organization advocating a different model of economic and social development using a certain interpretation of Islam to ensure the cohesion of its members and to represent their economic interest as an integral component of an ideological mission.[43] Consequently, MÜSIAD followed a discourse emphasizing the compatibility of EU membership with the 'Islamic and democratic identity' of the Turkish society,[44] a discourse which is quite similar to the arguments made by members of the JDP. On the other hand, the Europeanization process has produced two dynamics: firstly, economic Europeanization as a social learning process and political Europeanization as political opportunism and, secondly, ongoing Euro-scepticism.[45] Furthermore, one could also observe that there is an interesting shift from hard Euro-scepticism based on a civilizational divergence argument towards a soft Euro-scepticism expressed through national interest and a new Islamic rhetoric in line with the assumption that Turkey has become a 'soft power' in its region in the late 2000s. TUSKON (Turkey's Businessman and Industrialists Confederation), another business association, was founded during the 1990s. The association consisted of 7 federations based on more than 200 local associations and more than 55,000 entrepreneurs scattered all around the world. The most distinctive feature of TUSKON is its close ties with the Gülen Movement, which was an ally of Recep Tayyip Erdoğan until very recently.[46] The alliance between Erdoğan and the Gülen movement was literally terminated by the failed military coup organized by the Gülen-affiliated commanders in the Turkish army.[47]

In addition to business associations, it should be noted that the IKV (*Iktisadi Kalkınma Vakfı*, Economic Development Foundation) was established as an initiative of the Istanbul Chamber of Commerce in 1965 to inform the public about the internal affairs of the EU as well as the relations between Turkey and the EU. Similarly, TESEV (*Türkiye Ekonomik ve Sosyal Etüdler Vakfı*, Turkish Economic and Social Studies Foundation) is a non-governmental think tank focusing on social, political and economic policies in Turkey. Both IKV and TESEV have been very active in informing the public and the government on EU-related issues.[48] One should also note that there have been several other CSOs such as environmental groups (WWF, Regional Environment Centre), human rights organizations (Helsinki Citizens Assembly, TÜSEV, Anadolu Kültür), women rights organizations (KADER, KAGIDER), LGBT groups and international foundations (Heinrich Böll Foundation, Friedrich Ebert Foundation, Open Society Foundation, British Council, etc.) advocating the EU in Turkey.[49]

During and after the *Gezi* movement, the position of the above-mentioned business organizations largely differed from each other. TÜSIAD continuously criticized the JDP government on the issues of abortion, women's rights, freedom of press and fundamental rights. However, the clientalist and corporatist nature of state and business relations in Turkey put pressure on secular business circles to remain in alliance with the government. Business associations such as TÜSIAD, MÜSIAD and TOBB often tend to benefit from their co-operation with the state, rather than co-operation with other voluntary associations to pressure the state.[50] As these associations tend to campaign for state attention, subsidies and assistance, they prefer not to question the authority of the state. Business associations, whether their membership constituted conservative, devout Muslims, or modern, secular, establishment elites, avoided publicly commenting on the disproportionate use of force by the law enforcement units in Istanbul, Ankara, Izmir, Eskişehir, Hatay and Adana that has left eight minors dead and several hundreds injured.[51] However, despite the corporatist links with the state actors, most of the members of TÜSIAD took a supportive role for the democratic rights of the protesters. Taking a critical Europeanist position in his statement, the TÜSIAD chairman touched upon the disproportionate intervention of police forces against protesters that prompted the small protest into a full blown reaction towards the government. The declaration of TÜSIAD was as follows:

> While there is continuing public support for a new and civilian constitution as well as for the resolution process of violence and terror, what we all need is to ensure that *fundamental rights and freedoms* including the *right to peaceful meetings and demonstrations* will be secured. This is a prerequisite for the success of the process, and the responsibility belongs to all of us. When we all have such an expectation, extraordinary and disproportionate use of force and intolerance against the demonstrators in Taksim Gezi Park does not only hurt the public conscience, but also discourages the search for social cohesion. In such a critical time, when we are all in need of social cohesion, we want to invite all the public administrators and protesters to act in a deliberation, responsibility, transparency and creativity without using violence and force. (my translation and italics)[52]

The declaration of TÜSIAD was in line with that of the European Union, underlining the disproportionate use of force and the protection of fundamental rights and freedoms. Probably, the most explicit reaction among the members of TÜSIAD came from the Koç Family, who opened the doors of their Divan Hotel to groups of women, children and young people who had escaped tear gas and water cannons at the Elmadağ exit of *Gezi Park*.[53] It did not take long for PM Erdoğan to express his discomfort with regard to the explicit support of one of the members of TÜSIAD, the Koc Family of the protestors, and his critical remarks were followed by a delegation of tax authorities from the Ministry of Finance accompanied by about 20 police officers to raid Turkey's largest publicly traded company, the oil and energy giant TÜPRAŞ in Kocaeli.[54]

On the other hand, TUSKON remained silent during the *Gezi* protests. After then PM Erdoğan explicitly started to accuse the Gülen Movement about their involvement in the *Gezi* protests, the members of TUSKON took a new position. The association started to accuse the government as corrupt and oppressive with respect to the *Gezi* protests.[55] Mustafa Boydak, President of the Kayseri Chamber of Industry (*Kayseri Sanayi Odası*, KAYSO), released a statement three days after the TÜPRAŞ raid to support the Koç Family and to warn the JDP government not to authorize an unfair and McCarthyist push against pro-*Gezi* business circles. Highlighting the importance of the Koç Group for the Turkish economy, Boydak reminded the JDP government and the public that the fresh memory of the 28 February 1997 coup initiated against conservative Islamist groups and its aftermath should urge democratic leaders not to divide the business community into two oppositional groups.[56] Mustafa Boydak was later detained by Turkish authorities on 29 July 2016 as part of the investigation launched into the activities of the Fethullah Gülen Movement.[57]

Although the reactions of the Koç Family and the Boydak Family appear to back up the protestors and to criticize the brutality of security forces along the same lines as the European Union, one should be careful in assuming the main rationale for both sides. While the former family has traditionally followed a Kemalist genealogy, the latter was known to be linked with the Islamist genealogy in parallel with JDP, whose strategic alliance with the Gülen Movement has been severed in the aftermath of the *Gezi Park* protests. As opposed to the TÜSIAD and the Gülenist business circles, TOBB preferred to align with the state actors. In June 2013, TOBB published an announcement on the behalf of the chambers and other CSOs with which it had drafted a public statement, calling on a peaceful and democratic end to the *Gezi* protests:

> It is not a democratic right to insult our Prime Minister, his family, our Parliament, our institutions, and various segments of our society. Everyone should know that those who are committing such crimes are willing to cause chaos in our country. Our citizens are expected to raise their claims in accordance with the legal regulations. However, the latest events indicate that the protestors are willing to take our country into terror and chaos. *All our citizens should strongly respond to those* insulting *our national and moral values* by means of social media and billboards. Those using this insulting language will be considered responsible in the consciousness of our nation. (my translation and italics)[58]

The public announcement claimed that though the movement had been triggered by civilians and environmentalists with good intentions, it became quickly engulfed by 'marginalised groups,' mostly left-wing, which then politicized and securitized a civilian movement. The TOBB declaration matched the public statements made by members of the JDP government and was a clear sign that the business community sought a comfortable distance from the heated political and societal conflict, which was believed to be harming the economic stability in the country. There was unanimous agreement between TOBB and the JDP government that the protests were damaging Turkey's reputation and jeopardized business ventures of Istanbul's shop owners, artisans and service sector companies.[59] The other parallel between TOBB and the JDP government was their call for the civilian vigilantes to respond to protestors. PM Erdoğan followed a more straightforward way of inviting the vigilantes to take action against the protestors to save the dignity of the nation. By calling protesters 'scum and feral,' trying to get the support of devout Muslims by turning them into vigilantes fighting in the name of Islam, Erdoğan was actually trying to deflect from his disputed ways of doing politics and business as well as the rampantly feral nature of capitalism, which had already turned the big cities into endless lands of profit for the JDP elite and its followers.[60]

As for Islamist business associations other than TUSKON, which would later be banned by the JDP government due to its links with the Gülen Movement, MÜSIAD has always been supportive of the European integration process until the *Gezi Park* protests.[61] Through the Occupygezi movement, EU membership catalyzed the building of a brief but powerful coalition between secular and Muslim conservative business elites.[62] Associations of Turkey's Muslim conservative business circles warmed up to the process of Europeanization. Dilek Yankaya identifies three perspectives towards the European integration process: politically speaking, MÜSIAD and its members adopted an opportunist position, assuming that EU membership would guarantee broader democratic and civil rights and freedoms, particularly the freedom of faith and conscience. Simultaneously, MÜSIAD displayed a degree of Euro-scepticism as the Islamic character of the association impedes its full submission to European belief and value systems. Economically speaking, MÜSIAD's behavior is rather pragmatic because they assume that the process of social learning regarding European business patterns and culture contribute to the ways in which they discipline and efficiently regulate their way of doing business.[63] However, their appeal to the EU has been interrupted along with the *Gezi Park* protests, as their clientalist interests have led them to reposition themselves in line with the JDP government and against the European integration process.

Trade unions

In the Turkish context, it is often claimed that business associations have triggered the accession process while most of the labor unions have been critical towards the European integration process.[64] In comparison to the literature on CSOs and political parties, the literature on trade unions with respect to their role in the Europeanization of Turkey during the post-Helsinki period is rather limited. Nevertheless, it is possible to characterize the stances of trade unions as rather cautious and inconsistent. For instance, on the one hand they argue that the Europeanization process would cause unemployment and the disintegration of the country; on the other hand, EU membership is seen as providing an opportunity to move forward and to improve labor rights.[65] However, it is also noted by others that:

> many of the labour market problems currently experienced in Turkey emerge in a context of rapid structural change. Until quite recently, the bulk of employment was in the agricultural sector, whereas today the urban labour force in industry and services is much larger than the rural workforce.[66]

In reference to her in-depth interviews with members of labor unions, Zeynep Alemdar argues that although the literature expects them to appeal to the EU for better labor standards or workers' rights, Turkish domestic actors' use of the EU depends heavily on the domestic environment and their respective perceptions of the EU.[67] In fact, Alemdar's argument in general is also reflective of shifting views towards the EU, but she relies on the premise that the domestic environment, such as military coups, political party alliances and labor regulations, influences the ways in which trade unions perceive the EU. Consequently, the unions appeal to the EU when they are not satisfied with domestic politics.

In order to examine the perceptions of labor unions on EU membership and the reforms it necessitates, scholars tend to look at the cases of Türk-İş (*Türkiye İşçi Sendikaları Konfederasyonu*, Confederation of Turkish Trade Unions), DİSK (*Devrimci İşçi Sendikaları Konfederasyonu*, Confederation of Revolutionary Trade Unions), KESK (Confederation of Public Labourer's Unions) and Hak-İş (*Hak İşçi Sendikaları Konfederasyonu*, Confederation of Justice-Seekers' Trade Union). These Unions are all members of the European Trade Union Confederation. Alemdar describes TÜRK-İŞ as a state-centric labor union, showing that Türk-İş took an openly anti-EU stance after 2000 but has softened its position since 2005, when membership negations began. TÜRK-İŞ's position *vis-à-vis* the EU is very well explicated by Yıldırım Koç, who is one of the advocates of the syndicate:

> The European Union's demands for Turkey are in opposition to the Turkish Republic's unitary state system and its independence. Abiding by these demands would tear our country apart and divide it, creating a new Yugoslavia. Turkey is not going to solve its problems through the EU. Turkey is not going to be stronger because of the EU. Turkey is going to solve its problems despite the EU, and it will be stronger. Turkey's admittance to the EU is dependent on this strength.[68]

It is important to note that Koç's argument is similar to the political parties' concerns over territorial integrity as well as the unity of the Republic. While TÜRK-İŞ did not necessarily reflect the structure of its counterparts in the EU, the leftist DİSK reformulated itself in the 1990s in line with the European trade unions.[69] Consequently, DİSK has been adamant in pressuring the government and lobbying to harmonize Turkish labor regulations with those of the EU.[70]

Hak-İş, on the other hand, presents a different dynamic in the sense that Hak-İş' attitude towards the EU has been intricately linked with the organization's relationship with the government. When the government was pursuing the EU, the appeal of the EU was strong, and vice-versa.[71] In December 1999, Hak-İş declared its stance towards the EU as follows:

> A major challenge to integration with Europe is Turkey's Muslim population. Turkey, because of its historical, moral, philosophical, religious and national characteristics, is not Western. 'Westernisation' comes as a betrayal and alienation to Turkish culture … if membership in the EU is pushed, this would mean a total surrender [to Western values]. On the other hand, Turkey's application for EU membership means a heavy legal burden for the Constitution and other laws, and constitutes a threat to the state's sovereignty and the nation's unity … the fact that the government and the opposition parties are silent about this raises questions.[72]

However, as the Islamist political parties modified their perceptions of the EU and the notion of Westernization, Hak-İş also followed the same discourse, in line with the JDP.

During and after the *Gezi* movement, the labor unions generated different perspectives. A majority of the unions became critical Europeanists. Major trade unions such as DISK and KESK mobilized their members through the declaration of two general strikes during the protests in June 2013. Initially, KESK called for a national 24-hour strike on June 5th. On June 4th, DISK, TMMOB (the Union of Chambers of Turkish Engineers and Architects) and TTB (The Turkish Medical Association) declared their support for the strike on June 5th. This strike took place with significant participation of the public sector. It is estimated that between 400,000 and 500,000 workers participated in the strike throughout the country.[73] Although Hak-İş and large parts of TÜRK-IŞ did not support the uprising, some platforms within TÜRK-IŞ joined the strike to declare their support for the protesters against the brutality of state security forces.

In his study on left-wing labor unions such as DİSK and KESK, Can Büyükbay reveals that such labor unions identify the EU with both positive and negative nominations/predications. Accordingly, the EU is positively perceived by the leadership of such labor unions as the *provider of democracy, welfare state and social rights*. On the other hand, the EU is negatively perceived by the same actors as a *neoliberal, imperialist and colonialist* entity trying to assimilate Turkey into the capitalist free market economy.[74] The discursive construction of Europe as a capitalist center is realized through two major representations of Europe: Europe as a transformative and colonial power, and neoliberal Europe as the diluter of labor rights and enabler of privatization in partnership with the JDP government. Europe is commonly represented among leftist labor union leaders as a capitalist project that transforms the accession countries in accordance with neoliberal policies.[75]

Both labor unions are known to be Kemalist, laicist, state-centric, militarist and previously Euro-sceptic. They were also actively involved in the 2007 Flag demonstrations organized by the Association for Ataturkist Thought (*Ataturkçü Düşünce Derneği*, ADD) and the Association for the Support of Contemporary Living (*Çağdaş Yaşamı Destekleme Derneği*). In the spring of 2007, these two urban elite organizations called for a series of protest demonstrations throughout the main urban centers with the active support and participation of some other nationalist and state secularist associations – all of which were later active during the *Gezi Park* protests – such as DİSK and KESK. These two were also active prior to 2013 and organized at least three large-scale demonstrations in collaboration with local community organizations, protesting the redevelopment and commercialization projects in urban areas, especially in Istanbul. In the press conference organized at the Taksim *Gezi Park* on 3 March 2012, the Secretary General of DISK, Adnan Serdaroğlu, even suggested that PM Erdoğan was acting like an Ottoman Sultan and ignoring the opposition:

> The power of the JDP does not work out here. Taksim bears the footsteps of millions of workers from 1976, 1977 and 2000s. Taksim is the place where the powerless become powerful. Taksim is the place where we declared 1 May as holiday. Everyone seems to comply with whatever the Sultan asks. Everyone says 'Long live Sultan.' But we won't say that. This country will not be surrendered to pain, exploitation and pressure. We won't give in Taksim. (translated by the author)[76]

This statement made by the Secretary General of DISK was an early reminder of the attempt of oppositional CSOs to occupy the city center at the expense of the JDP government. Similarly, in the very first days of the *Gezi Park* protests, following the immediate reaction of German Chancellor Angela Merkel and the President of the European Parliament, Kani Beko, the leader of the DİSK trade union confederation called on workers to get together to put an end to 'oppression and persecution':

> If the government doesn't stop its war against the people, we will continue to take our *democratic reaction to the squares.* (my translation and italics)[77]

His call for a general strike was influential for other left-wing labor unions such as KESK and a small part of TÜRK-İş. During and after the *Gezi* protests, Kani Beko's discourse underlined a pro-European stance of left-wing labor unions who are in strong alliance with the European Trade Union (ETUC).[78] The rights-based approach of left-wing labor unions has brought them in closer contact with European integration, while Islamist and corporatist labor unions such as Hak-İş and larger groups of TÜRK-İŞ had to reposition themselves against the EU and adjacent to the JDP government and the President Erdoğan, who has repeatedly expressed his concerns about the way the European Union interprets developments in Turkey. Responding to a vote in the European parliament in Strasbourg during the early days of the *Gezi Park* protests, PM Erdoğan immediately responded to the EU with the following words:

> I won't recognise the decision that the European Union parliament is going to take about us. *Who do you think you are* by taking such a decision? (my translation and italics)[79]

Erdoğan's statements regarding the EU were a sign for some labor and business associations to reposition themselves *vis-a-vis* the European Union. Erdoğan has continued his populist discourse with regard to the EU after he became President in 2014. Just to give an example of one of his public speeches, which explicitly hit out the criticisms coming from the EU to the political leadership of a candidate country, one could be reminded of his rhetoric about the death penalty, which he brought back to debate in the aftermath of the failed coup of 15 July 2016 for the punishment of the perpetrators:

> If the nation makes such a decision [in support of death penalty], I believe political parties will abide by this decision. As the sovereignty unconditionally belongs to the nation and as you request the death penalty [for the coup leaders], the authority which is going to decide on this issue is Turkey's National Assembly. If our parliament takes such a decision, the necessary step will be taken. I am expressing in advance that I will approve such a decision coming from the parliament ... They say there is no death penalty in the EU. Well, the US has it, Japan has it, China has it, most of the world has it. So they are allowed to have it. We used to have it until 1984. *Sovereignty belongs to the people, so if the people make this decision I am sure the political parties will comply.* (my italics)[80]

The discourse of President Erdoğan highlights his populist style and invites the clients of the state to side with it. His Euro-sceptic discourse reinforces the Euro-scepticism of all kinds of CSOs, while the same discourse is likely to strengthen the pro-European position of those associations that are in opposition to the ways in which Turkey is being governed.[81]

The media

First and foremost, it should be noted that similar to the literature on trade unions, the literature on the role of the media in the process of modernization and Europeanization of Turkey is also very limited. Nevertheless, scholars have studied the nature of the Turkish media with regard to the European integration process. During the period between 1982 and 1993, it is possible to observe a proliferation in media outlets, which was a result of non-media-related capital in the sector altering the structure of the media to resemble industrial enterprises.[82] The technological developments during this period contributed to the establishment of numerous television and radio channels, both local and national. As the intensity of competition increased in tandem with the rise of capitalist ideology, media enterprises began to focus more on sales. In correlation with the increased competition, this period was marked by, among other things, the rise of monopolies in the sector, which in return created support for the government and politicians due to the growing need for 'incentives, credits, and public announcements.'[83]

The Turkish media could be categorized as a part of the Mediterranean model. In this model, journalists take sides as members of the political and literary elites. The Mediterranean, or Polarised Pluralist Model, is character-ized by an elite-oriented press with relatively small circulation and a corre-sponding centrality of electronic media. Freedom of the press and the development of commercial media industries generally came late; newspapers have often been economically marginal and in need of subsidy. Political par-allelism tends to be high in this model; the press is marked by a strong focus on political life and external pluralism, and the tradition of commentary-oriented or advocacy journalism persists more strongly than in other parts of Europe. Instrumentalization of the media by the government, political parties and industrialists with political ties is common. Professionalization of journalism is not strongly developed as in the other models. Journalism is not strongly differentiated from political activism and the autonomy of journalism is often limited.[84]

Turkish journalists have also been swinging between pro-Europeanness and Euro-scepticism while framing the EU beyond traditional institutional news coverage, like 'Turkey must fulfil its EU requirements by ... ' or 'the EU must fulfil its promises ... '[85] While Arsan depicts the problematic nature of journalists located in Brussels, it is also necessary to examine the nature of domestic sources of information. In terms of domestic television channels, Gencel Bek suggests that the Turkish media has also gone through a 'tabloidisation process.' As a part of her research, she analyzes the state-owned TRT (*Türkiye Radyo ve Televizyon Kurumu*, Turkish Radio and Television Corporation), and characterizes the quality of the news as follows:

> In general, the reports are quite bland accounts of cabinet meetings. There is no setting of context, interpretation, discussion or criticism. TRT just reports that such and such politicians met, in a formulaic way. The news gives no other

information such as who else talked in the meeting, who said what, what the main aim of the meeting was, etc … What TRT does achieve, however, is full coverage of all the national ceremonies, reminding the public of national history from the perspective of the official memory. One could call TRT news the 'news of the nation-state.'[86]

The above-mentioned argument is partly a result of the mentality followed by RTÜK (*Radyo Televizyon Üst Kurulu*, Radio and Television Supreme Council), which is a public legal entity that monitors television channels. On that issue, Gencel Bek criticizes the operations of the RTÜK for being in favor of the state. She argues:

> The peculiar characteristics of broadcasting regulation also have an effect on content: the RTÜK controls content to a far greater extent than media structure, concentration, increasing market mechanisms, etc. Content control and subsequent penalties are mainly directed towards the channels 'which are against the state.' Protecting the state takes precedence over the citizen's right to information.[87]

Even though Arsan and Gencel Bek examine different aspects of the Turkish media, it is possible to infer a common theme, which is that the news media – both journalists in Brussels and the TRT – filter the news before it reaches the public. In that sense, the lack of professional and extensive media coverage from Brussels and the domination of the public service channel by nationalist events indicate that the citizen's right to information about the EU and the process of Europeanization has been overshadowed by political and social interests. Moreover, media coverage depends highly on the relations of media ventures with the government in particular, and with the political parties in general.

The media continue to shift between Euro-scepticism and pro-Europeanness. The EU has always been a practical source of legitimacy for the media in Turkey. *Cumhuriyet* and *Sözcü*, for instance, are two Kemalist daily newspapers with Euro-sceptic coverage prior to the *Gezi* movement. In their coverage, they often represented the EU as a homogenous institution which was directly involved in the transformation of the Turkish political system leading to the replacement of the Kemalist state by an Islamist one.[88] However, in the second half of the 2000s, oppositional newspapers started to have difficulties with the JDP government. Media outlets were sometimes denied access to events and information for political reasons. For instance, in September 2012, seven publications, mostly Kemalist and leftist, such as *Cumhuriyet, Sözcü, Birgün, Evrensel, Aydınlık, Özgür Gündem* and *Yeniçağ*, were denied the accreditation needed to cover the JDP's Fourth Party Congress. In November 2014, the media was prohibited from disseminating information on the investigation commission of the 17 and 25 December corruption scandals related to the four ministers in the JDP government.[89] As a result of the escalation of the tension between the government and the oppositional news-papers, TV and radio channels, and some social media outlets, those media institutions also tried to align themselves with the EU and other domestic pol-itical institutions such as the Republican People's Party.

Following the statement of the European Parliament criticizing the PM and the official security forces, the Kemalist newspapers, Cumhuriyet and Sözcü, immediately changed their discourses on the EU in parallel with that of the Republican People's Party. Both papers have become more pro-European during and after the *Gezi* movement. One of the Kemalist columnists of *Cum-huriyet*, Nilgün Cerrahoğlu, explicitly criticized the JDP government and approved of the critics by the European Parliament towards the Turkish government:

> Apparently, the intervention of the European Parliament to invite the Turkish government to act properly has disrupted the chemistry of Erdoğan. He was not really expecting such an intervention from the European Parliament. PM Erdoğan has been so harsh against this intervention. *The EU has always devel-oped a very patronising relationship with the previous Turkish governments along with the requirements of the Copenhagen Criteria. However, so far, the EU has always supported Erdoğan's government as if the Copenhagen Criteria were no longer applied to Turkey ...* Turkey could intervene in 'internal affairs' of Syria, but it doesn't let the EU, a union with a five hundred million population, and a Union to which it has become 'a candidate for full membership', intervene in its internal affairs on the basis of international agree-ments, or it only communicates with the Union as long as it is admired by the EU. The JDP does not accept critics. The main distinctive element of the JDP's Turkey is that there is no longer any concern for 'consistency.' (my translation and italics)[90]

Nilgün Cerrahoğlu clearly refers to the discursive shift of the European Union with respect to its changing relationship with the JDP government, which has become obvious during the *Gezi Park* protests. Criticizing the patronizing position of the EU over previous governments and the privileges given earlier to Erdoğan's government, Cerrahoğlu implicitly appreciates the inter-vention of the EU in the JDP government. Aligning itself with the EU, a similar line of criticism towards PM Erdoğan came from the other Kemalist newspaper, *Sözcü*:

> PM Recep Tayyip Erdoğan Zeytinburnu had to address his constituents in a public meeting called 'Respect to National Will' organised by his party in Kazlı-çeşme [a district of the European part of Istanbul, away from the centre] under the shade of the sky-scrapers, which 'he tried to cut down a bit, but couldn't manage.' [Erdoğan said the following in his speech]: 'Now Gezi Park is evacu-ated, Taksim square is evacuated, our municipality has cleaned the park, plant-ing flowers, and now the environmental workers are on business ... I called the protestors as 'a few scums', and some people were offended ... We will legally interrogate those who drank alcohol in the Mosque ... International media and European Parliament don't see Gazza, or Syria ... ' (translation is author's) [91]

This extract is from a news coverage in *Sözcü*, and starts taunting Erdoğan for one of his failures. The news also implicitly refers to the fact that Erdoğan could not hold his speech in the center of the city, which was actually occupied by the protestors. In this extract, the newspaper aligned itself with the European Parliament and focused on the threats made by PM Erdoğan to the protestors.

Another very interesting newspaper, which is likely to instrumentalize European integration for its own use, is *Zaman*. It is publicly known that *Zaman* belongs to the Gülen Community, which was an ally of the ruling party JDP. Recently, the JDP rule has cut off its alliance with the Gülen Community, which was later found to be the main perpetrator of the 15 July 2016 failed coup attempt. The divide between the JDP and this community became visible when PM Erdoğan publicly declared in November 2013 that they will ban preparatory schools (*dershane*), specialized education centers that help prepare students for high school and university entrance examinations. The Gülen Community used to run hundreds of prep-schools all around the country, where teachers affiliated with the mission of the community indoctrinated students with a kind of moderate Islam while preparing them for university and high school exams. Interestingly, *Zaman* used Chapter 22 (Regional Policy) to spread its message out to its readers, saying that

> the government plan to close down Turkey's prep schools will widen the educational gap created by social and economic inequality and regional disparities in Turkey, and it may endanger the implementation of the recently opened Chapter 22 in Turkey's European Union accession process.[92]

Zaman has always been the main information channel for Eurocrats, European politicians, as well as for the rest of the international community interested in news about Turkey, Central Asia and the Middle East. However, when the JDP government decided to dealign itself from the Gülen Movement, *Zaman* also started to lose its popularity in and outside the country. Despite the fact that it continued to have a Europeanist discourse for its own vested interests, it was closed down in the aftermath of the 15 July 2016 coup attempt.

Conclusion: the future of the EU debate in Turkey

The analysis developed in this article points to the relevance of the discursive interaction between the European internal debate and the Turkish debate on the EU.[93] The article has shown that similar frames have been developed in the civil society debate both in the EU and in Turkey. The fact that these are (partly) overlapping is evidence in itself of the ideational exchange between the two sides. Such exchange is both subterranean, channeled through a myriad of people-to-people micro-practices that create a de facto link between EU civil society and its Turkish counterpart, and explicit and public as reported in the media, in the conventional political debates or in the fora of elites.

In this regard, a particularly significant case study has been provided by the *Occupygezi* movement and its role in transforming part of the Turkish public debate on Europe. The harsh responses of the EU to the brutal acts of the Turkish state have contributed, perhaps unintentionally, to a radical turn in the mind-sets of laicist/secular Kemalist groups, who were previously Euro-sceptic. After the protests, such groups have become more pro-European than the supporters of the JDP rule. In other words, some of the Turkish civil society actors and private individuals have started to critically embrace European values by underlining their critical Europeanism such as members of TÜSIAD, DISK, KESK and the readers of *Cumhuriyet* and *Sözcü*, as well as some other left-wing newspapers. This kind of transform-ation was explained in the article through the ideological and political divides becoming sharper among business associations, labor unions and the media. This confirms once again that the transformation of Turkish civil society is deeply intermingled with the European integration process. Sometimes it follows a linear trajectory, other times it may follow unexpected paths.

It is comprehensible that the Turkish democratization process can be expected to persist alongside a liberal, political and post-civilizational project of Europe that would be ready to welcome Turkey, whereas a cultu-rally and religiously defined Europe would possibly abstain from welcoming Turkey and would, thus, certainly interrupt the democratization process. Turkey's democracy is strongly linked to the ways in which the EU is being constructed and reconstructed. There are at least two definitions of Europe and the European Union. The first defines Europeanness as a static, retrospec-tive, holistic, essentialist and culturally prescribed entity. The latter empha-sizes the understanding of 'Europe' as a fluid, ongoing, dynamic, prospective, syncretic and nonessentialist process of becoming. While the first definition highlights a *cultural project*, the latter definition welcomes a *political project* embracing cultural and religious differences, including Islam. In the article, it was argued that the *Occupygezi* movement triggered the existence of a group of critical Europeanists in different sectors such as business associations, labor unions and the media, who have begun to under-line the importance of European values as well as a social Europe in opposi-tion to the Europe of markets. What is embraced by critical Europeanists is a more political Europe that is needed to counter the apolitical and elite-driven Europe that we have known so far.

Eventually, the *Gezi Park* protests with a peaceful content can be perceived as reflections of Europeanisation by Turkish civil society, who have learned to raise claims about pluralist democracy, individual liberties, freedom of speech and freedom of the media.[94] In the 2013 Progress Report of the Commission on Turkey, it was stated that

> the wave of protests in June 2013 is the result of the broad democratic reform that has taken place in the past decade and the emergence of a vibrant and diverse civil society that needs to be respected and consulted more systematically at every level of decision making.[95]

This article was also based on the same premise that the Europeanisation process has had a very strong impact on the transformation of Turkish civil society. The Europeanization of Turkish civil society can be interpreted as one of the explanatory factors of why the failed coup of 15 July 2016 did not have a popular support as opposed to previous military coups in Turkey.

Notes

1. Kaya and Marchetti, "Europeanisation."
2. Wodak, *The Discourses of Politics*.
3. Kaya and Marchetti, "Europeanisation."
4. Casanova, "The Long, Difficult, and Tortuous Journey," 245.
5. Özbudun and Yazıcı, *Democratisation Reforms*. For further discussion on the impact of the European integration process on the state of minorities in Turkey see Kaya and Tarhanlı, *Türkiye'de Çoğunluk ve Azınlık* Politikaları, and Yılmaz, "Is There a Puzzle?."
6. Kaya, *Europeanisation and Tolerance*, Chapter 1.
7. Ibid.
8. Öniş, "Turkish Modernisation," 12.
9. For further discussion on the decision of the ECtHR see Saktanber and Çorbacıoğlu, "Veiling and Headscarf Skepticism."
10. German Marshall Fund, 'Transatlantic Trends Survey.' *German Marshall Fund*, 2010, http://trends.gmfus.org/transatlantic-trends/country-profiles/.
11. European Commission, "Eurobarometer 2013." July 11, 2013. http://ec.europa.eu/public_opinion/archives/eb/eb79/eb79_en.htm.
12. According to a similar survey conducted by the IKV, Istanbul Development Association, in April 2015, public support for membership to the EU was 61 percent. For this comparison see the website of the IKV, http://web.ikv.org.tr/icerik_print.asp?id=1403.
13. See "Main Opposition Urges Merkel Not to Block Turkey's EU Path." *Hurriyet Daily News*, June 22, 2013. http://www.hurriyetdailynews.com/main-opposition-urges-merkel-not-to-block-turkeys-eupath.aspx?PageID=238&NID=49191&NewsCatID=338.
14. See, European Union, *Statement by the Spokesperson of High Representative Catherine Ashton on Violence in Turkey*, A 295/13, Brussels, June 2, 2013. Accessed September 12, 2016. http://www.consilium.europa.eu/uedocs/cms_Data/docs/pressdata/EN/foraff/137372.pdf.
15. European Parliament, *Debates: Situation in Turkey*, Strasbourg, June 12, 2013, Accessed March 19, 2014. Accessed September 12, 2016. http://www.europarl.europa.eu/sides/getDoc.do?pubRef=-//EP//TEXT+CRE+20130612+ITEM-015+DOC+XML+V0//EN.

16. See "World Socialists Discuss Gezi Protests in Istanbul." *Hurriyet Daily News*, November 11, 2013. http://www.hurriyetdailynews.com/world-socialists-discuss-gezi-protests-in istanbul.aspx?PageID=238&NID=57727&NewsCatID=338.
17. Badiou, *The Rebirth of History*.
18. Slavoj Žižek, "The Simple Courage of Decision: A Leftist Tribute to Thatcher." *New Statesman*, April 17, 2013. http://www.newstatesman.com/politics/politics/2013/04/simple-courage-decision-leftist-tribute-thatcher.
19. Hardt and Negri, Declaration.
20. Kaya, "Islamisation of Turkey."
21. Sitrin, "What Does Democracy Look Like?"
22. Hrant Dink Street, Ceylan Özkol Street, Pınar Selek Square and Mustafa Sarı Street are some of those names used by the protestors to demonstrate their solidarity with those who had been exposed to the discrimination of the state machinery either in the past or during the demonstrations. Naming the fictional streets of squares after those persons, the protestors aimed to restore justice which was not secured by the state. Personal interview with one of the activists, Yigit Aksakoglu, Istanbul, September 16, 2013.
23. Della Porta, "Critical Trust," 40.
24. Ibid., 41.
25. For further information on Zucotti Park see Craig Calhoun, "Occupy Wall Street."
26. Konda Public Survey, "Survey on Gezi Park," June 6–7, 2013, http://t24.com.tr/files/GeziPark%C4%B1Final.pdf.
27. Holston, *Insurgent Citizenship*.
28. Lefebvre, "The Right to the City," 158.
29. Ibid., 158.
30. Harvey, *Rebel Cities*, 4.
31. Lefebvre, "The Right to the City," 36.
32. For a more detailed discussion on the interchangeable use of the terms Europeanization, modernization, secularization and Westernisation see Kaya, *Europeanisation and Tolerance*, Chapter 1.
33. Özbudun and Yazıcı, *Democratisation Reforms,* 14–16.
34. Keyman and İçduygu, "Globalisation, Civil Society and Citizenship," 222–6.
35. Kubicek, "Turkish Accession," 762.
36. Keyman and İçduygu, "Globalisation, Civil Society and Citizenship," 222.
37. Kalaycıoğlu, "State and Civil Society in Turkey," 250–2.
38. Ibid., 258.
39. Ibid., 260.
40. Atan, "Europeanisation of Turkish Peak Business Organisations," 109.
41. Ibid., 107.
42. Follow-up reports have been published in 1999 and 2001. For complete texts of these reports please consult: http://www.tusiad.us/main_page.cfm?TYPE_ID=12.
43. Atan, "Europeanisation of Turkish Peak Business Organisations," 111.
44. Ibid., 112.
45. Yankaya, "The Europeanisation of MÜSİAD."
46. For further detail see Seufert, "Is the Fethullah Gülen Movement Overstretching Itself?", Turam, *Secular State and Religious Society*.
47. For further detail on the failed coup see Stevenson, "Turkey: The Attempted Coup."

48. See http://www.ikv.org.tr and http://www.tesev.org.tr.
49. For a list of some of these organizations see the website of the World Movement for Democracy, http://www.wmd.org/resources/whats-being-done/human-rights-democracy-turkey/list-turkish-ngos-working-human-rights-and-.
50. Kalaycıoğlu, "State and Civil Society in Turkey."
51. lhan, "Turkey's State-Business Relations."
52. "Gezi Park Statement from TÜSİAD," Accessed June 20, 2016. http://www.hurriyet.com.tr/ekonomi/23414830.asp.
53. İlhan, "Turkey's State-Business Relations Revisited," 211–2.
54. "TÜPRAŞ'a şok baskın" (A surprise raid on TÜPRAŞ), *Milliyet Online*. July 24, 2013, Accessed September 10, 2016. http://ekonomi.milliyet.com.tr/tupras-a-sok-baskin/ekonomi/detay/1741160/default.htm. For the response of the Koç Family to the raid see "Ali Koç sessizliğini bozdu" (Ali Koç ended his silence), available at http://www.cnnturk.com/2013/guncel/07/29/ali.koc.sessizligini.bozdu/717490.0/index.html. For a more detailed account of the responce of the Turkish associations to the Gezi Park protests see İlhan, "Turkey's State-Business Relations Revisited."
55. "The Businessmen that is Close to Gülen Anxious." Accessed June 18, 2016. http://www.wsj.com.tr/article/SB10001424052702303562904579223742211718068.html.
56. "Boydak'tan TÜPRAŞ çıkışı: 28 Şubat'taki hatayı tekrarlamayalım" (Boydak's TÜPRAŞ comment: Let us not repeat the same mistakes we made on February 28, 1997)', *T24. Online*. July 27, 2013. Accessed September 11, 2016. http://t24.com.tr/haber/boydaktan-tupras-cikisi-28-subattaki-hatayi-yapmayalim/235423.
57. "Turkey Detains 3 Businessmen Over Failed Coup Attempt," *Hurriyet Daily News*, July 29, 2016. Accessed September 12, 2016. http://www.hurriyetdailynews.com/turkey-detains-3-businessmen-over-failed-coup-attempt.aspx?PageID=238&NID=102226&NewsCatID=341.
58. "Gezi Parkı Protestolarına TOBB'dan Açıklama" (Declaration on the Gezi Park Protests). Accessed September 11, 2016. http://www.internethaber.com/gezi-parki-protestolarina-tobbdan-aciklama-543802h.htm.
59. For a more detailed analysis of TOBB's position vis-a-vis the Gezi Park protests see İlhan, "Turkey's State-Business Relations Revisited," 211. See also "TOBB'dan "Gezi Parkı açıklaması" (TOBB's Gezi Park opinion)' *Hürriyet Ekonomi*, Online. June 7, 2013. Accessed September 11, 2016, http://www.hurriyet.com.tr/ekonomi/23445815.asp.
60. In the present case of vigilantism, it is arguable that wherever people live within State structures, similar questions about the (un)satisfactory provision of law and order from that source frequently arise. Taking the law into their own hands is a common response of citizens to such problems of order. For further information on this debate see "Released footage shows no physical attack on headscarf-wearing woman during Gezi protests," *Hurriyet Daily News*, February 14, 2014. Accessed September 14, 2016. http://www.hurriyetdailynews.com/released-footage-shows-no-physical-attack-on-headscarf-wearing-woman-during-gezi-protests.aspx?pageID=238&nID=62479&NewsCatID=341.
61. Erdinç, "AKP Döneminde Sendikal."
62. İlhan, "Turkey's State-Business Relations Revisited," 145.
63. Yankaya, "The Europeanisation of MÜSİAD."

64. Keyman and İçduygu, "Globalisation".
65. Yıldırım et al., "Turkish Labour Confederations," 363.
66. Adaman et al., "Societal Context."
67. Alemdar, "Turkish Trade Unions," 3.
68. Cited in Ibid., 9.
69. Ibid., 15.
70. Doğan, "Sendikalar."
71. Alemdar, "Turkish Trade Unions," 19.
72. Cited in Ibid., 20.
73. International Communist Current. (2013, June 25). "Turkey: The Cure for State Terror Isn't Democracy". Accessed June 20, 2016. http://en.internationalism. org/icconline/201306/8371/turkey\x{FFFE}cure-state-terror-isnt-democracy.
74. Büyükbay, "Deconstructing the Neoliberal Character."
75. Ibid., 59
76. Accessed September 11, 2016. http://www.etha.com.tr/Haber/2012/03/03/ guncel/taksim-ayaklarin-bas-oldugu-yerdir/.
77. "Turkish Unions March to Protest Police Crackdown in Istanbul," *Bloomberg News*, June 17, 2013. http://www.bloomberg.com/news/articles/2013-06-17/ turkish-strikers-march-amid-threat-of-renewed-police-crackdown.
78. For further information on the activities of ETUC with regard to Turkey see https://www.etuc.org/issue/turkey.
79. "Erdoğan issues stark 'final warning' to Turkey's Gezi Park protesters", *The Guardian*, June 14, 2013. Accessed September 15, 2016. https://www. theguardian.com/world/2013/jun/13/turkey-gezi-park-protesters.
80. Turkey coup: President Erdogan backs reintroduction of death penalty," *The Independent*, August 8, 2016, Accessed September 14, 2016. http://www. independent.co.uk/news/world/europe/turkey-death-penalty-erdogan-coup-president-backs-capital-punishment-a7178371.html.
81. For a debate about the populist leadership style see Jan-Werner Müller "Trump, Erdoğan, Farage: The Attractions of Populism for Politicians, the Dangers for Democracy," *The Guardian*, September 2, 2016. Accessed August 10, 2016. https://www.theguardian.com/books/2016/sep/02/trump-erdogan-farage-the-attractions-of-populism-for-politicians-the-dangers-for-democracy.
82. Sağnak, *Medya-Politik*, 55–6.
83. Ibid., 51.
84. Arsan, *Avrupa Birliği ve Gazetecilik*.
85. Ibid., 72.
86. Gencel Bek, "Tabloidisation of the Turkish Media."
87. Ibid., 383.
88. Kaya, "Islamisation of Turkey."
89. Transparency International Turkey, "National Integrity System Assessment."
90. Nilgün Cerrahoğlu, "Avrupa Parlamentosu'ndan 'Balans Ayarı'" (Balance from the EU) *Cumhuriyet*, June 10, 2013. For another example of the pro-European coverage of *Cumhuriyet* see the issue dated June 18, 2013, which covers news about Angela Merkel as well as Martin Schulz, Elmar Broek, Hannes Swoboda and Andrew Duff from the European Parliament. As for *Sözcü* see the issues of June 17, 2013 and June 18, 2013, which cover the news about the leader of the Socialist Group in the European Parliament, Hannes Swoboda, and other members of the European Parliament criticizing the

Turkish government. See http://www.sozcu.com.tr/2013/ekonomi/ swobodadan-erdogana-yanit-317178/.
91. "Erdoğan yine tehdit etti" (Erdoğan again threatened), *Sözcü*, June 16, 2013, http://www.sozcu.com.tr/2013/gundem/erdogan-konusuyor-canli-yayin- 316476/.
92. See Nesibe Hicret Soy, "Ban on Prep Schools Deal Blow to EU's Chapter 22," *Today's Zaman*, November 24, 2013, http://www.todayszaman.com/news- 332130-ban-on-prep-schools-deals-blow-to-eus-chapter-22.html.
93. Kaya and Marchetti. "Europeanisation."
94. See Öner, "Internal Factors."
95. European Commission, "Turkey 2013 Progress Report," December 2013, avail- able at the EU Commission's webpage, http://ec.europa.eu/enlargement/pdf/ key_documents/2013/package/brochures/turkey_2013.pdf.

Acknowledgements

I would like to express my gratitude to Cristiano Bee and Bianca Kaiser for their invaluable criticisms and support during the process of writing this piece. I have learned a lot in the discussions we had together. I am also very grateful to two anon- ymous reviewers who made very constructive criticisms and suggestions for this article. And last but not the least, I am also very thankful to Paul Kubicek, who made it possible for me to share my insights on this particular issue with a distin- guished readership.

Disclosure statement

No potential conflict of interest was reported by the author.

Bibliography

Adaman, Fikret, Ayşe Buğra, and Ahmet İnsel. "Societal Context of Labour Union Strategy: The Case of Turkey." *Labor Studies Journal* 20, no. 10 (2008): 168–188.

Alemdar, Zeynep. "Turkish Trade Unions and the European Boomerang." *European Journal of Turkish Studies* no 9. 2009. Accessed November 2, 2016. https://ejts.revues.org/3774.

Arsan, Esra. *Avrupa Birliği ve Gazetecilik: Brüksel'den Bildirenlerin Gözünden Avrupalılık* [EU and Journalism: Europeanness from the Perspective of Those Reporting from Brussels]. Istanbul: Ütopya Yayınevi, 2007.

Atan, Serap. "Europeanisation of Turkish Peak Business Organisations and Turkey-EU Relations." In *Turkey and European Union Integration: Accession Prospects and Issues*, edited by Mehment Uğur and Nergis Canefe, 100–121. London: Routledge, 2004.

Badiou, Alain. *The Rebirth of History: Times of Riots and Uprisings*. London: Verso, 2012.

Büyükbay, Can. "Deconstructing the Neoliberal Character of the European Union: A Major Source of Leftist Dissent Over the EU in Turkish Civil Society." *Alternatives, Turkish Journal of International Relations* 14, no. 3 (2014): 54–73.

Calhoun, Craig. "Occupy Wall Street in Perspective." *British Journal of Sociology* 64, no. 1 (2013): 26–38.

Casanova, José. "The Long, Difficult, and Tortuous Journey of Turkey into Europe and the Dilemmas of European Civilisation." *Constellations* 13, no. 2 (2006): 234–247.

Cerrahoğlu, Nilgün. "Avrupa Parlamentosu'ndan 'Balans Ayarı'" [Balance from the EU] Cumhuriyet, June 15, 2013.

Council of the European Union. *EU Strategic Framework and Action Plan on Human Rights and Democracy*, Luxembourg (11855/12/2012).

Della Porta, Donatella. "Critical Trust: Social Movements and Democracy in Times of Crisis." *Cambio*, II, no. 4 (2012): 33–44.

Doğan, Erhan. "Sendikalar ve Türkiye'nin Avrupa Birliği Seyahati" [Trade Unions and Turkey's EU Journey]. *Akdeniz Universtiy IIBF Journal* 6 (2003): 19–43.

Erdinç, Işıl. "AKP Döneminde Sendikal Alanın Yeniden Yapılanması ve Kutuplaşma" [Reconstruction of Labour Union Space and Polarisation under the AKP Rule]. *Çalışma ve Ekonomi* 2 (2014): 156–174.

Gencel Bek, Mine. "Tabloidisation of the Turkish Media: An Analysis of Television News in Turkey." *European Journal of Communication* 19, no. 3 (2004): 371–386.

Hardt, Michael, and Antonio Negri. *Declaration*. New York: Melanie Jackson Agency, 2012, http://antonionegriinenglish.files.wordpress.com/2012/05/93152857-hardt-negri-declaration-2012.pdf.

Harvey, David. *Rebel Cities: From the Right to the City to the Urban Revolution*. London: Verso, 2012.

Holston, James. *Insurgent Citizenship*. Princeton, NJ: Princeton University Press, 2008.

İlhan, Ebru. "Turkey's State-Business Relations Revisited: Islamic Business Associations and Policymaking in the AKP Era." PhD diss., Kings College, London, 2014.

Kalaycıoğlu, Ersin. "State and Civil Society in Turkey: Democracy, Development and Protest." In *Civil Society in Muslim World: Contemporary Perspectives*, edited by Amyn B. Sajoo, 247–272. London, New York: I.B. Tauris Publishers, 2002.

Kaya, Ayhan. *Europeanisation and Tolerance in Turkey: The Myth of Toleration*. London: Palgrave, 2013.

Kaya, Ayhan. "Islamisation of Turkey Under the AKP Rule: Empowering Family, Faith and Charity." *South European Society and Politics* 20, no. 1 (2015): 47–69.

Kaya, Ayhan, and Raffaele Marchetti. "Europeanisation, Framing Competition, and Civil Society in the EU and Turkey." In *Global Turkey in Europe II: Energy, Migration, Civil Society and Citizenship Issues in Turkey-EU Relations*, edited by Senem Aydin-Düzgit, Daniela Huber, Meltem Müftüler Bac, Fuat Keman, Jan Tasci and Nathalie Tocci, 145–196. Roma: Edizioni Nuova Cultura, 2014.

Kaya, Ayhan, and Turgut Tarhanlı, eds. *Türkiye'de Çoğunluk ve Azınlık Politikaları: AB Sürecinde Yurttaşlık Tartışmaları* [Majority and Minority Policies in Turkey: Citizenship Debates on the Way to the EU]. Istanbul: TESEV Publications, 2005.

Keyman, Fuat, and Ahmet İçduygu. "Globalisation, Civil Society and Citizenship in Turkey: Actors, Boundaries and Discourses." *Citizenship Studies* 7, no. 2 (2003): 219-234.

Kubicek, Paul. "Turkish Accession to the European Union: Challenges and Opportunities." *World Affairs* 168, no. 2 (2005): 67–78.

Lefebvre, Henri. "The Right to the City," English translation of the 1968 text by Eleonore Koffman and Elizabeth Lebas, *Writings on Cities*. London: Blackwell, 1996.

Öner, Selcen. "Internal Factors in the EU's Transformative Power Over Turkey: the Role of Turkish Civil Society." *Southeast European and Black Sea Studies* 14, no. 1 (2014): 23–42.

Öniş, Ziya. "Turkish Modernisation and Challenges for the New Europe." *Perceptions* 9, no. 3 (Autumn 2004): 5–28.

Özbudun, Ergun, and Serap Yazıcı. *Democratisation Reforms in Turkey*. Istanbul: TESEV, 2004.

Sağnak, Mehmet. *Medya-Politik: 1983-1993 Yılları Arasında Medya-Politikacı İlişkileri* [Media-Politic: Relationships Between Media and Politics in the period of 1983 and 1993]. Ankara: Eti Kitapları, 1996.

Saktanber, Ayşe, and Gül Çorbacıoğlu. "Veiling and Headscarf Scepticism in Turkey." *Social Politics: International Studies in Gender, State & Society* 15, no. 4 (2008): 514–538.

Seufert, Guenther. "Is the Fethullah Gülen Movement Overstretching Itself? A Turkish Religious Community as a National and International Player." *SWP Working Paper 2*, Berlin (2014). http://www.swp-berlin.org/fileadmin/contents/products/studien/2013_S23_srt.pdf.

Sitrin, Marina. "What Does Democracy Look Like?" *The Nation* (April 2012). http://www.thenation.com/article/166824/what-does-democracy-look.

Stevenson, Jonathan. "Turkey: The Attempted Coup and Its Troubling Aftermath." *Strategic Comments* 22, no. 5 (2016): v–vii. doi:10.1080/13567888.2016.1217082

Transparency International Turkey. "National Integrity System Assessment." *Turkey Report*, 2016. Istanbul: Poen Society Foundation and Transparency International.

Turam, Berna, ed. *Secular State and Religious Society: Two Forces in Play in Turkey*. New York: Palgrave Macmillan, 2012.

Yankaya, Dilek. "The Europeanisation of MÜSIAD: Political Opportunism, Economic Europeanisation, Islamic Euroscepticism." *European Journal of Turkish Studies* [Online], 9 (2009): 1–9. Accessed November 2, 2016. http://ejts.revues.org/index3696.html.

Yıldırım, Engin, Suayyip Calış, and Abdurrahman Benli. "Turkish Labour Confederations and Turkey's Membership of the European Union." *Economic and Industrial Democracy* 29, no. 3 (2008): 362–387.

Yılmaz, Gözde. "Is There a Puzzle? Compliance with Minority Rights in Turkey (1999–2010)." *Working Paper* 23, Kolleg-Forschergruppe, The Transformative Power of Europe, Free University, Berlin, 2011.

Youth activists and *occupygezi*: patterns of social change in public policy and in civic and political activism in Turkey

Cristiano Bee ⓘ and Stavroula Chrona ⓘ

ABSTRACT
The research puzzle that our paper focuses on is the struggle of youth organizations to have their voice heard in public policy processes. We examine the implications of *occupygezi* in establishing, or not, a new relationship with the political domain and policy makers in Turkey. By drawing on a policy analysis framework, this paper looks at whether *occupygezi* opened up new windows of opportunities for social and political change for youth activists in Turkey. In doing so, we rely upon the results of a number of in-depth interviews conducted in 2015/16 in Turkey with representatives of youth organizations.

Introduction

In recent years, the literature studying the role of civil society organizations in fostering public policies and promoting active citizenship has grown exponentially.[1] Part of this discussion has focused on the factors that motivate citizens' engagement and participation in *organized civil society*.[2] In this article, we examine whether civil society determines the processes of change with respect to public policies by focusing in particular on youth policy in Turkey in the aftermath of the 2013 Gezi protest. This protest, as a key event, saw the mobilization of tens of thousands of young people[3] from diverse backgrounds, representing a wide array of interests.[4] The Gezi events brought to the fore 'a new threshold to democracy'[5] with protesters sharing a common denominator, the claim for public space, freedom, and ultimately public involvement in decision-making processes.

The scope of this article is not to evaluate the overall impact and achievements of the movement so far, as this would require a different research strategy,[6] but to investigate the impact of *occupygezi* in two specific directions. First, our aim is to gather information about the youth activists' views of *occupygezi*. In doing so, we want to understand its significance by looking at the narratives that were invoked during and after the protests. Second, we examine whether *occupygezi* has fostered a change of approach in youth policy, by looking at the core discourses and meanings associated with practices of participation in public policy by youth activists that are part of the so-called organized civil society.[7] By this, we refer to organizations of interests that have a well-defined structure and, normatively, a direct and established relationship with policy makers. As a category, organized civil society includes bodies such as volunteer groups, foundations, non-profit organizations, civil society organizations, to name just a few. Their peculiarity stands in the institutionalization of participatory practices with the political level, through the exercise of activities such as lobbying or consultations.

The research puzzle that our paper unpacks has to do with the struggle of youth organizations to have their voice heard in public policy processes. The choice of focusing specifically on young people is motivated by the fact that this social group has been commonly described as apolitical and disengaged.[8] In our analysis, we look at the significance associated with the Gezi Movement, by establishing whether this behavioral connotation characterized by passivity and disengagement has been challenged stimulating the assumption of more active behaviors. We argue that this broad social movement has exposed a generation characterized by the assumption of necessary conformist behaviors[9] to a new experience and relationship with the political domain, but also, more directly, with policy makers in Turkey.[10]

As we discuss extensively while presenting the results of our analysis, in the mindset of youth activists' *occupygezi* represents a turning point, challenging this conformism until the point that the experience has been met with violence. In this sense our research attempts to understand to what extent the dynamics inherent to such a social movement challenged and stimulated new points of view for youth activists in regards to the political arena in Turkey.

Our work is particularly relevant in a context characterized by persistent top-down dynamics of interaction between policy makers and civil society activists and that is more extensively characterized by an authoritarian turn.[11] Under the current authoritarian drift the way that activists perceive and engage with the political arena and policy-making processes can offer significant information about the incentives, aims and objectives but also the problems activists encounter in their positioning in the political arena.

In designing our research and before approaching our interviewees, we drew two opposite scenarios that contain our expectations.

Scenario 1: In the aftermath of *occupygezi*, youth activists have become more conscious and aware of their political power vis-à-vis public institutions in Turkey. By consequence, they seek to influence the agenda setting through various means and with increasing intensity. Because of their nature, that of being part of organized civil society, they mainly use formal instruments of participation, such as consultations and lobbying activities. At the same time, public institutions have become aware of their political power and have established means to listen to their concerns, opening up public policy processes in order to make them more transparent, accessible, and democratic. This is a scenario that we defined as *bidirectional political participation*, in so far as civil society organizations and public institutions benefit from this new interaction in policy making. This style of policy making is characterized by being outward looking, in the sense that is open to influences from the civil society and transparent and accessible to the public.

Scenario 2: As a consequence of *occupygezi*, public institutions have become more inward looking, leaving little or no space for the participation of organized civil society in public policy processes. Because of this approach, there is a consequent struggle for activists to proceed with processes of mobilizations and at the same time to attract new members in joining in their activities. Civic participation is an essential part of their work routine, but political participation, either in conventional or non-conventional forms, is not effective in terms of creating an impact on public policy. This is a scenario that we define as *unidirectional civic participation*, in so far as organizations are actively involved in various activities of social and civic nature (volunteering, empowerment, promotion of anti-discrimination, etc.), without counting on public support and at the same time avoiding engagement in political activities. In this scenario, organizations struggle to survive, and more explicitly look to financial and structural support outside of Turkey, for example, by applying for funding to supranational institutions such as the European Union (EU).

By referring to the scenarios that we established, our key research questions are the following: how do civil society activists relate to *occupygezi* and what is the significance attributed to this event, and what are the challenges that activists of Turkish organized civil society advocating for youth policy experienced in the aftermath of *occupygezi*? The first question has to do with an evaluation of the events linked with the uprisings of Gezi Park by interviewees. The second question is meant to evaluate activists' perceptions of the impact of *occupygezi* in terms of access to policy making, by focusing on whether this has become more or less accessible or, in other words, outward or inward looking.

In trying to answer these research questions, we unpack specific systems of meaning through the policy actors involved in the research. By adopting a discursive approach to policy analysis,[12] we investigate systems of values, ideas, beliefs and reactions by youth civil society activists in Turkey in the aftermath of the Gezi park protests. The analysis relies on forty in-depth interviews with members of civil society organizations representing young people in Turkey, including current and former volunteers, youth trainers, and policy officers.[13] Due to the qualitative nature of our research, we decided in the course of the design of the interviews to follow the suggestions of scholars such as Strauss and Corbin and opted for an *explorative* strategy with little pre-planned structure.[14] This approach let our participants touch upon the factors they considered more important and significant in determining the impact of *occupygezi* on their activities, both at the individual and collective level.[15]

In the sections that follow we start with an outline of the paradox of Turkey, by arguing that recent processes of governance and managerial reform, which, in principle, have enhanced the role and impact of organized civil society, have not offered a qualitative improvement in terms of political participation and impact on public policy making. Subsequently, we stress the importance to focus on organized civil society as a specific analytical category that has emerged in Turkey under the pressure of the Europeanization process and we outline the theoretical approach of our research. We then conclude our article by presenting the results of semi-structured interviews with members of Turkish youth organizations. The discussion on our results is divided into two categories. First, we look at a number of dimensions regarding the processes of social change resulting from the youth activists' experience of the Gezi movement. In other words, based on the evidence collected through interviews, we focus on the significance of the protest and the impact this experience had for challenging participatory behaviors. In addition, we look at the evaluation of the purposes of *occupygezi* and the impact it had in fostering (or not) social change. Secondly, we focus on the impact that *occupygezi* had for organized civil society with respect to two intertwined aspects: the enhancement of participatory behaviors and motivations for young people to get more involved in civic and political life as well as its impact on policy making, in particular by looking at whether, according to civil society activists, the Gezi Movement has played a role in enhancing or reducing spaces for political participation and possibilities to access the policy making for young people.

The paradox of Turkish civil society

This research establishes the ground for understanding the legacy of *occupygezi* in terms of opportunity structures for civil society organizations. As we will argue further in the paper, a major paradox dominates the Turkish socio-political context. On the one hand, the country is characterized by an on-going challenge to its strong state tradition and Napoleonic administrative structure.[16] This challenge has made public institutions permeable to processes of social and political change. In the Napoleonic administrative model, the state is considered as unitary and indivisible and is highly centralized, with 'direct imposition of central state authority over its citizens.'[17] It is rather important to note here that when looking more precisely into the sphere of state-society relations, the state is conceived as a means of integrating society, by consequence there is 'less of an autonomous role to society and to citizens with the state having an obligation to defend society.'[18] Public policies are therefore the outcome of highly technocratic and centralized processes that respond to public problems mostly perceived as such by the dominant political elite.

However, in the last 15 years, various processes of policy change have questioned this centralized administrative structure. Under the Justice and Development Party's (*Adalet ve Kalkınma Partisi*, [AKP]) governance since 2002,[19] Turkey has engaged in several reforms following the principles of *New Public Management*.[20] This includes a number of managerial reforms which have been implemented in order to improve the effectiveness of the public sector, promote decentralization and enhance the process of privatization that had started in the 1980s. Furthermore, reforms have been aimed at fostering better governance by improving transparency, accountability, and participation.[21] As a consequence, different pressures have been pivotal in bolstering a process of decentralization following key principles of openness towards civil society with the aim to increase transparency and accountability, to strengthen administrative capacity and productivity, and to encourage a participatory and results-oriented decision-making process.[22]

Intertwined with this agenda of reforms, the questioning of the state centric model of Turkey is enlightened by the discussion regarding civil society in this country. The emergence of a variety of actors, such as foundations and non-governmental organizations, has been central in enhancing a process of change in the bond between citizens and the state.[23] The growth of civil society in Turkey in terms of quantity[24] has radically put into question the passive and state-centered model of citizenship and brought forward new forms of civic and political activism undermining this unquestioned trust and dependency upon the state.

Yet, at the same time, and here stands the paradox, the persistent and solid state structure has not been subverted. Academic research still notes the lack of effective participation in public policy, as well as the scarce influence on the agenda setting exercised at various levels by different policy actors.[25] One example can be found in the institution of the city councils that serve as a platform to enhance inputs from organizations and interactions between these councils and policy makers at the local levels, without however being completely effective apart from some exceptions.[26] A second example refers to the practice of adopting formal instruments for guaranteeing participation such as consultations. Yilmaz[27] notes that the practice of consulting civil society has been recently implemented by the governing party, with certain limitations. In particular, he explains that these consultations have not become a practice in all policies and sectors of institutional activity, and that 'the impact of organized societal pressure via civil society in Turkey is still in the making.'

This paradox is enlightened when looking at the challenges that persist in the Turkish context. In the 2011, *Civil Society Monitoring Report*, the Third Sector Foundation of Turkey (TUSEV)[28] highlighted the obstacles to the emergence of civil society, first and foremost the lack of a solid approach regarding the issue of the relationships between institutions and civil society actors, because of the absence of a legal definition of civil society in Turkey. This absence is noted as a shortcoming that undermines the overall impact of civic and political participation.[29] More recently, TUSEV emphasized the impossibility to better define the outcomes of the new processes of consultation that started to take place with civil society.[30]

Active citizenship and its exercise appear therefore to be limited because of a vague definition of civil society, due to a lack of legislative measures that can regulate its role in policy making. This is an issue that has recently been noted by the EU in the 2014 and 2015 progress reports on Turkey, where the necessity to encourage active citizenship by allowing the full inclusion of civil society in policy processes is widely remarked upon.[31] The recommendations of the EU address a number of crucial issues that up to now have mostly remained untouched by Turkish public institutions, and directly point to the need to establish means of empowerment that are deliberative and entail the full openness of policy makers and the state towards inputs from civil society.

It can therefore be argued that spaces for participation in Turkey are still limited, especially for young people.[32] Even though there has been a constant increase in the number of organizations dealing with youth policy across the years, this rise has not corresponded to an increase in the quality of these groups in terms of their impact on the policy making.[33] This issue is a rather important point to note, since it undermines the scope of the development of a civil society that participates, civically and politically, in the country. The emergence of active citizenship in Turkey is therefore strongly affected by the political context that has been described above and is still dependent upon a highly centralized structure.

Locating organized civil society as an analytical category

Organized civil society is a category that has emerged prominently in European studies, where the literature has mostly been concentrated on the functions performed by civil society organizations active both at the EU level and transnationally, for the improvement of standards in terms of input legitimacy to public policies and by consequence on the promotion of outputs based on participatory approaches.[34]

It can be argued that the process of development of Turkish organized civil society in the last 15 years has proceeded hand in hand with the Europeanization process, and has been critically enhanced by the support of the EU,[35] bringing into discussion the process of *top-down Europeanization* of citizenship in Turkey.[36] Additionally, the financial support of the EU for key programs has been an essential factor that has facilitated the internationalization of Turkish civil society organizations. This process has enhanced the structuring of organized forms of civil society groups in a way similar to what has been happening in many other European countries, but at the same time is directly linked to a process of democratization and political socialization.[37] In these terms, the emergence of an organized civil society as a specific analytical category is a consequence of a process of cultivation of democracy from below.[38] As Kubicek stresses when explaining this logic:

> (…) non-governmental organizations (NGOs) can play a crucial role in preventing the state from dominating society by both challenging undemocratic practices and providing information to elites so that democratic shortcomings can be corrected. Beyond cultivating the quantitative growth of non-governmental actors in civil society, part of EU's tasks in these endeavours is political socialization through implanting and fostering democratic norms.[39]

The emergence of such groups, and their relevance, is thus to be located in respect to the democratic functions they exercise vis-à-vis public institutions as well as towards the general public.

Based upon these considerations, the theoretical framework that we refer to in order to study Turkish organized civil society as an analytical category refers to insights and suggestions put forward as part of the 'discursive turn' in public policy analysis.[40] We refer to the literature that has been advocating for the emergence of a new vocabulary that rejects state centric approaches as a consequence of the increased relevance of policy networks,[41] with the scope of understanding the structures of power and systems of meaning prevailing in accessing public policy making.[42]

In this regard, public policy is not the result of top-down mechanisms set by, for example, a government, but the result of a complex interaction between a variety of policy actors that intervene and express their critical voice at various stages of the policy process. Taking into account this stance and accounting for the emergence of new systems of governance where power is fragmented and dispersed across different levels, we need to consider various political and social struggles where different articulations of discourse are taking place. In a nutshell, we need to account for new sites, actors, and themes in the development of key policies and their objectives. This approach is particularly useful for the analysis presented here, because it allows us to assess how civil society discourses develop in order to shape meaning around specific narratives regarding the direct experience of *occupygezi* by civil society activists, but also with respect to the impact of this macro-event for NGOs' everyday practices and the engagement with policy makers in Turkey.

The implications for the emergence of an organized civil society in Turkey are to be seen in conjunction with specific bottom-up dynamics that brought forward patterns of civic participation and non-conventional political participation.[43] Political socialization[44] in this case plays a central role, because in our view the injection of normative values – the respect for human rights, the promotion of equality and social solidarity, freedom of speech, freedom of thought above all – that are now commonly recognized as fundamental to youth organizations, have on the one side emancipated civil society organizations and at the same time offered valid alternatives for mobilization challenging the effectiveness of conventional forms of political participation, such as voting. The emergence of networks of civil society that represent interests, promote initiatives of solidarity, lobby for gender equality and the reduction of discrimination, and promote youth exchanges and initiatives of empowerment, implies a renewed attention on the mechanisms that account for forms of dispersion of legitimacy, power, and authority as it is in the logic of multi-level governance systems of public policy.[45] Due to the remarkably high voter turnout in Turkish elections, we do not argue that this undermines the relevance and impact of voting behavior, but it showcases the fact that Turkish civil society is now offering credible options for representation, especially to young people, aside of the realm of conventional politics. This representation, however, happens within the frame of the dominant paradox that we outlined above. The recent protests linked with the *occupygezi* movement are representative of the emergence of different bottom-up dynamics of mobilization, both of a civic and political nature. As part of the demands, the wide protests consequent to *occupygezi* can be interpreted as a movement that had the broad scope to produce a process of radical social change in the country,[46] but more specifically, in our view, to highlight this emancipation from the political elite of civil society organizations.

Occupygezi and processes of social change

The interviews with activists of organized civil society reveal a number of common patterns with regards to the positioning of youth organizations in respect to the events linked with *occupygezi*. Some, but not all the participants in our research, directly participated in the occupation of the Gezi Park, in most of the cases as individual citizens rather than in representation of the organization they belong to. This participation is a quite important issue to note, because it sheds light on the processes that motivated individual agency, as well as – in the case of those not directly involved in the protest – the actual impact in terms of individual understanding of the experience of Gezi.[47] At the same time, in our view, it is an important aspect because it sheds light on the processes of learning accumulated during the days of Gezi. In other words, it is worthwhile to focus on the reflections activated by the direct or indirect participants at the protest, by looking at what young people inherited from this experience, and the heritage they transmitted, as activists, to their organizations. Ultimately, we are interested in the process of political socialization consequent to the Gezi movement, focusing in particular on the accumulation of new experiences that signify the shaping of a new relationship with the political domain.

Explanatory dimensions and the experience of Gezi

A good deal of the interviews had to do with the activists' perceptions of the underlining factors that led to the emergence of *occupygezi*. It is particularly important to point out, that most of the interviewees reject the vision that Turkish youth are apolitical and disengaged, and consider themselves committed to playing a central role in Turkish society, both from a civic and political point of view. This stance, in our view is a direct consequence of their involvement in civil society organizations that deal with different matters that are, on the one side, of social nature, but at the same time have a rather significant political dimension.

Interviewees, when asked to provide an explanation of why such a big and heterogeneous movement took to the streets, focus on different interrelated dimensions. Initially, they consider Gezi as a response to the current socio-political structure, claiming that this reaction has come from a process of social, economic and political change that has been first of all promoted by specific elite groups in the country. In this term, the overall feeling is one that refers to a highly polarized society, where spaces for cooperation and engagement are dramatically reduced and overall high levels of fragmentation persist. In their narratives, *occupygezi*, represents the struggle of citizens to emerge and have a say in Turkish society and in politics. In a nutshell, young people describe it as the attempt to gain ownership of a public space, from which they feel to have been excluded. The vindication of their own representative power is one factor, therefore, that motivated them to sustain *occupygezi*, either via direct or indirect participation in the protests. On this account, one interviewee argued that:

> Gezi has been the result, in my view, of a transformation that happened too quickly, I mean from the top down, where no one had a say, apart from the elite. And when you transform too quickly, then the people react. It showed that there is a counter power in Turkish society, an alternative. And in the mindset of many young people many things changed. (Interview n. 2)

Besides this recurrent argument in the interviews, there has been a discussion regarding freedoms, and the persistent lack of these in Turkey. Gezi represents, in this term, the necessity to express voices of dissent towards the limitation of basic fundamental rights. *Occupygezi*, according to interviewees, is an indicator of a need to reaffirm such rights from the bottom:

> You know ... Turkish people are very, how can I say this, very patient, the bar needs to be raised a lot, a lot before they react. They will always be silent, silent, silent ... but at one point if you are trying to block our freedoms and everything, then there will be a consequence about that. And yes, we had more than 10 years of these kind of policies that made people blind, I mean you know that Turkey is the worst in terms of freedom of speech, freedom of press and everything. (Interview n. 17)

Besides this, *occupygezi* is also associated with a process of *realization*, a term that has often been used in order to describe the activation of the processes of awareness with regards to the development of the situation in the park, but also to address, more broadly, a new consciousness regarding various political and social aspects of the country, gained thanks to passive or active exposure to the events. The infamous image of the penguin documentary shown on CNN-Turk,[48] while international media were instead focused on the reporting of the protest is, in this regard, recalled by an activist as a peculiar important aspect that is connected to an individual and collective process of learning that brought about a *realization* regarding the manipulation of the media:

> Personally Gezi has changed my point of view ... for me it was difficult to understand, our media was showing penguins, I had to follow it through international media, because I was not in Istanbul, I was out. So for me it was difficult to understand at the beginning. It helped us understand the manipulation, the fact that media, for example, are, ok, they are obviously biased. This was one of the learning moments for me but also for others, for most of the people that were with me. (Interview n. 4)

Gezi is thus seen as a turning point where different issues regarding the self-realization of Turkish people come into play. On this account, the examples addressed above need to be seen in conjunction with the images that are evoked in remembering the experiences of Gezi. In this sense, interviewees clearly connect different narratives that are – in our view – extremely important in order to shape meaning about the importance of specific values in their mindsets, such as freedom of expression, freedom of thought, and freedom of speech. In other words, the experience of Gezi, either experienced in the field or without direct involvement, stimulates the recollection of different images that are extremely important in order to shape the collective memory of a movement that is seen as unitary and capable to put an end to the radical divisions persisting in Turkish society. In the following extract, for example, an activist refers to the otherwise unbridgeable gap between football fans that, in compliance with the movements' claims, took to the streets and protested together at Gezi. What is peculiar in the extract is the connection between the event and the personal experience of the activist as a practitioner directly involved with an NGO of participating in projects addressing this phenomenon:

> (…) it was incredible. Even for instance, I mean, do you follow football? Just imagine Milan and Juventus, their supporters. In Turkey this is so, so strong. The rivalry, I mean. For instance, you support Fenerbahce and I support Gala-tasaray, we can even end up fighting, violently. But during Gezi park, yes, we were each carrying the flags of our teams but we were together. This is also another success for me, I mean, because we are also working on this fair play issue, football fanaticism, there are different projects on this. Thanks to Gezi park these people from Besiktas, Galatasaray, Fenerbahce, they were walking together. (Interview n. 14)

The evocation of unitary images as a peculiar aspect regarding the personal experiences of activists during *occupygezi* is therefore to be interpreted as a breaking point towards the persistent dichotomies that are inherent to Turkish society. In another example, an activist connects his/her current experience as a youth practitioner, by reminding the 'spirit of Gezi' and what it meant, to reframe his thinking of the *others* within a highly polarized society:

> (…) when I see the work that I am doing, yes, to me young people are more united now, no matter what our colors are, no matter what our ideas are. I mean, I was there, as a republican person, but at the same time there was a Kurdish person, a democratic person, an Islamic person, all different kinds of people. The people during Gezi were united as one, and we saw that if we put our differences aside, we can be there as human beings. So in that respect I think, it was important for me. If you put differences aside, you can be a single unity and we can speak a common language. (Interview n. 26)

The experience of *occupygezi* also recalls the importance the movement had for young people in order to identify and compare the salience of non-conventional forms of political participation and civic participation with respect to conventional political participation. This is a particularly important element, in order to redefine the relationship with the political domain as well as the potential impact that alternative instruments of participation can have:

> Gezi has been important. It means a lot of things to us. We defined our rights and we came together. There was a lot of cooperation with others, and politi-cally we needed it. Because ok, there are elections, there are those mechanisms, but sometimes they don't work, especially for young people. We showed our response at Gezi. I think it is going to be very important for our history because our way of behaving changed after that. (Interview n. 33)

To sum up, it is important to note that on the one side youth activists are recalling and widely remarking on the importance of Gezi, by connecting their own understanding and processes of learning with respect to their changing perceptions of the political domain and the possible alternative ways to participate in politics. On the other side, however, they appear to be divided with regards to the evaluation of the actual impact of the movement in terms of social and political change. This is the specific aspect that we address in the following section.

The utopia of an unfinished revolution?

Most of the interviewees claim to have supported, directly as participants or indirectly as observers, the movement in the initial phases, especially until the violence by the police erupted on 28 May 2013. In the following extract, an activist talks about his/her direct experience as a participant during the initial occupation:

> My organization did not take part in it because we are non-political and non-governmental but, as a person, I was there, as a young person of Turkey who doesn't like the system. We decided to stand against, not with violence but, for example, by reading books. Until that part, I have to say, it was awesome, all the people were bringing food, we were discussing, reading, deciding, getting informed, we were together. It was like … how can I say, it was like a utopia, you know, we were living like a heaven. In that part, at the beginning, it was like a good start, like a dream. (Interview n. 5)

This extract interestingly unpacks a specific issue that looks at the process of disengagement from current politics. Barrett and Zani[49] focus on two core categories that address this, the apolitical and antipolitical:

> Individuals can be disengaged for a variety of reasons. Some people may be passively and quietly apolitical while others may be actively and strongly antipolitical. In other words, some disengaged individuals might think that politics is uninteresting and boring and feel no desire or need to participate or to make their voices heard, while others might refuse to engage with or participate in politics by any means, perhaps because they think that politics is fundamentally objectionable, corrupt and dishonest.[50]

The anti-systemic positioning of the activist therefore fits in the second category, with a consideration, by reflex, of the positive and open experience represented by the participation in the public space occupation. Disengagement from politics, in this case, results in the active participation in various experiences of collective deliberation, that provides a direct experience of democracy. Yet, as the interviewee defined it, this represented a *utopia* in the case of Gezi.

Several activists defined the experiences of *occupygezi* as an *unfinished revolution* that came to an end when a combination of factors undermined the scope and the impact of the movement itself. By looking at our interview data, we can identify at least three critical dimensions that brought the movement to a dead-end – at least for individual participants of *organized civil society*. In the first instance, the increasingly violent response by the authorities that repressed the movement:

> (…) the police got very hard on the people, they used gas and force. I have many friends who were at Gezi, and it was so bad. I mean some friends of mine … they were beaten up and they were just crying, I think it was too hard for all Turkish people. (Interview n. 19)

Another particular important dimension that, according to civil society activists, undermined the reach and practical impact of *occupygezi* was the lack of a clearly identifiable set of aims. If on the one side the movement can be considered as being focused around different claims for social justice and a radical social change in the country,[51] on the other side activists recall the fact that a wider reach was not evident because of the lack of clear leadership in the absence of clearly identifiable objectives. The following extract addresses these points:

> The Gezi park protest did not have any leadership, did not have any certain aim, it was simultaneous action. Some of the people did not even understand what was going on, some protesters wanted to take leadership of the protest, but some people did not let that happen. So a revolution did not occur because there was not a certain aim or a certain leadership. (Interview n. 23)

When questioned about the actual legacy of the movement nowadays – and the possibilities for another event similar to Gezi to emerge – youth activists pointed at the volatility of the Turkish political context in order to explain the continuous shifts of events and priorities. In this regard, this volatility of course undermines the actual establishment of common patterns:

> What I believe is that Turkey is a very complicated country. Our memories easily change because we have so many issues in Turkey. At the moment we have this refugee issue, this Syria issue, we are at the beginning of a war and we don't know what will happen, a conflict with Russia perhaps, there is the PKK issue as well, and so many problems, it's so difficult for people to focus on so many things. Today, I don't know, we might be focusing on the problems of youth but tomorrow we might be speaking about what happened to the Russian flights, the other day we will speak about something else. So yes, there are so many issues to discuss and each day some new things are happening and the topics are changing easily. So this is one reason why we are not talking about Gezi now. (Interview n. 35)

As argued above, *occupygezi* can be interpreted as a movement that brought together a set of important elements regarding a renewed sense of unity between those who supported the protests, as well as it provided important bases for the activation of the processes of self-consciousness with regards to the importance of freedoms and for changing the mindset of young people with regards to political issues. At the same time, however, its impact is challenged by important contextual elements that undermined its scope, such as the lack of clear leadership, the eruption of violence by the police together with the volatility persistent in the Turkish context. It is worth to investigate further at this stage the perceived impact of *occupygezi*, focusing in particular on youth organizations.

Impact on organized civil society

The analysis reveals two diverging patterns with regards to the positioning of organized civil society with respect to the movement. In this part of the article, therefore, we reflect upon the challenges for NGOs in the aftermath of Gezi.

Civic and political participation: demands for active citizenship

In terms of impact, activists clearly argue that the legacy of *occupygezi* relies on the wide consequences it had in activating the political behavior of young people and in bringing forward new demands for active citizenship from below. On this account, *occupygezi* is well established in the mindset of activists that consider it a milestone in order to produce a process of change in the exercise of civic and political participation in Turkey. In a nutshell, it can be argued that *occupygezi* has been a central factor in stimulating the process of awareness building that can be classified as civic and political engagement and, at the same time, is seen as a key driver for establishing active citizenship in society, both at the civic and political level. Most actors that were interviewed refer to their own activities as being of both a civic and political nature, and most importantly consider themselves as part of a civil society that has the ambition to act independently and autonomously. During this time period, *occupygezi* has been key, according to the interviewees, in order to establish mechanisms of non-conventional political participation that are, however, to be seen as instruments that need to be further institutionalized. Most activists, therefore, recall the importance to improve, as their main objective, clear and working modalities of interaction with public institutions, that need to be established and become effectively transparent. Hereby, the importance of reflecting upon the structure of a civil society that is organized and impactful upon public policy is seen as essential in order to improve the Turkish democratic bases.

Civil society actors agree on the fact that *occupygezi* has been an extremely important event in the history of Turkey and more specifically for Turkish youth. This belief is reflected in the increase of interest towards civic and political participation. It corresponds to an ever-growing interest in joining civil society groups and to be part of various organizations. In other words, according to our interviewees, the importance of Gezi relies on the activation of a new civic consciousness diffused within young people in Turkey. One youth activist, for instance, puts emphasis on the changing behavior of young people in the country in the aftermath of Gezi, relating this to their willingness to assume participatory behaviors:

> Well ... if I think about political participation, active citizenship ... you saw what happened with Gezi. Gezi has been a turning point for us, because young people realized what they can do, that there is something different. It was not only about the trees ... it was about something else. It has also changed a lot for us, for the organizations, people want to be involved more, they are not scared. Yes, for sure Gezi was important for us. (Interview n. 39)

It is important to note that this trend touches upon various dimensions of political life in Turkey, from participation in local politics to the necessity to find ways to have a say in decision-making. In the following extract, the interviewee argues that, as a consequence of *occupygezi*, young people have shown a willingness to become more active, to participate in policy making as well as in local politics. The extract is significant in the sense that it connects rather efficiently the issue of participation with the new acquired sense of ownership of democratic processes by young people:

> Especially after Gezi Park there is a new participatory trend, where the youth became more active in the local bodies. As an organization, we also see a stronger commitment of Turkish youth to have their voices heard in the decision making processes, to be involved politically and also in acting like they were a watchdog of Turkish democracy, and I think that this comes from the understanding that you don't have the luxury to be out, you know, of social issues, not only of politics, but also of social issues. So I think yes, there has been a breakthrough that led Turkish youth to be more active and I think this is going to be more and more visible in the coming years. (Interview n. 1)

The statement above corroborates the idea that the social and political domains are strictly interconnected, according to civil society organizations, through a pattern that grows parallel to conventional politics, and develops across various and complex dimensions of participation that are meant to be key in order to extend the basis of democracy in the country. In light of our theoretical framework – that looks at the transformation of domains of policy making thanks to the emergence of networks that represent and reflect certain political needs emerging from specific discourses put forward by groups of interests in the society – we believe that this is a rather important finding. The willingness to reduce the bases for conflict and the unitary spirit of Gezi generates therefore more or less stable networks that act aside of the political system, attempting to express narratives that bring together the necessity to remark on the importance of primary rights and freedoms. This legacy of *occupygezi* is therefore an important element that signifies a radical change in the way young people relate to politics, channeling their demands into organizations of interest that represent their views, ideas, and values, and provide new spaces for social and political action.

Institutional responses and civil tactics

It is important, however, to note that this increase in civic consciousness – that in our case signifies an increased interest in the activities of civil society and in the willingness to participate – does not correspond, according to the interviewees, to an opening of the policy making. In other words, the evidence collected through our interviews shows that as a result of *occupygezi*, policy making in Turkey has become more inward looking and not open to the participation of civil society organizations. In this sense, our research confirms all the difficulties that organized civil society in Turkey has in its emergence, with a situation that has clearly deteriorated in the aftermath of *occupygezi*. Turkish public institutions have maintained their traditional solid-state structure and impermeability. An activist, clearly addresses this point, by remarking on the fact that, if on the one side the Gezi Movement had surely positive effects in activating active behaviors, on the other side it has corresponded to a more selective attitude by current political leaders:

> In Turkey we are not like other countries, I don't know, like in the northern countries, for example, they increase the price of bus tickets, maybe just one cent, and the people are allowed to take to the streets and protest, and the government says, ok, this is what the people are asking for and we shouldn't ignore them. In Turkey it is not like that, and after Gezi things have become much more difficult, not only for my organization, but for everybody. It's more difficult to cooperate now. (Interview n. 8)

It is clearly important to address the issue, at this point, regarding the actual impact with regard to youth civil society organizations vis-à-vis public institutions. Here, the key issue that is considered fundamental for organizations is funding. Most NGOs are non-profit and therefore the main modality to sustain their activities is to rely partially on public funding in order to implement specific projects. It is important to note that, in countries such as the United Kingdom for instance,[52] this practice has been key in order to pave the way for the flourishing of civil society organizations under the logic of *New Public Management*. This is based on the rationale that the third sector can be key – because of its proximity to the population at the local level for instance – to provide specific services and in order to raise accountability. In other words, the proximity with civil society organizations is seen as a key modality to inject input legitimacy in public policy processes. The scenario emerging in Turkey is rather different, and at this stage far away from this situation. In the aftermath of *occupygezi*, the engagement with policy makers is described in the following way by a youth activist:

> If you have contacts with specific branches, with specific policy makers, yes, as an organization you can be influential. If you do not offer much in the way of criticism, yes they listen to you, but if you have a critical point of view, that is more difficult. For example, you can of course be active without working

directly with the state institutions but things are more difficult. If you are not very critical, you can work for them, if you criticize, then things can be a bit different, I mean, you don't get any funding. This does not mean that state institutions do not do anything about active citizenship of course, but it means that they control more, who wins projects for example, and who does certain activities. (Interview n. 22)

In this sense, the development of a properly functioning governance system where organizations are all independent and can play a key role, using their voices in policy making, seems unrealistic in the present state. The balance between freedoms, on the one side, and state control, on the other, lead to the assertion that, in terms of benefits for Turkish youth, Gezi is to be better placed as a momentum rather than a full revolution. Activists, for example, refer quite clearly to the second scenario that we delineated in our introduction:

I hope anything like Gezi will not happen again in the future. I hope not, and I will tell you why. I believe that, or worse, I fear that any new event such as Gezi will have a huge negative impact on Turkish youth. Because I think, you know, what the policy makers are looking forward to, is to find new excuses to take the liberties, to take the freedoms, to … you know … to alter the agenda. So I think a new event, a new protest such as Gezi or something similar would definitely cause a fairly bad effect on Turkish youth organizations. (Interview n. 1)

It is important here to reflect as well on the way forward, as it is delineated by the organizations of civil society. In a nutshell, what are the strategies put in place in order to circumvent the growing control over their activities? Civic activism and civic participation, throughout the stimulation of the processes of engagement at the grassroots level are seen not just as an activity, but as a tactic in order to guarantee the survival of civil society organizations in the present context but also to connote forms of active citizenship outside the realm of conventional political participation:

I think no we should not be confrontational, so this can be a tactic. I think repressing and oppressing the protesters is the strongest point of the political elite right now, so more civilian tactics would be helpful to push democratization in Turkey now and in the future. (Interview n. 27)

After observing the closure of the political system, civil society activists are fully committed to finding new ways and modalities to have an impact on Turkish society. In our way, a specific communitarian pattern emerges, where young people see themselves as active citizens fully committed to ensuring and increasing the well-being of the society they live in, considering civic participation as central and as an important alternative way to exercise their commitment to improving Turkish society. This is an important element to note. Ekman and Amnå,[53] for example, explain very well that various forms and experiences of civic engagement and participation contain important and significant *latent* elements. The authors argue that these elements are based 'on the simple observation that citizens actually do a lot of things that may not be directly or unequivocally classified as political participation but at the same time could be of great significance for future political activities.'[54] Hereby, we argue that *civil tactics* reflect this importance. As another interview stated:

> In Turkey for some reason somehow, protests run violent very fast and ok, we know it, there are deep reasons for that. So we need to find alternatives. There is not only protesting, but if you see a problem in your city, in your street, and try to find a solution somehow also this is a way of lobbying, actually if you talk about that with other people and you find that they think it's also a problem, then there are ways to change things. Usually those kind of non-violent responses don't see a violent response. So changes might take time and it might not be as simple as I expressed, but at least people should know that there is in some way a way of creating a difference. I think most civil society organizations now are trying to do this. (Interview n. 34)

In conclusion, it is worth to note here that, in rejecting the use of violence, civil society organizations provide viable solutions to finding viable pathways for social change. These pathways involve forms of lobbying based on the diffusion of a collective sense of responsibility towards the common good. Hereby, we believe that Turkish organized civil society, within many constraints, can play a key role in promoting participation through the usage of non-conventional means.

Conclusion

When referring to the scenarios that we drew attention to in our introduction, we feel confident to argue that the analysis reveals many patterns that are similar to what we defined as *unidirectional civic participation*. Evidence based on our analysis, as it has been presented in the final part of our article, shows that, according to the interviewees, policy making, as a result of *occupygezi*, has become inward looking, rather than more transparent and accessible.[55] Interviewees argue that opportunities for engagement and participation seem to be reduced, and capabilities to express critical voices in policy making limited. Organized civil society, however, mostly acts aside of formal politics, and various experiences testify that policy solutions are put forward in order to gain ownership of the public space, following principles that look at the establishment of communitarian principles of active citizenship. Latent dimensions of political participation are expressed on the one side by the refusal to protest as a tool for social change, and on the other side, through the exercise of civil tactics, there is a wide involvement in social activities that brings about a consideration of the emergence of bottom up processes of participation. In light of this, our research shows two things, on the one hand, the strong state tradition of Turkey has been revitalized as a consequence of *occupygezi*. On the other hand, this has happened within a process that sees the maturation of a civil society struggling to be active, and seeking for viable and alternative solutions to participate, despite everything. Common values, that are driving this willingness to participate and contribute to the process of Turkish democratization, are those of human rights, freedoms, solidarity, etc. The self-reflectivity of the members of youth organizations that we interviewed – as well as their commitment to finding bottom up answers to public and social problems – shows that they are ready to be full participants in future possible modalities of *bidirectional political participation* should windows of opportunities for political change coherent with the present values embodied in the Turkish Constitution open up in the future.

Notes

1. Balme and Chabalet, *European Governance*; Smismans, *Civil Society and Legitimate*; Smismans, "European Civil Society."
2. Boje, "Commentary"; Hoskins and Mascherini, "Measuring Active Citizenship."
3. According to the survey results by KONDA the average age of Gezi participants was 28 with the majority from the 21–30 age group (2014: 8–9). Also only a minority of the participants (21.2 percent) indicated that had an affiliation with a political or non-governmental organization whereas the majority indicated that they did not have any affiliation (78.9 percent) (2014: 16). Interestingly the 55.6 percent of the KONDA survey sample said they had participated in a form of protest before Gezi whereas the 44.4 percent had not participated before (2014: 17).
4. Acar and Ulug, "Prejudice Reduction among Gezi Protesters"; Damar, "The Secular/Islamic Divide after Gezi."
5. Göle, "Gezi-anatomy of a Movement."
6. Giugni, *Social Protest and Policy Change*.
7. Kendall, *Handbook on Third Sector Policy*; Ruzza, *Europe and Civil Society*.
8. Neyzi, "Object or Subject?"; Lüküslü, "Constructors or Constructed."
9. Lüküslü, "Necessary Conformism."
10. This is a point advanced in the article by Pinar Gümüs in this special issue as well.
11. White and Herzog, "Examining State Capacity"; Akkoyunlu and Öktem, "Existential Insecurity"; Somer, "Understanding Turkey's Democratic Breakdown"; Chrona and Capelos, "The Political Psychology of Participation"; Esen and Gumuscu, "Rising Competitive Authoritarianism"; Iğsız, "Brand Turkey and the Gezi Protests."
12. Hajer, "Discourse Analysis"; Fischer, *Reframing Public Policy*.
13. In our research, we specifically focus on members of youth organizations that are either part of transnational networks thanks to project funding sponsored by the EU in programmes such as Youth in Action and Erasmus +, or have been attempting to put forward proposals to join such networks. The areas of activity of such organizations regard democratization, human rights, social

inclusion, education and youth exchanges. In this sense, we look at one but yet significant side of the coin regarding the emergence of the organized civil society in Turkey, by taking a stance on civil society groups that have been active in the light of the Turkish Europeanization process. Our research and the findings of our research are not meant to generalize conclusions in regard to other typologies of organizations (i.e. religious organizations).

14. Strauss and Corbin, *Basics of Qualitative Research*. See also Kvale and Brinkmann, *InterViews*, 106.
15. Participants at the interviews were young people in the age 18–28. All of them are either university students or have obtained a university degree. They are currently involved in their organizations as policy officers or youth trainers. Being directly involved in the activities of their organizations under these roles they are representatives of the organizations of belonging. Participants were selected following a snowball sample technique. The transcripts of the interviews were coded following an open-coding process that led to the definition of specific analytical categories. It is important to note that the fieldwork was carried on following very specific ethical standards. All participants have been approached with the provision of all necessary information regarding our ethical procedures and guaranteed the right to stay anonymous. From the extracts reported in this article we therefore removed any reference such as names or organization of belonging.
16. Demirkaya, *New Public Management in Turkey*.
17. Peters, *Four Main Administrative Traditions*.
18. Peters, "The Napoleonic Tradition," 121–2.
19. Yilmaz, "EU Conditionality."
20. Demirkaya, *New Public Management in Turkey*; Sözen, "Recent Administrative Reforms."
21. Sözen, "Recent Administrative Reforms."
22. Göymen, "Dynamics of Changes," 10.
23. Keyman and Icduygu, "Globalisation Civil Society and Citizenship," 231; Navaro-Yashin, *Faces of the State*.
24. Şimşek, "The Transformation."
25. Göksel and Güneş "The Role of NGOs"; Ergun, "Civil Society in Turkey"; Zihnioğlu, *European Union Civil Society*.
26. Karakurt Tosun and Keskin, "City Councils."
27. Yilmaz, "EU Conditionality," 308.
28. TUSEV, *Civil Society Monitoring Report*.
29. Ibid., 4–5.
30. TUSEV, *Strengthening Civil Society*, 89.
31. CEC, *Turkey 2014 Progress Report*; CEC, *Turkey 2015 Progress Report*.
32. Bozkurt, Cok, and Şener, "Government Perspectives"; Şener, "Civic and Political."
33. Şimşek, "The Transformation."
34. Kohler-Koch and Rittberger, *Debating the Democratic Legitimacy*; Greenwood, *Interest Representation*.
35. Yilmaz, "EU Conditionality"; Marchetti and Kaya, "Europeanisation"; Ergun, "Civil Society in Turkey."
36. Çakmaklı, "Active Citizenship."
37. Kubicek, "Political Conditionality."
38. Ibid.

39. Ibid., 913.
40. Hajer, "Discourse Analysis"; Fischer, *Reframing Public Policy.*
41. Hajer and Wagenaar, *Deliberative Policy Analysis.*
42. Ingram and Schneider, "Policy Analysis for Democracy."
43. For definitions of these terms, we refer to Barrett and Zani, "Political and Civic Engagement"; Ekman and Amnå, "Political Participation."
44. Warleigh, "Europeanizing Civil Society."
45. Kohler-Koch and Rittberger, *Debating the Democratic Legitimacy.*
46. Gül, Dee, and Cünük, "Istanbul's Taksim Square"; Karasulu, "If a Leaf Falls."
47. In this sense, our analysis is meant to look at the process of political socialisation and learning of youth activists through the direct or indirect exposure to the events linked to *occupygezi*, as well as at the impact this experience had in changing attitudes and patterns of participatory behaviours.
48. Tufekci, "Social Movements and Government in Digital Age."
49. Barrett and Zani, "Political and Civic Engagement."
50. Ibid., 6.
51. Acar and Ulug, "Prejudice Reduction among Gezi Protesters"; Abbas and Yigit, "Scenes from Gezi Park."
52. Bee and Villano, "Active Citizenship in the UK."
53. Ekman and Amnå, "Political Participation."
54. Ibid., 287.
55. This is mainly explained on the basis of the authoritarian drift of Turkey. For more information on the development of authoritarianism in Turkey see White and Herzog "Examining State Capacity"; Akkoyunlu and Öktem, "Existential Insecurity"; Somer, "Understanding Turkey's Democratic Breakdown"; Esen and Gumuscu, "Rising Competitive Authoritarianism"; Iğsız, "Brand Turkey and the Gezi Protests."

Acknowledgements

We would like to thank Ayhan Kaya for his valuable comments on earlier versions of our article. We are also grateful to the two anonymous reviewers for their constructive insights. Their feedback has proved to be essential in order to improve our manuscript.

Disclosure statement

No potential conflict of interest was reported by the authors.

Funding

This work was supported by EEA Grants [grant number Marie Curie IEF 2013/625977].

ORCID

Cristiano Bee ⓘ http://orcid.org/0000-0003-2370-074X
Stavroula Chrona ⓘ http://orcid.org/0000-0002-0914-4938

Bibliography

Abbas, Tahir, and Ismail Hakki Yigit. "Scenes from Gezi Park: Localisation, Nationalism and Globalisation in Turkey." *City: Analysis of Urban Trends, Culture, Theory, Policy, Action* 19, no. 1 (2015): 61–76.

Acar, Yasemin Gulsum, and Özden Melis Uluğ. "Examining Prejudice Reduction Through Solidarity and Togetherness Experiences Among Gezi Park Activists in Turkey". *Journal of Social and Political Psychology* 4, no. 1 (2016): 166–179.

Akkoyunlu, Karabekir, and Kerem Öktem. "Existential Insecurity and the Making of a Weak Authoritarian Regime in Turkey". *Southeast European and Black Sea Studies* 16, no. 4 (2016): 505–527.

Balme, Richard, and Didier Chabanet. *European Governance and Democracy: Power and Protest in the EU.* Lanham, MD: Rowman & Littlefield, 2008.

Barrett, Martyn, and Bruna Zani. "Political and Civic Engagement: Theoretical Understandings, Evidence and Policies." In *Political and Civic Engagement: Multidisciplinary Perspectives*, edited by Martyn Barrett and Bruna Zani, 3–25. London: Routledge, 2015.

Bee, Cristiano, and Paola Villano. "Active Citizenship in Italy and the UK: Comparing Political Discourse and Practices of Political Participation, Civic Activism and Engagement in Policy Processes." In *Political and Civic Engagement: Multidisciplinary Perspectives*, edited by Martyn Barrett and Bruna Zani, 436–455. London: Routledge, 2015.

Boje, Thomas P. "Commentary: Participatory Democracy, Active Citizenship, and Civic Organizations-Conditions for Volunteering and Activism." *Journal of Civil Society* 6, no. 2 (2010): 189–192.

Bozkurt, Sümercan, Figen Çok, and Tülin Şener. "Government Perspectives on Civic and Political Participation of Youth and Women in Turkey: Deriving Insights from

Policy Documents." In *Political and Civic Engagement: Multidisciplinary Perspectives*, edited by Martyn Barrett and Bruna Zani, 420–435. London: Routledge, 2015.

Çakmaklı, Didem. "Active Citizenship in Turkey: Learning Citizenship in Civil Society Organizations." *Citizenship Studies* 19, no. 3–4 (2015): 421–435.

Chrona, Stavroula, and Tereza Capelos. "The Political Psychology of Participation in Turkey: Civic Engagement, Basic Values, Political Sophistication and the Young." *Southeast European and Black Sea Studies* (2016): 1–19. doi:10.1080/14683857. 2016.1235002.

Commission of the European Communities (CEC). *Turkey 2014 Progress Report*. Brussels: European Commission, 2014.

Commission of the European Communities (CEC). *Turkey 2015 Progress Report*. Brussels: European Commission, 2015.

Damar, Erdem. "Radicalization of Politics and the Production of New Alternatives: Rethinking the Secular/Islamic Divide after the Gezi Park Protests in Turkey." *Journal of Contemporary European Studies* 24, no. 2 (2016): 207–222.

Demirkaya, Yüksel, ed. *New Public Management in Turkey: Local Government Reform*. London: Routledge, 2016.

Ekman, Joakim, and Erik Amnå. "Political Participation and Civic Engagement: Towards a New Typology." *Human Affairs* 22, no. 3 (2012): 283–300.

Ergun, Ayça. "Civil Society in Turkey and Local Dimensions of Europeanization." *Journal of European Integration* 32, no. 5 (2010): 507–522.

Esen, Berk, and Sebnem Gumuscu. "Rising Competitive Authoritarianism in Turkey". *Third World Quarterly* 37, no. 9 (2016): 1581–1606.

Fischer, Frank. *Reframing Public Policy: Discursive Politics and Deliberative Practices*. Oxford: Oxford University Press, 2003.

Giugni, Marco. *Social Protest and Policy Change: Ecology, Antinuclear, and Peace Movements in Comparative Perspective*. Lanham, MD: Rowman and Littlefield, 2004.

Göksel, Diba Nigar, and Rana Birden Güneş. "The Role of NGOs in the European Integration Process: The Turkish Experience." *South European Society and Politics* 10, no. 1 (2005): 57–72.

Göle, Nilüfer. "Gezi-anatomy of a Public Square Movement." *Insight Turkey* 15, no. 3 (2013): 7–14.

Göymen, Korel. "Dynamics of Changes in Turkish Local Governance." *Society and Economy* 28, no. 3 (2006): 245–266.

Greenwood, Justin. *Interest Representation in the European Union*. Basingstoke: Palgrave Macmillan, 2007.

Gül, Murat, John Dee and Cahide Nur Cünük. "Istanbul's Taksim Square and Gezi Park: The Place of Protest and the Ideology of Place." *Journal of Architecture and Urbanism* 38, no. 1 (2014): 63–72.

Hajer, Marteen. "Discourse Analysis and the Study of Policy Making." *European Political Science* 2, no. 1 (2002): 61–65.

Hajer, Marteen, and Hendrik Wagenaar, eds. *Deliberative Policy Analysis: Understanding Governance in the Network Society*. Cambridge: Cambridge University Press, 2003.

Hoskins, Bryony, and Mascherini Massimiliano. "Measuring Active Citizenship Through the Development of a Composite Indicator." *Social Indicators Research* 90, no. 3 (2009): 459–488.

Iğsız, Aslı. "Brand Turkey and the Gezi Protests: Authoritarianism in Flux, Law and Neoliberalism." In *The Making of a Protest Movement in Turkey #Occupygezi*, edited by U. Ozkirimli, 25–49. Basingstoke: Palgrave Macmillan, 2014.

Ingram, H., and A. L. Schneider. "Policy Analysis for Democracy." In *The Oxford Handbook of Public Policy*, edited by M. Moran, M. Rein, and R. E. Goodin, 169–189. Oxford: Oxford University Press, 2008.

Karakurt Tosun, Elif, and Enes Battal Keskin. "City Councils as a Means of Local Participation in Turkey During the EU Membership Process: The Investigation of the Awareness of the Bursa City Council." *Yönetim ve Ekonomi Araştırmaları Dergisi* 13, no. 3 (2015), 362–376.

Karasulu, Ahu. "'If a Leaf Falls, They Blame The Tree': Scattered Notes on Gezi Resistances, Contention, and Space." *International Review of Sociology: Revue Internationale de Sociologie* 24, no. 1 (2014): 164–175.

Kendall, Jeremy, ed. *Handbook on Third Sector Policy in Europe: Multi-level Processes and Organized Civil Society*. Cheltenham: Edward Elgar, 2009.

Keyman, E. Fuat, and Ahmet Icduygu. "Globalization, Civil Society and Citizenship in Turkey: Actors, Boundaries and Discourses." *Citizenship Studies* 7, no. 2 (2003): 219–234.

Kohler-Koch, Beate and Berthold Rittberger, eds. *Debating the Democratic Legitimacy of the European Union*. Lanham, MD: Rowman and Littlefield, 2007.

KONDA. "Gezi Report." Public perception of the Gezi Protests. 2014. Accessed December 2, 2016. http://konda.com.tr/en/raporlar/KONDA_Gezi_Report.pdf.

Kubicek, Paul. "Political Conditionality and European Union's Cultivation of Democracy in Turkey." *Democratization* 18, no. 4 (2011): 910–931.

Kvale, Steinar, and Brinkmann, Svend. *InterViews: Learning the Craft of Qualitative Research Interviewing*. 2nd ed. Thousand Oaks, CA: Sage, 2009.

Lüküslü, Demet. "Constructors and Constructed: Youth as a Political Actor in Modernising Turkey." In *Revisiting Youth Political Participation. Challenges for Research and Democratic Practice in Europe*, edited by Joerg Forbrig, 29–35. Strasbourg: Council of Europe, 2005.

Lüküslü, Demet. "Necessary Conformism: An Art of Living for Young People in Turkey." *New Perspectives on Turkey* 48, (2013): 79–100.

Marchetti, Raffaele, and Ayhan Kaya. "Europeanization, Framing Competition and Civil Society in the EU and Turkey." IAI Istituto Affari Internazionali, *Working Paper* N. 6 (2014). Accessed July 15, 2015. http://Www.İai.İt/Sites/Default/Files/GTE_WP_06.Pdf.

Navaro-Yashin, Yael. *Faces of the State. Secularism and Public Life in Turkey*. Princeton, NJ: Princeton University Press, 2002.

Neyzi, Leyla. "Object or Subject? The Paradox of 'Youth' in Turkey." *International Journal of Middle East Studies* 33, no. 3 (2001): 411–432.

Peters, Guy B. *Four Main Administrative Traditions*. Washington, DC: World Bank, 2000. Accessed July 1, 2016. http://go.worldbank.org/8W85CKFC80.

Peters, Guy B. "The Napoleonic Tradition." *International Journal of Public Sector Management* 21, no. 2 (2008): 118–132.

Ruzza, Carlo. *Europe and Civil Society: Movements Coalitions and European Governance*. Manchester: Manchester University Press, 2004.

Sener, Tulin. "Civic and Political Participation of Women and Youth in Turkey: An Examination of Perspectives of Public Authorities and NGOs." *Journal of Civil Society* 10, no. 1 (2014): 69–81.

Şimşek, Sefa. "The Transformation of Civil Society in Turkey: From Quantity to Quality." *Turkish Studies* 5, no. 3 (2004): 46–74.

Smismans, Stijn, ed. *Civil Society and Legitimate European Governance*. Cheltenham: Edward Elgar, 2006.

Smismans, Stijn. "European Civil Society and Citizenship: Complementary or Exclusionary Concepts?" *Policy & Society* 28, no. 4 (2009): 59–70.

Somer, Murat. "Understanding Turkey's Democratic Breakdown: Old vs. New and Indigenous vs. Global Authoritarianism." *Southeast European and Black Sea Studies* 16, no. 4 (2016), 481–503.

Sözen, Süleyman. "Recent Administrative Reforms in Turkey: A Preliminary Assessment." *International Journal of Business and Social Science* 3, no. 9 (2012): 168–173.

Strauss, Anselm, and Juliet Corbin. *Basics of Qualitative Research: Grounded Theories and Techniques.* 2nd ed. Thousand Oaks, CA: Sage, 1990.

Tufekci, Zeynep. "Social Movements and Governments in the Digital Age: Evaluating a Complex Landscape". *Journal of International Affairs* 68, no. 1 (2014): 1–18.

TUSEV. *Civil Society Monitoring Report 2011.* Istanbul: TUSEV, 2011.

TUSEV. *Strengthening Civil Society Development and Civil Society-public Sector Dialogue in Turkey.* Istanbul: TUSEV, 2015.

Warleigh, Alex. "Europeanizing Civil Society: NGOs as Agents of Political Socialization." *Journal of Common Market Studies* 39, no. 4 (2001): 619–639.

White David, and Mark Herzog. "Examining State Capacity in the Context of Electoral Authoritarianism, Regime Formation and Consolidation in Russia and Turkey." *Southeast European and Black Sea Studies* 16, no. 4 (2016), 551–569.

Yilmaz, Gözde. "EU Conditionality Is Not the Only Game in Town! Domestic Drivers of Turkey's Europeanization." *Turkish Studies* 15, no. 2 (2014): 303–321.

Zihnioğlu, Özge. *European Union Civil Society Policy and Turkey. A Bridge Too Far?* Basingstoke: Palgrave, 2013.

Stand-in as a performative repertoire of action

Özge Derman

ABSTRACT

Numerous rallies, gatherings and occupations in public squares of large cities have occurred since 2010. They constitute a new guideline to new social movements, which embrace a transformation in public spaces through interaction, shared experience and art so that a collective energy is generated within a given context and time. They therefore propose an alternative form of acting and living together in the light of the equality of all individuals involved. The re-creation of this new active citizenship, both individually and collectively, is also highly connected with the appropriation of a performative repertoire of action within everyday life. This paper focuses on the active, yet unorganized participation of Turkish citizens across the country to the protestation and/or performance of the Standing Man. Standing still and silent offers thus a performative action, which has become collective through social networks. This unpredicted act has been a pioneer in terms of the transformation of a singular creative intervention to a collective performative action.

Introduction

Artistic and performative actions in new Occupy movements carry significant weight thanks to the re-creation of active citizenship under violent circumstances. The Gezi Uprising took place in Turkey in May and June 2013, subsequent to Occupy movements all around the world. They therefore have similar characteristics such as the occupation of public spaces, shared experience, experimentation of alternative living and acting together, horizontal organization during resistance, considerable use of social media and performative action and ultimately artistic intervention. Considering the immediacy and unpredictability of the latter, those movements including Gezi, embrace a transformation of political action repertoire[1] as they all elicit a non-organized and spontaneous form of resistance. Therefore, Occupy movements reveal alternative forms of solidarity and creativity in the light of social and political contemporary issues.

The present paper mainly focuses on the protestation and/or performance of the Standing Man and the active, yet unorganized participation of Turkish citizens to this act all over Turkey. Following 19 days of protest movement and the occupation of Gezi Park in Istanbul in May and June 2013, the country and the world witnessed a new form of protest action, that of a single man standing still and silent for eight hours in Taksim Square on 17 June 2013. An artist and performer Erdem Gündüz – a fact understood around the end of his act – stood without speaking and moving in the square beside Gezi Park in order to protest police violence during the demonstrations. Soon afterwards, he was not the only one standing still.

Standing still and silent would, on the one hand, propose a nonviolent direct action related to political protest and, on the other hand, it would put forth a creative and performative action, which makes use of contemporary artistic repertoires. The intervention of the Standing Man thus represents a new way of artistic expression as well as political resistance. Such interpenetration of art and politics in the contemporary world indicates an era of creative tactical resistance starting from the protests against the World Trade Organization (WTO) in Seattle in 1999. However, it would be hard to deny that there has been a significant inspiration from the Situationists and the happenings in the 1960s as well as the political repertoire of nonviolent action of the Indian anti-colonial resistance and the African-American Civil Rights Movement in the United States.

In this regard, I would suggest that the nonviolent performative action and 'stand-in' of the Standing Man not only exhibits a close relationship between art and politics, but it also incorporates the transformation of a singular and individual creative act into a collective performative intervention. Hence, it enriches both political and artistic repertoires by utilizing a tactical small gesture of everyday life.

Since this act introduces an extensive concept that necessitates an exploration of interdisciplinary knowledge, this paper will firstly provide an overview of the theoretical framework of new social movements (NSMs), alter-globalization movements and active citizenship along with the description of Occupy movements and the Gezi Uprising. Then it will discuss the relationship between art and politics in accordance with the concept of performativity and its roots in political repertoire of action. Afterwards, the act of Standing Man will be described. The research reposes on a qualitative methodology, which puts forward the understanding of the principal actor's experience and the interpretations in the media. Accordingly, a comprehensive interview is conducted with the artist to understand his sensible and corporal experience and an investigation of mainstream and social media is made. Finally, the analysis of the paper through a hermeneutic-interpretative approach will be presented, supported with the theories of previous sections as well as the new theoretical guidance on which findings of the research will be built.

Active citizenship: from NSMs to post-2010 occupy movements

Since this article analyzes the Gezi Uprising and the new forms of active citizenship as integral to the Occupy movements, it is indispensable to present a brief theoretical framework of NSM theory starting from the protests of 1968 and then moving on to the alter-globalization movements of 1990s. This historicization is fundamental in order to be able to comprehend the core concepts of current Occupy movements and their transformation, especially regarding the transition from post-industrial to global society.

NSM is developed from the idea that it represents a diversification from conventional social movements, which are identified principally by class conflict such as labor movements. In this respect, NSMs firstly refer to a new wave of protest action related to the rise of post-industrial society during the 1960s, and then they mark a considerable transformation concerning the participation of new actors and new groups.[2] In general terms, NSMs represent decentralized forms of organization, alternative values or claims such as quest of identity or lifestyle issues and a transformation regarding the relationship to politics of the actors and groups.[3]

Touraine emphasizes the capacity of 'self-production and self-transformation'[4] of the actor within NSMs as they are 'less sociopolitical and more sociocultural'[5] such as women's movement and actions against the use of nuclear energy. Likewise, Melucci points out a shift 'from the political form to a cultural ground'[6] in relation with the transformation in the sphere of information. He stresses that the quest for identity, the body, the emotions, the daily experiences, that is to say the 'individual' by discovering 'the capacity to reject the dominant codes'[7] becomes more of the core of those movements in which the system's overall logic is concurrently questioned.[8] Regarding the new 'political paradigm' analyzed by Offe,[9] the values such as 'autonomy, identity and opposition to manipulation'[10] is related to the new space of action representing 'a space of noninstitutional politics,' which seems to be a third universe of action alongside the private and institutional politics spheres.[11] Within this new paradigm, he underlines the environmental, human rights, peace and feminist movements, which represent the demands 'strongly universalistic or, to the contrary, highly particularistic.'[12]

Those movements articulated within the post-industrial society lead to a proliferation of non-governmental organizations (NGOs) since 1970s, however, the 'NGO boom'[13] of the 1990s in several countries around the globe represents an intense institutionalization of those organizations. As a result of the transformation of the society through neoliberal globalization, NGOs are introduced as compensatory elements with the abdication of the state from its traditional role[14] and the promoters of civil society. However, the debates around the NGO-ization reveal the two poles of those organizations: their utility for change as a development discourse to fill the gap of retreating states on the one hand, and on the other hand, their cooperation with the governments, multinational corporations and international organizations such as World Bank, which results in the depoliticization and danger for resistance.[15] That latter point is critical, as several authors point out, that NGOs turn 'confrontation into negotiation'[16] since they became 'a sort of buffer between (...) Empire and its subjects'[17] by entailing 'national and global neo-liberalism's active promotion.'[18] Within the NGO/INGO professionalization process, a new class of activist/lobbyists generates, a fact that consequently 'pushes towards upward vertical participation and not downward horizontal participation.'[19]

Following a period of institutionalization of former actors and withdrawal of cultural actors into their identities in 1980s and 1990s, begins a new phase of mobilizations across the globe towards the end of 1990s: global movements.[20] In this regard, Pleyers[21] investigates those global justice movements, in other words alter-globalization movements, which constitute a cooperative global movement developed as an opposition to the negative effects of economic globalization. Firstly, the local and national mobilizations against neoliberalism such as Zapatista Movement in Mexico in 1994 emerged, which consequently became visible in global level with the Seattle Protests against WTO Conference in 1999. With the initiation of civil society networks such as ATTAC, the gatherings in World Social Forums (WSF) starting from the first WSF in Porto Alegre in 2001, in Florence in 2002 and Mumbai in 2004 and the mobilizations against WTO in Seattle, in Cancun and against G8 in Genoa, in Evian etc., the global justice movement extended geographically.[22] G8, G20, World Bank, IMF and WTO have been the main targets of the global activists as these organizations represent the economic model of neoliberalism against which they rallied. Despite the global targets, those movements managed to combine, according to Wieviorka, the 'requests for cultural recognition with demands for social justice and forms of behaviour contributing to the opening up of new political spaces.'[23]

Therefore, it is not surprising that the recent 'Occupy' or 'post-2010' mobilizations around the world give equally reference to social justice, dignity and democracy.[24] Touraine equally points out 'the dignity of human being'[25] as the core concept of these movements, which emerge as a continuation of Berkeley in the 1960s, later on in Tiananmen in 1989 and recently in Tunisia, in Cairo, in Chile in 2011. He describes all as 'ethicodemocratic' movements through which the actors become 'the creators of their history and destiny.'[26] Even though the impact of globalization and social, cultural and political contexts are not identical all over the world, the recent mobilizations appear to 'speak to one another.'[27]

The Occupy movements that have taken place throughout the world since 2011 strongly embrace a transformation of political and social action in the public sphere. The rallies and occupations of public spaces directed against economic, political, social and/or cultural inequalities started off with the 'Arab Spring' in December 2010, prompting a series of protests against authoritarian regimes in several Arab countries. Inspired by and along with those protests, the gatherings extended through European countries and the United States: in May 2011 the 'indignados' claimed their right to dignity, freedom and democracy in Madrid; in May 2010 and 2011 the anti-austerity movement emerged in Athens due to the public debt crisis; in September 2011 the citizens occupied Zuccotti Park which is in the Wall Street financial district in New York and many other protests occurred in Asia and South America. Without underestimating the local specificities of each one of them, all those rallies reveal several common characteristics such as the democratic and horizontal organization of different interest groups, absence of a particular leader, presence of police violence, non-violence of most of the demonstrators and considerable use of social networks.[28] The encampment or occupation of public spaces constitutes the most evident commonality, which differentiates those from previous 'nomadic' alter-globalization movements.[29] Moreover, as Hardt and Negri asserts, there exists a struggle for the common even though it is expressed by a variety of ways. For Pleyers, 'the transformation of the individual's subjectivity (…) across fences and borders'[30] appears to be an outcome through which people faced the fear and experienced their creativity. The actors shape thus their own trajectories, produce their own experiences, invent their own creativities along with their contribution to the collective action.[31]

Furthermore, the distinguished feature of the Occupy movements, or 'networked social movements'[32] as Castells puts it, results from the considerable use of digital communication platforms in order to share information. The crucial transformation in current global movements takes place through the rise in the use of the Internet and wireless networks for communication.[33] Social networking tools such as Twitter, Facebook and YouTube transformed the way those movements organized in relation with the physical face-to-face interaction during the occupations.[34] The rapid diffusion of the information at national and international levels facilitates both the propagation of movements and specific themes in the movements through the use of hashtags (#) on Twitter.

The occupied public space and the digital space constitute an interactive and non-hierarchical sphere of action.[35] According to Juris, besides determining emerging forms and structures, 'networking technologies (…) shaped new political subjectivities based on the network as an emerging political and cultural ideal.'[36] The social media constitutes thus a heterogeneous and open cultural sphere, which politicizes subjects in everyday life by which a less formal practice of citizenship comes into being.[37] What is more, the linking of ideas and topics through hashtags could apparently bring people together 'offline' as it appeared during the initiation of every Occupy movement and also around specific actions throughout those demonstrations.

The Gezi Uprising

The Gezi Uprising in Turkey as a part of this global resistance wave[38] portrays one of the local contexts in relation to the globally interconnected mobilizations. Depending on the circumstances under which every single protest took shape, motivations and demands unique to each of them existed as well. According to Yörük and Yüksel,[39] those movements could be divided into three categories. While the first one involves the Occupy Wall Street, Indignados and Greek protests representing anti-austerity and anti-liberal demands, the second category projects anti-authoritarian and pro-democratic protests such as the Arab Spring and the demonstrations in Russia and Hong Kong. The third one is characterized by inflation, policies of expansion and construction in countries such as Brazil and India. They suggest that the Gezi Uprising in Turkey does not fit the first category, just as Özatalay[40] who also differentiates the motivations of Occupy Wall Street and the Gezi resistance. Moreover, it is not possible to frame the latter in classical class codes,[41] but rather the main trigger of Gezi seems to be political.[42] According to Tugal,[43] while the main trigger of protest in the USA was the commodification of money, in Turkey it was that of nature and in Egypt, in Tunisia, in Brazil and in southeastern European countries it was the commodification of labor. In addition to that, he asserts that in Turkish and Brazilian cases the leading aspect is urban right issues and he outlines the proximity of Greek and Spanish uprisings as they present a discontent towards the corruption within the state bodies. There certainly exists a distinction between national and local conditions and demands, nevertheless a frustration towards global structures were articulated on broader perspective as it is previously discussed in this article.

As a part of the protest wave mentioned above, the Gezi Uprising in Istanbul represents resistance against the ongoing repression of the Turkish government whose decisions acutely affect the lifestyle of several citizens[44] even though the protests initiated as an environmental concern. Gezi Park in Taksim is one of the green spaces which is intended to be destroyed by the municipality of Istanbul following the neoliberal policies of urbanization that constantly destroy green areas in major cities. The project to pedestrianize Taksim[45] thus aims to demolish this small park in order to build a shopping mall inspired by a historical palace, by which several civil society organizations such as 'Taksim Solidarity,'[46] became concerned, alongside environmentalists and citizens. This attempt of the municipality provoked the occupation of the park by peaceful environmentalists starting on 28

May, so that they set up tents and protested against the destruction of Gezi Park. The occupation following this environmental and urban concern constitutes the origin of the Gezi Uprising during which citizens claimed their right firstly to the city and consequently to freedom and dignity. Throughout the occupation of the park for 18 days, activists 'experienced simultaneously the peaks of ecstasy and the depths of sorrow'[47] as Gambetti puts it, since the experience of being and acting together and the experimentation of direct democracy interlaced with the violence of the police.

An atmosphere of festive resistance in order to prevent the destruction of a small park in the center of Istanbul in Taksim Square transformed into a battlefield following the closure of the park by the police. The repression of the government and the growing police violence conduced to the propagation of the movement, extending the issues against which citizens protested during the demonstrations. Besides the police violence and several offensive discourses made by the government, the blindness among mainstream media regarding the whole movement strongly bothered its participants and supporters. As a consequence of this blindness, citizens began to use social networks such as Facebook and Twitter not only to get information from Taksim Square, but also to communicate and organize. The Gezi Uprising mainly lasted for 20 days in May and June 2013 until the police violently evacuated the park on 16 June.[48]

The Gezi Uprising, considered as a part of the Occupy movements, displays a new era in which people claim their democratic rights in Turkey. This awakening from political apathy emphasizes a democratic awareness of fundamental principles such as 'equal rights and voice, accountability of each individual; respect for the dignity of people; development of the autonomy of individuals; defense of pluralism of lifestyles.'[49] The physicality of people pervading the public places and claiming their rights transforms those spaces into alternative spaces of interaction and experience. Within this new collectivity, people experience the multiplicity, heterogeneity, difference and inclusion in order that new social relationships and new ways of acting and living together are created. Consequently, the 2013 Turkey Report of European Commission accentuates that 'the Gezi Park protest in Istanbul and related protests across Turkey from May–June reflected the emergence of vibrant, active citizenry.'[50]

Moreover, those Occupy movements including Gezi, transform the nature of social and political movements by generating a new way of doing politics, as they break off the idea of a homogeneous community. Chomsky[51] accentuates the understanding and learning process through participation and experience of people and he states that 'the most exciting aspect of the Occupy movement is the construction of the associations, bonds, linkages and networks that are taking place all over – whether it is a collaborative kitchen or something else'.[52] Therefore, every singular orientation or experience constitutes a significant part of the collectivity that embraces an experimental active citizenship.

Active citizenship

Within the space of Occupy movements and Gezi Uprising, the presence of active citizenship constitutes a remarkable element. The notion of 'active citizenship' differentiates from the concept of 'citizenship' with its reference to the traditional meaning of membership of a nation state as a legal status. While the conventional form of citizenship relies on the belonging to a national community as a full membership of a community[53] depends upon the citizen's passive acquirement of responsibilities and rights, the active citizenship features an 'active involvement and engagement in the practices of citizenship.'[54] In this context, the latter involves the civic participation of the citizens in groups of civil society, independently from the political party organizations. The blurring of the traditional citizenship concept occurs through the recent formulations such as post national citizenship[55] by moving out of the frontiers of the nation state, group-differentiated citizenship by exposing the difference-blindness of universalist approach, multicultural citizenship[56] and universalist citizenship[57] by expressing a global morality.

Byrony Hoskins[58] analyzes the active citizenship within the European Union context by which she addresses the significance of the word 'participation.' She defines the concept of active citizenship as 'participation in civil society, community and/or political life, characterized by mutual respect and non-violence and in accordance with human rights and democracy.'[59] According to her, it comprehends both the new forms (non-conventional forms such as participating in a protest event) and the traditional (conventional) forms of participation: that is to say, a range from responsible consumption to voting, in any case limited by ethical boundaries.

Therefore, the active citizenship incorporates primarily the civic engagement of individuals by developing a participatory democracy consciousness. Putnam[60] argues that there exists a close relationship between active citizenship and civic engagement through which the formation of social capital takes shape in accordance with the shared values and experience. For Meehan, practicing active citizenship requires the combination of 'voluntary action and experiential learning'[61] while Zaff et al. proposes the concept of Active and Engaged Citizenship which identifies 'an active and engaged citizen as someone who has a sense of civic duty, feeling of social connection to their community, confidence in their abilities to effect change, as well as someone who engages in civic behaviors.'[62]

The context of active citizenship includes equally the participation of marginalized, disadvantaged, divergent and minority groups in order to expand both the sense of togetherness and self-actualization. At the individual level, self-actualization involves a process of autonomous self-production and self-creation concerning the experiences and awareness of every individual in strong relation with the proper identities, values, interests and skills. The individual level of active citizenship constitutes a leading point in this article since the act of Standing Man during the Gezi Uprising emerges from a very individual point of view. However, it results in a particular position where people put into practice an active citizenship experience. However, the purpose of this article is certainly not to assert that the Standing Man nor the standing men and women all over Turkey represent the one and only act of active citizenship. On the contrary, this act portrays an extraordinary example that reveals the capacity of one creative actor to mobilize a collective active citizenship.

The non-conventional and unorganized forms of civic and political activism were highly experienced during the Gezi Uprising. As in the case of Standing Man, it is possible to say that in that period of intense political environment, a bottom-up introduction of active citizenship emerged mostly from individual viewpoints and actions, yet the collective reproduction becomes a key process to get the voices of citizens heard. The propagation of that act all over Turkey occurred through social media. Barrett and Zani mention as non-conventional political participation both protest/demonstration and 'using social networking sites on the Internet to distribute or share links which have a political content to friends and contacts.'[63] Hence, the bodily and digital presence of people supporting the Standing Man action of disobedience enriches the context of active citizenship as well as civic engagement and political participation. Those enable the citizens to individually broaden their 'personal empowerment and (...) sense of subjective well-being'[64] and ensure the democratic structure and means in decision-making of the authorities and governments.

For that matter, the act of Standing Man appears to be 'latent political participation,'[65] a term by which Ekman and Amnå suggests the actions 'not directly or unequivocally classified as "political participation", but (...) [with] great significance for future political activities.'[66] They determine thus the 'latency' in comparison with the formal and extra-parliamentary political participation. From their perspective, such 'pre-political actions' may bring about political consequences even if they do not aim at pressuring directly the authorities in power. This article aims thus to point out that both the individual and collective levels of the act of Standing Man illustrate an action grounded in personal interests in social and political issues, which reveals the performativity and active citizenship of singularities during the Gezi Uprising as it was in all the Occupy movements.

The dynamic relation of art and politics: performative repertoire of action

During the Occupy movements, alternative methods of individual or collective participation and resistance revealed a performative repertoire of action within everyday life as well as an inheritance of creative resistance vocabulary.

The notion of 'performativity' is derived from the lectures of the linguist J.L. Austin[67] on 'performative utterances' in 1955 and from the work of sociologist Goffman[68] on theatrical performance as a metaphor of social interactions in 1959. In this context, 'performance' appears to be in between the spaces of the real and the fictional act.[69] Subsequently, starting from 1966, Schechner[70] develops his 'performance theory' through which he acknowledges everyday life, arts, sports, business, ritual and play as performances. For him, 'there is nothing inherent in an action in itself that makes it a performance or disqualifies it from being a performance',[71] then there exists performativity in everything. Theories of performativity, which are later on reshaped by post-structuralism in philosophy and aesthetics, feminist and post-colonialist studies present an anti-authoritarian vision. All actions are performative for Butler[72] who reconstitutes the notion of performativity in the process of constitution of the gender. She states that 'the gender reality is performative, which means, quite simply, that it is real only to the extent that it is performed.'[73]

The notion of performativity in the Gezi Uprising as in other Occupy movements resides not merely in the fact that every action incorporates a performative act. Artistic creation as resistance, which refers to performance art, also embodies an experimentation of alternative methods within the movements' collective energy. During those movements, new forms of creative expression elicit a dynamic relationship between art and politics through an action of tactical intervention. Several artistic expressions realized within the Gezi Uprising reflect creativity and performativity of individuals and reveal an immediate and spontaneous nature, related to subjective action and collective energy all at once. As Göle mentions 'the political significance and effectiveness [of Gezi] is rooted in its public performativity.'[74] Gezi protesters appear to be 'artists in action' who practice 'action art' according to Yalçıntaş, who designates the creativity as the 'bio-political survival strategy of intellectually disobedient protesters willing to engage in a new political discourse.'[75]

In this respect, in those movements there exists an intertwined relationship between art and politics considering the creativity and performativity of the interventions. Rockhill states that art and politics 'are differentially constituted sociohistorical practices'[76] instead of the assumption that there exists a stable relationship or a sort of ontological separation. Within their dynamic relationship, he stresses that 'various relations are constructed and dismantled in the social sphere through a series of ongoing battles.'[77] In this matter, he suggests that art 'might embody strategies for transformation'[78] rather than an inherent political force.

With the emergence of global movements against neoliberal capitalism starting with demonstrations against the WTO in Seattle in the late nineties, art is reintroduced as a tactical action that challenges the course of global capitalism. Christian Scholl[79] argues that in moments of madness, such as the exhibition of giant puppets of world leaders during the rally in Seattle, there exists an interpenetration of instrumental action and expressive articulation. Disruption and confrontation are the key features of revolutionary change as he discusses, that would transform the making of classical protest.

Within this context, it is important to consider the historical artistic movements that can also be observed in the context of global uprisings today. The avant-garde movement of the 1960s, the Situationist International,[80] organized by intellectuals and artists intended to create 'situations' through which temporal ruptures were put in practice. This movement based on creating unexpected artistic situations introduces concepts such as anonymous and collective production in order to reinforce interaction. Moreover, Hakim Bey, the author of TAZ (Temporary Autonomous Zone) emphasizes the notions like spontaneity and unpredictability for tactical artistic interventions. Following that, he proposes 'a guerilla operation which liberates an area (of land, of time, of imagination) and then dissolves itself to re-form elsewhere, before the State can crush it.'[81] This kind of spontaneous creation of spaces and situations interrupts the normal course of things and involves a survival strategy by acknowledging the gradual transformation of the system.

'Bed-ins for peace'[82] by John Lennon and Yoko Ono in spring 1969 may be observed as a notable meeting point of performance and protest. Ono and Lennon initiated this bed-in performance during the Vietnam War to protest against war and violence and to become the voice of peace. They remained in bed dressed in white during their honeymoon and welcomed the international press into their hotel room. A more recent performance in public space is that of the Cuban artist Tania Bruguera.[83] During her performance, Bruguera offered a stage and a microphone to Cuban citizens on Revolution Square in Havana, in order to allow them to express their views about the future. One minute of freedom of expression caused the arrest of the artist on 30 December 2014 by the Cuban authorities, so that she was held in detention in Cuba until July 2015. Furthermore, the acts of civil disobedience of 'Tute Bianche' during the protests against the G8 in Genoa in 2001[84] and the tactical frivolity interventions of 'Pink & Silver' during the protests against the IMF and World Bank in Prague in 2000[85] are some other examples of creative nonviolent actions vis-à-vis the police force.

Within the Gezi Uprising, creativity and performativity led to a particular shift of the political action in Turkey towards a more humorous and performative repertoire of action. The new forms of expression that were mostly performed in a spontaneous way during the uprising, brought along an experience of politics as art through the carnivalesque ambience. The Standing Man has become a very substantive performative action and one of the best-known symbols of Gezi Uprising since it was more effective in terms of reproduction through the propagation on social media.

Methodology

The methodology adopted in this paper is qualitative[86] in two senses: firstly, the data is obtained from the testimony of the artist and the texts of interpreters in the mainstream and social media and the data is interpreted in a qualitative manner that emphasizes the meaning[87] constructed within the experience rather than statistical data. Secondly, the process of the research relies on a qualitative basis that leads to the interpretation and understanding of practices and experiences. The meaning is perceived within the encounter between the occurrences pertaining to the research subject and their comprehension, which requires a hermeneutic approach. Hermeneutics as a process of understanding, and interpretation implies a productive attitude[88] within which the meaning is in the course of continuous becoming. As Ameigeiras stresses, 'the meaning is constructed by the actor and reconstructed within the interpretation.'[89]

Qualitative analysis thus refers to the meeting point of the sensibility of the researcher and the experiences of the interviewee(s). Considering that there is a principal author of the act of Standing Man, it appears necessary to conduct a process, which mainly consists of the testimony of the artist in order to examine the meaning that he gives to his action. As the interpretive-hermeneutic and comprehensive approach would provide a better understanding of the sensible and corporal experience of the artist, a comprehensive interview[90] was conducted with Erdem Gündüz in Istanbul on 3 January 2015. After the transcription and the translation of the interview, a rearrangement of the data obtained has been made in order to categorize the moments and specific experiences, and draw a path for the interpretation.

In addition to that, the data provided by the participatory observation of the author of this paper assisted in reconstructing the shared experience within the given context of the Gezi Uprising. However, the author is also bound to maintain a critical reflexivity vis-à-vis the research subject. In other words, it is critical that the author becomes aware of her prejudices, values and emotions as well as those of the interviewee. In this regard, Bourdieu[91] warns about the 'biographical illusion' which may provoke an 'official self-introduction.' Being capable of introspection and emotional disengagement, and recognizing the affiliations and the social surface is of assistance in controlling the data analysis. It is therefore imperative to preserve a reflexive practice considering that the interviewee identifies himself by his emotions and subjectivity as well as his socially constructed identity.

Furthermore, an exploration in regard to national and international media such as BBC, *The Guardian*, CNN, *Hürriyet*, *Radikal* and *Milliyet* has been made due to the fact that the affirmations of several authors indicate a significant point of reference for multiple definitions given to this act. In order to observe the propagation of the act, an analysis has been made following the headlines and the contents of the articles from 17 to 18 June 2013 in national and international media such as *Hürriyet*, *Radikal*, *Milliyet*, sendika.org, CNN International and *The Guardian*. In addition to that, since the social networks served as space for the propagation of the spontaneous participation of people to the act of the artist, an enquiry based on hashtag ethnography[92] is conducted on Twitter. The latter includes a research on specific hashtags such as #duranadam, #standingman, #direnduranadam and #durankadin between 17 and 18 June 2013.[93]

The 'standing man'

Erdem Gündüz,[94] a Turkish performance artist and dancer, stood still for eight hours, motionless and silent in the middle of Taksim Square in Istanbul on 17 June 2013. His performative protest against police and state violence profoundly affected the participants and supporters of the Gezi Uprising due to the fact that it appeared during a particularly hopeless moment towards the end of the resistance, that is to say after the evacuation of the park by police. As he created a space of liberty in the heart of an oppressive situation, his act spread first nationwide and then worldwide through social media, taking on the hashtag *#duranadam* (*#standingman*) on Twitter. *#duranadam* was the sixth most shared hashtag of the Gezi Uprising, which was used more than one million times on Twitter on June 17. On that day, while 73.6 percent of the tweets had *duranadam* hashtag, the succeeding hashtags were *#direnduranadam* (resist standing man) and *#durankadin* (standing woman).[95] Numerous tweets with those hashtags including photos and videos demonstrate the propagation of this act all over the country.

The mainstream media reacted manifestly to this act, which spread widely throughout Istanbul and then Turkey via social media. Starting from Taksim Square, people occupied the public spaces all around Turkey so that the protest became an 'epidemic' as it is described in Hürriyet, one of the mainstream Turkish journals on 18 June 2013.[96] Some members of the Turkish parliament performed Standing Man protest in the parliament such as deputies Pervin Buldan, İdris Baluken, Sebahat Tuncel, Nursel Aydoğan and Sırrı Sakık from the Kurdish-oriented Peace and Democracy Party (BDP), and deputy Oktay Vural of the Nationalist Action Party (MHP) during his party's press conference.[97] Moreover, 22 members of the press put into practice the Standing Man act during the European Commission meeting called 'Speak Up' in Brussels on 20 June 2013.[98] Even as a counter-protest to the Standing Man, 'Standing Men against the Standing Man' took the streets during which they stood still in front of standing people.[99]

The moment, the place and the time of the realization of this act have a great significance given that the artist appeared in Taksim Square the day after the park was violently cleared from demonstrators by police, which terminated the community life and resistance in the park. The spirit of hope that predominated the resistance therefore came to an end and Gezi Park was closed to all public entrance. On the afternoon of 17 June 2013, a man in a white shirt and with a backpack suddenly appeared in Taksim Square and began to stand still and silent despite the ongoing harassment of the police, he paved the way for a space of freedom among the citizens who supported the resistance. He stood still and silent in the middle of Taksim Square for eight hours. Throughout these eight hours he conquered not only the public square, but also the public sphere on social media.

> It was simple. When I got there, there was nothing to do. When I decided to stop, it wasn't like I had decided or wanted to stand. At that point, there was nothing to do. But the thing that happened was, as if I had conquered the square because I was standing. Square, occupy. Alone, but you master the square.[100]

Those words of the artist point out the spirit of the Occupy movements as well as the creative and unpredictable nature of performative action. Considering the fact that Erdem Gündüz, the principal auteur of this act is a dancer and performer who works on stillness and temporality, his act is also observed as performance in the sense of performance art. Various sources consider this act as a 'silent performance (…) form of creative protest–endurance art as activism,'[101] 'disproportionate creativity'[102]; Tunç asserts that 'this time there was no word, no text, no leader in this performance. It was simple, calm, gentle, aesthetic, yet intense. This micro-seized moderate act made the whole grand political narratives look ridiculous.'[103] Others call it 'silent protest,'[104] 'passive resistance'[105] and 'civil disobedience.'[106] However, before the mentioned denominations in the traditional media, his act spread immediately through social networks, especially through Twitter, which provoked the propagation of the act of Standing Man first around Taksim Square, then all around Turkey and finally around the world.

As a matter of fact, through the act of Erdem Gündüz, presumed boundaries between art and politics collapsed so that standing still and silent profoundly disrupted political and police order during the course of the Gezi Uprising. Moreover, unexpected and artistic interventions such as Standing Man portray the tactical utilization of art under politically sensitive circumstances. His gesture puts forward a new way of protesting to be heard, through the spontaneous existence of his body. The reproduction of his act suddenly transforms a subjective experience into a collective disobedience.

> Whoever stood, did something original, since each of them had different intentions and opposed the power or fought for freedom, he/she resisted. This is the reason that each time it was original. They shared. I never said it was my performance or my protestation. (…) This incident is not an incident of a single person; it is something that affects everyone. And therefore it is something that belongs to everyone.[107]

On that day and the following days, his act was reproduced by other people in different ways and spaces giving rise to a collective performative action. The bodily immobile presence represents firstly a nonviolent act considering the violence executed by the police forces. Secondly, it embodies a legal and easily copied act so that each person could put it into practice related to his/her own intentions or motivations. However, a mass action is formed by the subjective presences and motivations manifesting a nonviolent resistance beyond the spatial existence of Gezi Park.

Resisting bodies

As the act of Erdem Gündüz transformed into a mass action of resistance all around Turkey, incorporating both artistic and political repertoires, the collective power of resisting bodies determines a new mode of civil disobedience and redefines the meaning of active citizenship through the occupation and performative action. Hence, it becomes an 'unappropriated act'[108] by which the Standing Man represents the multitude of the resisting singular bodies. This singular 'stand-in' of a man transmutes accordingly into a collective, intra-generational, multi-gender direct action.

The 'stand-in' is defined by Gene Sharp as 'the act of persistently standing and waiting at a certain place to gain an objective,'[109] which constitutes a method of nonviolent direct action. The well-known stand-in of 'Tank Man' of China who stood in front of military tanks, carrying a simple shopping bag during the Tiananmen movement in 1989 represents this kind of nonviolent action facing an extremely violent and unequal situation. Erdem Gündüz also recognizes the resemblance of his act to this unpredicted stand-in of Tank Man and the Civil Rights Movement of African-Americans against segregation. Those actions indicate the strong connection of his act to the political repertoire of action along with its performative character as mentioned previously.

> Everything is connected. I'm not the first person who opposes the power or injustice, and I will not be the last. Like the demonstrations of African-Americans, like the man in Tiananmen Square and many others that oppose the government. I am neither the first nor the last.[110]

Such iconic moments of resistance and nonviolent action put forward a framework of a new form of doing, thinking and resisting, by evoking a sense of freedom in the long term without reaching grand immediate changes. Such acts constitute recognition of resistance in other individuals. During the Civil Rights Movement, the sit-ins were held to uphold the rights of African-Americans against racial segregation and discrimination in the sixties. These were the occupations of restaurants and theatres during which the demonstrators were waiting for hours to be served in order to receive equal treatment. Likewise, the nonviolent resistance in

India was constituted by a spiritual power and the nonviolent moral ideology of Gandhi's principles, such as *ahimsa* (non-violence) *and satyagraha* (truth force).[111] The latter may consist of temporary work stoppage, strikes, boycotts, non-payment of taxes, non-cooperation and civil disobedience.[112]

The choice of non-violence puts into practice a refusal to fight against the state on its own terms, which is violence.[113] The artist therefore chooses a nonviolent action by his 'stand-in' and rejects any violent situation at all, not only for himself but also on behalf of other individuals who reproduce this act of resistance. As a matter of fact, he puts an end to his protest in order to prevent men and women beside him in Taksim Square from incurring any kind of violence, while the police got ready to attack people in the square.

> About two o'clock in the morning, the police were getting ready to attack, they began to put on their helmets and shields. I went a little behind, but they were still coming, so I took my bag and started to walk toward İstiklal. Why? Because, what I did was an act without violence. It was a peaceful one. No insult, nothing destructive. (...) If someone confronted violence, then this protest wouldn't be successful.[114]

As a consequence, the artist receives several prizes for his nonviolent performative action such as the 'Potsdam Media International M100 Media Award' from Germany in 2013, the 'Václav Havel Prize for Creative Dissent' from the Oslo Freedom Forum and the 'Standing Man Prize' from Italy in 2014. In his Oslo speech, he defines himself as a citizen performing 'a silent protest, an activism, a performance at the right time and the right place.'[115]

Performative action through a small tactical gesture

'Standing Man' contributes to the new language by implicating his silence and immobility, even though those elements seem at first to be the subject of a compromise. Since verbal and moving action against injustice are habitually considered as tools of resistance to be heard in political action, Standing Man goes beyond the ordinary and presents some sort of impediment to the government and the police force. By a reinvention of this creative and performative language in the Gezi Uprising, the solidarity and shared experience transcended the occupation of the park.

In this respect, it is important to bear in mind that the act of Standing Man occurs thanks to a simple everyday gesture: standing still. 'The politics of small gestures'[116] to which Hannula refers, envisions 'art as a partner in crime.' He argues that 'a small gesture is a political act that is either visible or embedded in works of art.'[117] Once those gestures that belong to everyday experience emerge in the public sphere, they could make a difference and restructure these spheres as the act of Standing Man did. In addition to that, Citton[118]

197

claims that the politics of gestures elicits a dynamic and unpredictable experimentation of micro-political practices. However, while Hannula suggests an idea of politicization instead of politics, which becomes a possibility to create and imagine alternatives, Citton lays emphasis on 'unexpected gesture' as 'a deviation, a shocking image, an ambiguous signal'[119] that would trigger the dynamic for a reversal.

Citton's approach strongly points out the political power of gestures given the fact that they reveal an immediate relation to everyday experience. The author stresses that the first gesture, which goes off unexpectedly, could awaken 'hyper gestures' in social movements, as it is in the case of Standing Man. Within public spheres of Occupy movements across the world, creative subjects and anonymous artists continuously put into practice a politics of gesture. A single gesture transforms into hyper gestures that bring out a performative and emancipating energy in order to express shared or varied vulnerabilities and inequalities. The 'stand-in' of the artist, on 17 June 2013 generates this sort of creative energy by a simple gesture, so that many people in Turkey and all over the world could reproduce it in several public spheres.

The artist himself describes his small and simple gesture like 'eating, drinking, sitting, listening.'[120] However, with his stillness and silence he creates one of the iconic tactical gestures of the Gezi Uprising; he sets 'the rules of the game' by which a hyper gesture engenders:

> Rule one: do not talk! Rule two: Do not move! Very simple, but since the police didn't know these rules, they did not know how to play this game. If you don't know how to play the game, it is difficult to win.[121]

Through this gesture of standing still and silent, a new political vocabulary emerges, not for the purpose of overthrowing all the existing systems, but rather to create pressures to break off the feeling of impuissance. It becomes a small 'exemplary gesture',[122] a generator of 'micro-political pressure'[123] without the use of violent means, which interrupts not only the exhaustion of hope but also the ordinary fluidity of everyday life in Taksim Square.

The singular 'stand-in' of Standing Man transforms into a collective action through social networks and is reproduced by people with several intentions. In connection with the new society in which ephemeral, liquid[124] and unpredicted action comes into prominence, this act offers a performative protestation that reflects the nature of the era of fugacity. It stands still in a world of constant movement. It owns its era as well as it is tactical so that it appears all of a sudden and then it disappears until somebody else suddenly appears somewhere else. It becomes a network of bodies of women and men silently standing still.[125] At last, it simultaneously contradicts and appropriates the principles of existence of today's reality as it evolves into a collective tactical intervention, both artistically and politically.

Conclusion

This paper draws attention to the recreation of active citizenship by virtue of a singular performative act that generates collective action. The 'stand-in' of Standing Man and its reproduction throughout Turkey and the world point out a very significant use of unconventional forms of resistance and participation to social conflicts during Occupy movements. That act as a singular example that reflects the citizens' engagement and participation in those movements reveals a considerable influence and contribution of creative interventions to the political repertoire of action. The regenerative impact of this performative act occurs through the construction of autonomous spaces and the subjective experiencing so that it questions the conventional political action. Consequently, it enounces a different kind of relationship with politics. The participation of autonomous actors appears to develop in a horizontal non-institutionalized space of politics to the extent that the emphasis is tended to be on personal resistance against whatsoever representing interference on human rights. Therefore, one self-initiated resistance generates a social connection even though it creates at first an autonomous space of tactical performative intervention.

Each performed 'stand-in' following the initial Standing Man, manifests a spontaneous and informal statement of self-perspective and experience by which an active citizenship and experiment of a new kind of interaction of singularities come into existence. These non-organized collectivities engendered by means of social networks eventually have noteworthy impact on political space by nourishing the understanding and experiential learning processes, even while they remain as ephemeral performative actions. Moreover, the reproducibility of Standing Man owes to its proposition of a creative protest by means of a small everyday gesture, which is standing still and silent. The transformation of the singular spontaneous act of nonviolent resistance into a collective reconstitution of subversive situations brings out the political power of a simple gesture by becoming a hyper gesture. Collective reproduction of the 'stand-in' of Standing Man conquers both the space of artistic and political repertoires of action by rejuvenating the strategies for transformation.

In the light of latest events in Turkey, that is to say coup attempt on 15 July 2016,[126] the concept of active citizenship extends even further. The people going out against heavily armed soldiers in order to block the coup d'état opens up a new kind of political engagement. Those who went out that night were presumably the supporters of the government and President Erdoğan, following his call on CNNTürk to go out and resist against the military forces. The sound of muezzins from the mosques all over Turkey accompanied the call of their leader Erdoğan, which created an unexpected and brave, yet semi-institutionalized resistance. In other words, contrary to the Gezi Uprising, it appears to be a hierarchical social movement organized around a leadership. Nonetheless, it cannot be overlooked the fact that a different kind of relationship with politics has emerged for those 'democracy watchers'[127] since throughout the religiously oriented political tradition in Turkey people do not have much experience in unconventional forms of political action. It appears that this time it was not enough just to vote for democracy as Erdoğan had previously stated, but rather to take the streets protecting the 'will of the people.'[128]

The mobilization of the people occurred mainly by means of the political power so that it cannot be presented as a self-initiated and spontaneous resistance, however it represents an intense subjective experience throughout the practice of taking the streets. Therefore, it develops the 'savoir faire' of resistance among those people and a new kind of active citizenship experience. Nevertheless, it is still an ongoing process and it is also a brand-new research area to explore more, considering the encounter between the dominant term utilized during this resistance, the 'democracy' and the declaration of the 'state of emergency' by the Turkish state.

Notes

1. See Tilly, *La France conteste de 1600 à nos jours* for his notion of 'repertoire of contention,' which refers to a set of shared means (tools or action) in a protest movement.
2. See Touraine, *La Voix et le Regard*; Melucci, *L'invenzione del Presente*; and Offe, "New Social Movements."
3. See Neveu, *Sociologie des Mouvements Sociaux*.
4. Touraine, "An Introduction," 778.
5. Ibid., 780.
6. Melucci, "A Strange Kind of Newness," 114.
7. Ibid.
8. See Melucci, "The Symbolic Challenge"; "A Strange Kind of Newness."
9. See Offe, "New Social Movements." 'Political paradigm' is a notion which is borrowed and redefined by Offe from Joachim Raschke.
10. Ibid., 829.
11. Ibid., 826, 832.
12. Ibid., 831.
13. See Alvarez, "Beyond NGO-ization?"
14. See Roy, "Public Power."
15. See Jad, "The NGOisation of Arab Women's Movements"; Roy, "Public Power"; Alvarez, "Beyond NGO-ization?"; Jad, "NGOs."
16. See Roy, "Public Power."
17. Ibid.
18. Alvarez, "Beyond NGO-ization?" 176.
19. Jad, "NGOs," 627.
20. Wieviorka, "After New Social Movements."
21. Pleyers, *Alter-Globalization*.
22. Ibid. ; see Pleyers, "The Global Justice Movement."

23. Wieviorka, "After New Social Movements," 11.
24. See Glasius and Pleyers, "The Global Moment of 2011."
25. Touraine, *Le Nouveau Siècle Politique*, 11.
26. Ibid., 181.
27. Hardt and Negri, *Declaration*, 4.
28. See Ogien and Laugier. *Le Principe Démocratie* and Castells, Khosrokhovar, and Touraine, "L'unité des Grandes Contestations Contemporaines."
29. Hardt and Negri, *Declaration*, 4–5.
30. Glasius and Pleyers, "The Global Moment of 2011," 554.
31. See Wieviorka, "After New Social Movements."
32. Castells, *Networks of Outrage and Hope*, 4.
33. See Castells, Khosrokhovar, and Touraine. "L'unité des Grandes Contestations Contemporaines."
34. See Juris, "Reflections on #Occupy Everywhere."
35. See Castells, *Networks of Outrage and Hope*.
36. Juris, "Reflections on #Occupy Everywhere," 260.
37. See Park, Lim, and Park, "Comparing Twitter and YouTube Networks in Information Diffusion."
38. See Tuğal, "Resistance Everywhere"; Capitaine and Pleyers , ed. *Mouvements Sociaux*; Özkırımlı, ed. *The Making*.
39. See Yörük and Yüksel, "Class and Politics."
40. See Özatalay, "Gezi Direnişi."
41. Ibid.
42. See Yörük and Yüksel, "Class and Politics."
43. See Tuğal, "Resistance Everywhere."
44. Derman, "Un Stand-in Créateur des Contre-publics."
45. The Municipality of Istanbul announced the Taksim pedestrianization project in 2007, though the construction work began on 31 October 2012.
46. Taksim Dayanışması (Taksim Solidarity) includes more than 100 NGOs and associations http://taksimdayanisma.org/?lang=en
47. Gambetti, "Occupy Gezi," 90.
48. See note 44 above.
49. Ogien and Laugier. *Le Principe Démocratie*, 7.
50. European Commission Turkey 2013 Progress Report, p. 11. http://ec.europa.eu/enlargement/pdf/key_documents/2013/package/brochures/turkey_2013.pdf
51. Chomsky, *Occupy*.
52. Ibid., 45.
53. See Marshall, *Citizenship and Social Class*.
54. Mansouri and Kirpitchenko, "Practices of Active Citizenship," 311; Turner, "Outline of a Theory of Citizenship."
55. Soysal, *Limits of Citizenship*.
56. Kymlicka, *Multicultural Citizenship*.
57. Linklater, *Critical Theory and World Politics*.
58. Bryony, "Draft Framework for Indicators on Active Citizenship."
59. Ibid. and see Mascherini and Hoskins, "The Characterization of Active Citizenship."
60. See Putnam, *Bowling Alone*.
61. Meehan, "Active Citizenship," 115.
62. Zaff et al., "Active and Engaged Citizenship," 737.
63. Barrett and Zani, "Political and Civic Engagement," 5.

64. Ibid., 8–9.
65. Ekman and Amnå, "Political Participation."
66. Ibid., 287.
67. Austin, *How to Do Things with Words*.
68. See Goffman, *The Presentation of Self*.
69. Spielmann, "L'événement-spectacle."
70. See Schechner, *Performance Theory*, and Schechner, *Performance Studies*.
71. Schechner, *Performance Studies*, 38.
72. See Butler, *Gender Trouble*.
73. Butler cited in Schechner, *Performance Studies*, 151.
74. Göle, "Gezi – Anatomy of a Public Square," 12.
75. Yalçıntaş, "Intellectual Disobedience in Turkey," 19. The concept of "action art" mentioned by Yalçıntaş in his text is taken from Pavlina Morganova, who uses the term as a form of expression under the political suppression of Cold War.
76. Rockhill, *Radical History*, 225.
77. Ibid., 226.
78. Ibid.
79. See Scholl, "Bakunin's Poor Cousins."
80. See Knabb, ed. *Situationist International Anthology*.
81. See Bey, *T.A.Z. Temporary Autonomous Zone*.
82. See https://www.youtube.com/watch?v=mRjjiOV003Q
83. See http://www.taniabruguera.com and http://www.latimes.com/entertainment/arts/miranda/la-et-cam-artist-tania-bruguera-detained-cuba-20141231-column.html
84. See http://www.repubblica.it/online/politica/gottosei/bianche/bianche.html
85. See http://www.youtube.com/watch?v=xgfjgFqkCao and https://www.youtube.com/watch?v=GIVvBF_7JDo
86. See Paillé and Mucchielli, *L'Analyse Qualitative*.
87. Ibid., 61: 'The meaning can be defined as the human experience (real or imagined), which may be related to an utterance (word or set of words) that allows the understanding.'
88. See Gadamer, *Vérité et Méthode*.
89. Ameigeiras, "L'herméneutique," 39–40.
90. See Kaufmann, *L'entretien Compréhensif*.
91. See Bourdieu, "L'illusion Biographique."
92. See Bonilla and Rosa, "#Ferguson."
93. An example of the formula used for the research: *#duranadam since: 2013-06-17 until 3013-06-18 :) include: retweets*.
94. http://www.erdemgunduz.org (artist's website) and see https://www.youtube.com/watch?v=hQ1vRjJHWZE video on You Tube for the beginning of the protest of Standing Man.
95. See Banko and Babaoğlan, *Gezi Parkı*; "The Gezi Park Incident Evaluation Report," SiegeArts, https://siegearts.com/reports/tr/geziparki/index_en.php; "Gezi Olayları Sosyal Medya Analizi," July 8, 2013, http://insightradar.com/tr/gezi-olaylari-sosyal-medya-analizi/; and "Gezi Direnişinin Ekşi Sözlükteki Yansımaları", July 23, 2013, https://ssgpp.wordpress.com/2013/07/23/gezi-direnisinin-eksi-sozlukteki-yansimalari/
96. Yıldırım and Ural, "Duran Adam Salgını"; "Toma'ya karşı Duran Adam," *Radikal*, June 19, 2013, http://www.radikal.com.tr/turkiye/tomaya-karsi-duran-adam-1138271/; "Herkes Duran Adamı Konuşuyor" [Everybody Talks

About Standing Man], *Milliyet*, June 18, 2013, http://www.milliyet.com.tr/
herkes-duran-adam-i-konusuyor-/gundem/detay/1724339/default.htm;
Tüysüz, Penhaul, and Lee, "Hundreds of Turks"; and 140journos tweet, June 18,
2013, 5:26 a.m.; https://twitter.com/140journos/status/346816032985473025;
"Duran İstanbul ... Taksim'de Gece boyu Durma Eylemi" [Standing Istanbul
... Standing Act in Taksim through the Night], http://www.radikal.com.tr/
turkiye/duran-istanbul-taksimde-gece-boyu-durma-eylemi-1138079/. See also
note 104,105 and 125.

97. "Meclis'te Duran Adam Eylemi," NTV, June 18, 2013, http://www.ntv.com.tr/
turkiye/mecliste-duran-adam-eylemi,qZzA3rE0-0ytKpl-nC2RJA?_ref=infinite
and "MHP Grup Başkanvekili Vural'ın Basın Toplantısı," *MeclisHaber*, June 19,
2013, http://www.meclishaber.gov.tr/develop/owa/haber_portal.aciklama?p1=
125673.

98. "AB Toplantısında 'Duran Adam' Eylemi," *Radikal*, June 20, 2013, http://www.
radikal.com.tr/dunya/ab-toplantisinda-duran-adam-eylemi-1138467/

99. "Duran Adam'in Antitezi Sokağa Çıktı!", *Radikal*, June 19, 2013, http://www.
radikal.com.tr/turkiye/duran-adamin-antitezi-sokaga-cikti-1138289/

100. Interview with Erdem Gündüz, Istanbul, 03.01.2015.

101. Roffino, "How One Turkish Artist's."

102. Güllü, "Duran Adam."

103. Tunç, "#Standing Man."

104. BBC News, "Turkey's 'Standing Man' Silent Protest Spreads," June 18, 2013.
http://www.bbc.com/news/world-europe-22962526

105. *Democracy Now*, "Defiant Turkish Demonstrators,"; Seymour, "Turkey's
'Standing Man.'"

106. *Hürriyet Daily News*, "Standing Man Inspires a New Type of Civil Disobedience
in Turkey," June 18, 2013.

107. See note 100 above.

108. Ibid.

109. Sharp, *Sharp's Dictionary*, 282.

110. See note 100 above.

111. See Gandhi, *Non-violence in Peace & War Vol.I.*

112. See Sharp, "The Meanings of Non-violence."

113. See Hardman, "Towards a History."

114. See note 100 above.

115. Gündüz, Speech in Oslo Freedom Forum.

116. See Hannula, *The Politics of Small Gestures.*

117. Ibid., 7.

118. See Citton, *Renverser l'insoutenable.*

119. Ibid., 144.

120. See note 100 above.

121. Ibid.

122. See Scholl, "Bakunin's Poor Cousins."

123. See Citton, *Renverser l'insoutenable.*

124. See Bauman, *La vie liquide.*

125. See Sendika.org, "Direnişin Yeni Simgesi #duranadam ve #durankadınlar çoğa-
lıyor" [The New Symbol of Resistance #standingmen and #standingwomen
Multiply], June 18, 2013, http://sendika10.org/2013/06/direnisin-yeni-
simgesi-duranadam/; *The Guardian*, "Turkey's 'Standing People' Protest
spreads amid Erdoğan's crackdown," June 18, 2013, http://www.theguardian.

com/world/2013/jun/18/turkey-taksim-standing-protests-erdogan and *The Independent*, "Turkey's 'Standing Man' Captured Attention, but Protest doesn't Stand Still – It forms Assemblies," June 25, 2013, http://www.independent.co.uk/voices/comment/turkeys-standing-man-captured-attention-but-protest-doesnt-stand-still-it-forms-assemblies-8672456.html

126. See Gambetti, "Failed Coup Attempt."
127. See the official site of Presidency of the Republic of Turkey, "National Will is the Strongest Antidote to Coup," July 22, 2016, https://www.tccb.gov.tr/en/news/542/49722/national-will-is-the-strongest-antidote-to-coup.html and "Tekbir Eşliğinde Demokrasi Nöbeti" [Democracy Watch accompanied with Allahuekber], *Cumhuriyet*, July 16, 2016, http://www.cumhuriyet.com.tr/haber/turkiye/568682/Tekbir_esliginde__demokrasi__nobeti..._Meydanlar_ayakta.html
128. See Çubukçu, "It's Will of the Turkish People."

Disclosure statement

No potential conflict of interest was reported by the author.

Bibliography

Alvarez, Sonia E. "Beyond NGO-ization? Reflections from Latin America." *Development* 52, no. 2 (2009): 175–184.

Ameigeiras, Aldo. "L'herméneutique dans L'approche Ethnographique. Du Labyrinthe de la Compréhension au Défi de l'Interprétation [Hermeneutics in Ethnographic Approach. From the Labyrinth of Comprehension to the Challenge of Interpretation]." *Recherches Qualitatives* 28, no. 1 (2009): 37–52.

Austin, John Langshaw. *How to Do Things with Words*. Oxford: Clarendon Press, 1962.

Banko, Meltem, and Ali Rıza Babaoğlan. *Gezi Parkı Sürecinde Dijital Vatandaşın Etkisi* [The Impact of Digital Citizen during Gezi Park], 2013.

Barrett, Martyn, and Bruna Zani. "Political and Civic Engagement: Theoretical Understandings, Evidence and Policies." In *Political and Civic Engagement: Multidisciplinary Perspectives*, edited by Martyn Barrett and Bruna Zani, 3–26. New York: Routledge, 2015.

Bauman, Zygmunt. *La Vie Liquide* [Liquid Life]. Paris: Arthème Fayard, [2005] 2013.

Bey, Hakim. *T.A.Z. Temporary Autonomous Zone: Ontological Anarchy, Poetic Terrorism*. New York: Autonomedia, 1985.

Bonilla, Yarimar, and Jonathan Rosa. "#Ferguson: Digital Protest, Hashtag Ethnography, and the Racial Politics of Social Media in the United States." *American Ethnologist* 42, no. 1 (2015): 4–17.

Bourdieu, Pierre. "L'illusion Biographique [Biographical Illusion]." *Actes de la Recherche en Sciences Sociales* 62–63 (1986): 69–72.

Bryony, Hoskins. "Draft Framework for Indicators on Active Citizenship." Developed by CRELL research network "Active Citizenship for Democracy", 2006. http://citeseerx.ist.psu.edu/viewdoc/download?doi=10.1.1.132.1723&rep=rep1&type=pdf.

Butler, Judith. *Gender Trouble: Feminism and the Subversion of Identity*. New York: Routledge, 1990.

Capitaine, Brieg, and Geoffrey Pleyers, eds. *Mouvements Sociaux: Quand le Sujet Devient Acteur* [Social Movements: When the Subject Becomes Actor]. Paris: FMSH, 2016.

Castells, Manuel. *Networks of Outrage and Hope: Social Movements in the Internet Age*. Cambridge: Polity Press, 2012.

Castells, Manuel, Farhad Khosrokhovar, and Alain Touraine. "L'unité des Grandes Contestations Contemporaines [Unity of Grand Contemporary Contestations]." *Socio* 2 (2013): 139–167.

Chomsky, Noam. *Occupy*. London: Penguin Books, 2012.

Citton, Yves. *Renverser l'Insoutenable* [Overturn the Unsustainable]. Paris: Seuil, 2012.

Çubukçu, Ayça. 2016. "It's Will of the Turkish People, Erdogan Says. But Which People?" *The Guardian*, July 26. https://www.theguardian.com/commentisfree/2016/jul/26/turkish-people-erdogan-democracy.

Democracy Now. "Defiant Turkish Demonstrators 'Finding New Ways to Protest' in face of Relentless State Crackdown." Accessed June 19, 2013. http://www.democracynow.org/2013/6/19/defiant_turkish_demonstrators_finding_new_ways.

Derman, Özge. "Un Stand-in Créateur des Contre-publics: La Protestation Performative de l'Homme Debout [A Stand-in Creator of Counter-publics: the Performative Protestation of Standing Man]." MA diss., Galatasaray University, 2015.

Ekman, Joakim, and Erik Amnå. "Political Participation and Civic Engagement: Towards a New Typology." *Human Affairs* 22 (2012): 283–300.

Gadamer, Hans-Georg. *Vérité et Méthode. Les Grandes Lignes d'une Herméneutique Philosophique* [Truth and Method. The Outlines of a Philosophic Hermeneutics]. Paris: Seuil, 1996.

Gambetti, Zeynep. "Occupy Gezi as the Politics of the Body." In *The Making of a Protest Movement in Turkey: #occupygezi*, edited by Umut Özkırımlı, 89–102. London: Palgrave, 2014.

Gambetti, Zeynep. "Failed Coup Attempt in Turkey: The Victory of Democracy." Open Democracy / ISA RC-47: Open Movements, July 18, 2016, https://www.opendemocracy.net/zeynep-gambetti/failed-coup-attempt-in-turkey-victory-of-democracy.

Gandhi, Mahatma. *Non-violence in Peace & War Vol.I*. Ahmedabad: Narajivan Publishing House, 1942.

Glasius, Marlius and Geoffrey Pleyers. "The Global Moment of 2011: Democracy, Social Justice and Dignity." *Development and Change* 44, no. 3 (2013): 547–567.

Goffman, Erving. *The Presentation of Self in Everyday Life*. New York: Anchor Books, 1959.

Göle, Nilüfer. "Gezi – Anatomy of a Public Square." *Insight Turkey* 15, no. 3 (2013): 7–14.

Güllü, Fırat. "Duran Adam: Post-Avangard bir Direniş Estetiğine Doğru mu?" [Standing Man: To an Aesthetics of Postavangard Resistance?] Mimesis, June 21, 2013. http://mimesis-dergi.org/2013/06/duran-adam-post-avangard-bir-direnis-estetigine-dogru-mu/.

Gündüz, Erdem. "Speech in Oslo Freedom Forum, 2014." Accessed April 25, 2016. https://www.youtube.com/watch?v=xlkW1qGE488.

Hannula, Mika. *The Politics of Small Gestures: Chances and Challenges for Contemporary Art*. Istanbul: art-ist, 2006.

Hardman, David. "Towards a History of Non-violent Resistance." *Economic&Political Weekly* 48, no. 23 (2013): 41–48.

Hardt, Michael, and Antonio Negri. *Declaration*. New York: Argo, 2012.

Jad, Islah. "The NGOisation of Arab Women's Movements." *IDS Bulletin* 35, no. 4 (2004): 34–42.

Jad, Islah. "NGOs: Between Buzzwords and Social Movements." *Development in Practice* 17, no. 45 (2007): 622–629.

Juris, Jeffrey S. "Reflections on #Occupy Everywhere: Social Media, Public Space, and Emerging Logics of Aggregation." *American Ethnologist* 39, no. 2 (2012): 259–279.

Kaufmann, Jean-Claude. *L'entretien Compréhensif* [Comprehensive Interview]. Paris: Armand Colin, 2011.

Knabb, Ken, ed. *Situationist International Anthology*. California: Bureau of Public Secrets, 2006.

Kymlicka, Will. *Multicultural Citizenship: A Liberal Theory of Minority Rights*. Oxford: Oxford University Press, 1996.

Linklater, Andrew. *Critical Theory and World Politics: Citizenship, Sovereignty and Humanity*. London: Routledge, 2007.

Mansouri, Fethi, and Liudmila Kirpitchenko. "Practices of Active Citizenship among Migrant Youth: Beyond Conventionalities." *Social Identities* 22, no. 3 (2016): 307–323.

Marshall, Thomas Humphrey. *Citizenship and Social Class: And other Essays*. Cambridge: University Press, 1950.

Mascherini, Massimiliano, and Hoskins Bryony. "The Characterization of Active Citizenship in Europe." 2009. http://ec.europa.eu/eurostat/documents/1001617/4398416/S11P2-THE-CHARACTERIZATION-OF-ACTIVE-MASCHERINI-HOSKINS.pdf.

Meehan, Elisabeth. "Active Citizenship: For Integrating the Immigrants." In *Active Citizenship: What Could It Achieve and How?* edited by Bernard Crick and Andrew Lockyer, 112–128. Edinburgh: Edinburgh University Press, 2010.

Melucci, Alberto. *L'invenzione del Presente: Movimenti Sociali nelle Societa Complesse* [Invention of the Present: Social Movements in Complex Societies]. Bologna: Il Mulino, 1982.

Melucci, Alberto. "The Symbolic Challenge of Contemporary Movements." *Social Research* 52, no. 4 (1985): 789–816.

Melucci, Alberto. "A Strange Kind of Newness: What's New in New Social Movements?" In *New Social Movements: From Ideology to Identity*, edited by Enrique Larana, Hank Johnston, and Joseph R. Gusfield, 101–130. Philadelphia, PA: Temple University Press, 1994.

Neveu, Erik. *Sociologie des Mouvements Sociaux* [Sociology of Social Movements]. Paris: Découverte, 1996.

Offe, Claus. "New Social Movements: Challenging the Boundaries of Institutional Politics." *Social Research* 52, no. 4 (1985): 817–868.

Ogien, Albert, and Sandra Laugier. *Le Principe Démocratie: Enquête sur les Nouvelles Formes du Politique* [The Principle of Democracy: Inquiry on the New Forms of Politics]. Paris: Découverte, 2014.

Özatalay, Cem. "Gezi Direnişi: Antikapitalist mi, Alter-Kapitalist mi? [Gezi Resistance: Anticapitalist or Alter-Capitalist?]." In *Gezi ve Sosyoloji: Nesneyle Yüzleşmek, Nesneyi Kurmak* [Gezi and Sociology: Facing the Object, Building the Object], edited by Vefa Saygın Öğütle and Emrah Göker, 170–185. Istanbul: Ayrıntı, 2014.

Özkırımlı, Umut, ed. *The Making of a Protest Movement in Turkey: #occupygezi*. London: Palgrave, 2014.

Paillé, Pierre, and Alex Mucchielli. *L'Analyse Qualitative en Sciences Humaines et Sociales* [Qualitative Analysis in Human and Social Sciences]. 3rd ed. Paris: Armand Colin, 2012.

Park, Se Jung, Yon Soo Lim, and Han Woo Park. "Comparing Twitter and YouTube Networks in Information Diffusion: The Case of the 'Occupy Wall Street' Movement." *Technological Forecasting & Social Change* 95 (2015): 208–217. doi:10.1016/j.techfore.2015.02.003.

Pleyers, Geoffrey. *Alter-Globalization: Becoming Actors in the Global Age*. Cambridge: Polity Press, 2010.

Pleyers, Geoffrey. "The Global Justice Movement." *Globality Studies Journal,* 19 (2010): 1–14.

Putnam, Robert David. *Bowling Alone: The Collapse and Revival of American Community*. New York: Simon and Schuster, 2000.

Rockhill, Gabriel. *Radical History & The Politics of Art*. New York: Columbia University Press, 2014.

Roffino, Sara. "How One Turkish Artist's Silent Performance Kept the Protests Alive." *Blouinartinfo*, June 20, 2013. http://www.blouinartinfo.com/news/story/919754/how-one-turkish-artists-silent-performance-kept-the-protests#.

Roy, Arundhati. "Public Power in the Age of Empire: Arundhati Roy on War, Resistance and the Presidency." *Democracy Now*, August 23, 2004. https://www.democracynow.org/2004/8/23/public_power_in_the_age_of.

Schechner, Richard. *Performance Theory*. New York: Routledge, 1988.

Schechner, Richard. *Performance Studies: An Introduction*. New York: Routledge, 2002.

Scholl, Christian. "Bakunin's Poor Cousins: Engaging Art for Tactical Interventions." *Thamyris/Intersection* 21 (2010): 157–178.

Seymour, Richard. "Turkey's 'Standing Man' Shows How Passive Resistance can Shake a State." *Guardian*, June 18, 2013. http://www.theguardian.com/commentisfree/2013/jun/18/turkey-standing-man.

Sharp, Gene. "The Meanings of Non-violence: A Typology (Revised)." *Conflict Resolution* 3, no. 1 (1959): 41–64.

Sharp, Gene. *Sharp's Dictionary of Power and Struggle: Language of Civil Resistance in Conflicts*. New York: Oxford University Press, 2012.

Soysal, Yasemin Nuhoglu. *Limits of Citizenship: Migrants and Postnational Membership in Europe*. Chicago: University of Chicago Press, 1994.

Spielmann, Guy. "L'Evénement-spectacle: Pertinence du Concept et de la Théorie de la Performance [The Event-spectacle: Pertinence of the Concept and Theory of Performance]." *Communications* 92 (2013): 193–204.

Tilly, Charles. *La France Conteste de 1600 à Nos Jours* [The Contentious France]. Paris: Fayard, 1986.

Touraine, Alain. *La Voix et le Regard* [The Voice and the Eye]. Paris: Seuil, 1978.

Touraine, Alain. "An Introduction to the Study of Social Movements." *Social Research* 52, no. 4 (1985): 749–787.

Touraine, Alain. *Le Nouveau Siècle Politique.* Paris: Seuil, 2016.

Tuğal, Cihan. "Resistance Everywhere: The Gezi Revolt in Global Perspective." *New Perspectives on Turkey* 49 (2013): 157–172. doi:10.1017/S0896634600002077.

Tunç, Aslı. "#Standing Man: Aesthetics of Nonviolent Resistance." *Mediacommons*, March 6, 2014. http://mediacommons.futureofthebook.org/imr/2014/03/06/standing-man-aesthetics-nonviolent-resistance.

Turner, Bryan Stanley. "Outline of a Theory of Citizenship." *Sociology* 24, no. 2 (1990): 189–217.

Tüysüz, Gül, Karl Penhaul, and Ian Lee. "Hundreds of Turks Emulate 'Standing Man' in Protest", *CNN*, June 19, 2013. http://edition.cnn.com/2013/06/18/world/europe/turkey-protests/.

Wieviorka, Michel. "After New Social Movements." *Social Movement Studies* 4, no. 1 (2005): 1–19.

Yalçıntaş, Altuğ. "Intellectual Disobedience in Turkey." In *Creativity and Humour in Occupy Movements: Intellectual Disobedience in Turkey and Beyond*, edited by Altuğ Yalçıntaş, 6–29. New York: Palgrave, 2015.

Yıldırım, Hasan, and Ozan Ural. "Duran Adam Salgını [The Epidemic of Standing Man]." *Hürriyet*, June 18, 2013. http://www.hurriyet.com.tr/duran-adam-salgini-23530185.

Yörük, Erdem, and Murat Yüksel. "Class and Politics in Turkey's Gezi Protests." *New Left Review* 89 (2014): 103–123. https://newleftreview.org/II/89/erdem-yoruk-murat-yuksel-class-and-politics-in-turkey-s-gezi-protests.

Zaff, Jonathan, Michelle Boyd, Yibing Li, Jacqueline V. Lerner, and Richard M. Lerner. "Active and Engaged Citizenship: Multi-group and Longitudinal Factorial Analysis of an Integrated Construct of Civic Engagement." *Journal of Youth and Adolescence* 39 (2010): 736–750. doi:10.1007/s10964-010-9541-6.

Index

Confederation of Public Labourer's Unions
(KESK) 109, 141–3, 149
Confederation of Revolutionary Trade
Unions (DİSK) 141–3, 149
Confederation of Turkish Trade Unions
(Türk-İş) 136, 141–2
Congosto, M. 104
conventional forms of political
participation 1, 5, 33, 164
Cowart, Joseph 17
critical Europeanist frame 126–7
Cumhuriyet 126, 146, 149
cyber activism 102

digital activism: defined 102; framing
efforts 107–8; literature review
103–8; oppressive and prohibitive
environment and 120; optimistic
perspective of 104–5; persistent
perspective of 106–7; pessimistic
perspective of 105–6; political system
and economic system, role of 106; pro-
government 109–10; risk with
102–3; terms developed for 102; transformative power of the internet and
105; in Turkey 107–8, 117–20; Turkish
activists and 102–3
digital activism, understanding of: analysis
110–12; efficacy scores **112**, 112–17,
119; Gezi Park protests and 107,
117–20; methods 108–9; perspectives of
activists **113**, 113–17; research questions
108; sample 109–10, **111**
digital activists, defined 104
digital technologies 104–5; economic
limitations of 106
Dink, Hrant 57, 59, 62–4, 71n17
Doetsch-Kidder, Sharon 57, 62

e-activism 102
Economic Development Foundation (IKV)
137
Education and Science Workers' Union
(Eğitim-Sen) 109
Ekman, Joakim 173
electronic civil disobedience 102
Erasmus + 175n13
Erdoğan, Recep Tayyip 118–19, 144
e-revolution 102, 118–20
Erikson, Robert 17
Eröncel, Borak 6
ethicodemocratic movements 185
EU Helsinki Summit, 1999 126

Euro-enthusiastic attitudes in Turkey
126–8
European Commission's 7th Framework
Programme 5
European integration' (EUROCS) 5
Europeanization process of Turkey 5,
125–6, 175n13; civil society
organizations, perception of
135–40; Erdoğan's statements regarding
144; future of debate 148–50; media
coverage 144–6; shift between Euro-
scepticism and pro-Europeanness 137,
145–6; trade unions/labor unions,
perceptions of 140–4
European Trade Union (ETUC) 144
European Union (EU) 125
Euro-sceptic attitudes in Turkey 127–9
Evrensel 146

Facebook 109, 134, 186, 188
Farrell, H. 119
Fethullah Gülen Movement 139–40
Foucault, Michel 126
Frames 107
Friedrich Ebert Foundation 137

Gambetti, Zeynep 188
Gandhi, Mahatma 197
generation phenomenon on political
activism 15
Gerbaudo, P. 106
German Marshall Fund 129
Gezi Park protests, 2013 4, 10, 33, 40, 42,
46, **47**, 50, 77–8, 107–8, 117, 160, 182–3,
187–8; average age of Gezi participants
175n3; case of utopia in 168–70; civil
society organizations involvement in
138–9, 149–50; experiences of activists
during 165–8; interpretive-hermeneutic
and comprehensive analysis 193–4; labor
unions and 142; lessons 96–7; Nor
Zartonk in 57, 65–7; notion of
performativity in 190–2; rising
participatory Gezi generation 25; Twitter
usage 104, 120; young people's
participation in 77–8, 81–4; *see also*
young people's participation in politics,
study of
Ghannam, J. 105
Goldthorpe, John H. 17
Gramsci, Antonio 126
Grant Agreement No: 625977 6
Greek protests 187

INDEX

www.ingramcontent.com/pod-product-compliance
Ingram Content Group UK Ltd.
Pitfield, Milton Keynes, MK11 3LW, UK
UKHW020353010325

455677UK00021B/437